Gender and Politics

Series Editors

Aims of the Series

The Gender and Politics series celebrates its 5th anniversary at the 4th European Conference on Politics and Gender (ECPG) in June 2015 in Uppsala, Sweden. The original idea for the book series was envisioned by the series editors Johanna Kantola and Judith Squires at the first ECPG in Belfast in 2009, and the series was officially launched at the Conference in Budapest in 2011. In 2014, Sarah Childs became the co-editor of the series, together with Johanna Kantola. Gender and Politics showcases the very best international writing. It publishes world class monographs and edited collections from scholars – junior and well established – working in politics, international relations and public policy, with specific reference to questions of gender. The 15 titles that have come out over the past five years make key contributions to debates on intersectionality and diversity, gender equality, social movements, Europeanization and institutionalism, governance and norms, policies, and political institutions. Set in European, US and Latin American contexts, these books provide rich new empirical findings and push forward boundaries of feminist and politics conceptual and theoretical research. The editors welcome the highest quality international research on these topics and beyond, and look for proposals on feminist political theory; on recent political transformations such as the economic crisis or the rise of the populist right; as well as proposals on continuing feminist dilemmas around participation and representation, specific gendered policy fields, and policy making mechanisms. The series can also include books published as a Palgrave pivot.

More information about this series at
http://www.springer.com /series/14988

Susanne Zwingel

Translating International Women's Rights

The CEDAW Convention in Context

palgrave
macmillan

Susanne Zwingel
Politics and International Relations
Florida International University
Miami, Florida, USA

Gender and Politics
ISBN 978-0-230-29097-6 ISBN 978-1-137-31501-4 (eBook)
DOI 10.1057/978-1-137-31501-4

Library of Congress Control Number: 2016943530

Printed on acid-free paper

This Palgrave Macmillan imprint is published by Springer Nature
The registered company is Macmillan Publishers Ltd. London

Acknowledgements

If I should name one single person who has triggered my interest in CEDAW, it would be Dr. Hanna-Beate Schöpp-Schilling, longstanding expert on the CEDAW Committee from Germany. She was the first person I ever interviewed about the Convention in the late 1990s, and until her early death, she remained a strong intellectual presence in the field of international women's rights. I am deeply grateful to have met Dr. Schöpp-Schilling, a brave and, in the true sense of the word, *radical* advocate for the rights of the world's women. As the global work for gender equality is a collective endeavor, I have had the honor to get to know and learn from many other admirable women's rights activists. This book is dedicated to them, collectively.

During the course of writing this book, I was employed at two institutions: the State University of New York (SUNY) at Potsdam and Florida International University. I would like to thank SUNY for granting me the Dr. Nuala McGann Drescher leave for faculty on tenure track as well as a sabbatical shortly after I got tenure; both helped tremendously in developing this project. I also received decisive personal support, in particular from my friends Phil Neisser, chair of the Politics department, and Liliana Trevizan, like-minded transnational feminist in the Modern Languages department. At Florida International University, my thanks go in particular to Becky Salokar, chair of the department of Politics and International Relations, for her encouragement. In 2010, I was kindly hosted for six months by the Chair for Human Rights and Human Rights Policy at Friedrich Alexander Universität Erlangen-Nürnberg in Germany. I enjoyed a wonderful intellectual environment thanks to inspiring debates with Heiner Bielefeldt, Michael Krennerich, and Imke Leicht.

For reading the manuscript in parts or as a whole, I am indebted to Imke Leicht, Kathryn Sikkink, Annegret Staiger, and an anonymous reviewer. Their feedback has helped me improve this book significantly. Three students—Ashley Balbian (at SUNY Potsdam) as well as Katherine Castro and Mark Pacho (at FIU), have worked on CEDAW with me—Ashley on US–CEDAW relations, Katherine on trends of States Parties' affinity to CEDAW, and Mark on the online bibliography on CEDAW implementation literature. I would like to thank them for this collaboration as it has helped me tremendously in rounding the scope of the book. Another big thank you goes to Kaitlyn Baker and Amanda Barrett (both at SUNY Potsdam) for interview transcription and collection of statistical data, and to Kevin Modlin (at FIU) for thorough copy editing.

The content presented in this book is partly based on interviews. I am grateful to everybody who took time out of their busy schedules to talk to me and share their wisdom. I further benefited from the knowledge of several academic experts and thank them for their friendly responses to my inquiries. I would also like to thank Jemima Warren and Imogen Gordon Clark from Palgrave MacMillan as well as Johanna Kantola and Sarah Childs, the editors of the *Gender and Politics series.* They have been patient, generous, and supportive, knowing the challenges of producing a publishable manuscript. For allowing me to use her artwork and give the book a wonderfully creative touch, I thank Fehmi Baumbach.

In a broad sense, I have felt supported by the growing community of feminist international relations scholars. While I was working on this book, I co-edited a volume on Feminist Strategies in International Governance with Gülay Çağlar and Elisabeth Prügl. I can't put in words how much energy and inspiration I took out of this project. It felt like a long, passionate conversation with some of the world's smartest women on the gendered nature of global affairs. Also, I am grateful for the CEDAW-specific collaboration I have had with Debra Liebowitz over the last years. For me, this thinking and writing about CEDAW was not only analytically innovative and politically relevant but also an immensely pleasant experience based on trust and respect. On three different occasions, I was invited to contribute to policy- or advocacy-oriented meetings as an academic expert on CEDAW; these meetings took place in Loccum, Germany (2011), Taipei, Taiwan (2011), and Kuala Lumpur, Malaysia (2015). I am grateful to the organizers of these meetings—Ursula Rust, University of Bremen, and Joachim Lange, Evangelische Akademie Loccum; Shih-I Yen from the Foundation for Women's Rights Promotion and Development, Taipei; and the entire team of IWRAW Asia Pacific, Kuala Lumpur—both because they contribute to making CEDAW a better known tool for advocacy and because they create a connection between women's rights scholarship and activism. I feel honored to be part of this important bridge-building endeavor.

Finally, I would like to thank my partner George Gonos, who has been a wonderful intellectual and emotional supporter throughout the process of writing this book (as well as a great cook!), and my daughter Celeste, who is growing into a creative young lady who does not tolerate sexism. There is no better outlook for the future.

Contents

List of Acronyms

BPFA	Beijing Platform for Action
CAT	Convention against Torture and Other Cruel, Inhuman or Degrading Treatment or Punishment
CCD	Common Core Document
CCPR	Covenant on Civil and Political Rights
CED	Convention on the Protection of all Persons from Enforced Disappearance
CEDAW	Convention on the Elimination of All Forms of Discrimination against Women
CEDAW SEAP	CEDAW Southeast Asia Program
CERD	Convention on the Elimination of All Forms of Racial Discrimination
CESCR	Covenant on Economic, Social, and Cultural Rights
CHR	Commission on Human Rights
CIDA	Canadian International Development Agency
CRC	Convention on the Rights of the Child
CRMW	Convention on the Rights of Migrant Workers and their Families
CRPD	Convention on the Rights of Persons with Disabilities
CSW	Commission on the Status of Women
DAW	Division for the Advancement of Women
DAWN	Development Alternatives with Women for a New Era
DEDAW	Declaration on the Elimination of Discrimination against Women
DEVAW	Declaration on the Elimination of Violence against Women
ECOSOC	Economic and Social Council of the United Nations

EU	European Union
FAO	Food and Agricultural Organization
FGM	Female Genital Mutilation
FWLD	Forum on Women, Law and Development
GA	General Assembly of the United Nations
GII	Gender Inequality Index
GR	General Recommendation (issued by the CEDAW Committee)
HDI	Human Development Index
HRC	Human Rights Committee
ICW	International Council of Women
IFI	International Financial Institution
ILO	International Labour Organization
INSTRAW	International Research and Training Institute for the Advancement of Women
IPU	Inter-Parliamentary Union
IR	International Relations (the discipline of)
IWRAW	International Women's Rights Action Watch
IWRAW AP	International Women's Rights Action Watch Asia Pacific
LBT(I)	Lesbian, Bisexual, Transgender (and Intersex)
MDG	Millennium Development Goal
NGO	Non-governmental organization
NHRI	National Human Rights Institution
NYTKIS	Coalition of Finnish Women's Associations
OHCHR	Office of the High Commissioner for Human Rights
OIC	Organization of Islamic Cooperation
OP	Optional Protocol to CEDAW
OSAGI	Office of the Special Adviser to the Secretary-General on Gender Issues and Advancement of Women
SA	Specialized Agency
SERNAM	Servicio Nacional de la Mujer (Chilean WPA)
TAN	Transnational Advocacy Network
TSM	Temporary special measure
UDHR	Universal Declaration of Human Rights
UN	United Nations
UNDP	United Nations Development Programme
UNESCO	United Nations Educational, Scientific, and Cultural Organization
UNICEF	United Nations Children's Fund
UNIFEM	United Nations Development Fund for Women

UN Women	UN Entity for gender equality and the empowerment of women
VAW	Violence against Women
VCLT	Vienna Convention on the Law of Treaties
WIDF	Women's International Democratic Federation
WILDAF	Women in Law and Development in Africa
WILPF	Women's International League for Peace and Freedom
WIPSU	Women in Politics, Zimbabwe
WPA	Women's policy agency

List of Figures

List of Tables

CHAPTER 1

Introduction

The idea that women should have the same rights as men has long been internationally recognized, but does this recognition make a difference for the world's women? In this book, I aim to answer this question by exploring how far the Convention on the Elimination of All Forms of Discrimination against Women (CEDAW), the centerpiece of the international women's rights discourse, can reach.

There is a significant tension in this question. Given the pertinent nature of discrimination against women globally, or in other words, given the magnitude of the problem, it seems that studying gender equality mechanisms created in the context of international governance is not the most relevant focus. As readers will learn throughout the chapters, CEDAW is an international human rights treaty that was created in intergovernmental gatherings, was first not taken all too seriously by the world's states, but later rose to an adequate level of authority and visibility, mostly due to the work of its monitoring committee of experts and transnational women's rights advocates. In itself, the Convention seems far removed from the everyday human rights violations many women experience. How could it make a difference?

The one thing that has stood out to me while studying CEDAW is the incredible effort activists have made to use the Convention and turn it into an instrument of social transformation. Their norm translation activism, as I call it, has connected previously separated contexts; it has made CEDAW

S. Zwingel, *Translating International Women's Rights*,
Gender and Politics, DOI 10.1057/978-1-137-31501-4_1

relevant in global and many national and local discourses. I have come to believe that this connecting activism is foundational for a global justice project. In the following, I draw on Judith Butler's and Gayatri Spivak's work to explain why.

In their writings on human rights, both Butler (2004) and Spivak (2004) develop their views from the vantage point of traumatized and marginalized collectives, who arguably would benefit most from human rights but are not reached by them. Spivak's thinking famously builds on the subaltern, on human beings who are cut off from social mobility by layers upon layers of historical and contemporary exclusions. On the other side is the "rightening subject," one that she constructs as "fit enough to help." In her view, there is a divide "between those who right wrongs and those who are wronged," and it is not clear whether a connection can ever be established in a way that is empowering for the subaltern (Spivak 2004, p. 563). Butler also sees a divide; in a heteronormative social order, some fit the criteria of heterosexual normal-ness, and this "fitting in" qualifies and protects them as humans. All others do not belong. They are silenced, perceived as threats, and often denied their humanity.

Butler envisions the building of a truly inclusive human rights discourse as a chance to overcome such divisions of belonging and not belonging. She proposes to open our understanding of humanness as something that we do not fully know and can never be sure about; something that is not just us but also something besides ourselves. If we then engage in the project of "cultural translation," in connecting to what we do not know, in allowing disorientation/insecurity rather than domination/autonomy, then we can pursue a normative project that includes *and* goes beyond our own truths and convictions. Spivak is more pessimistic in regard to the reach of the human rights discourse, but she sees education as a possibility to connect what seems too far apart to be connected. The subaltern need education that works against the many layers of exclusion in which they find themselves (the education they typically have access to rather reinforces such exclusion). It needs to be attentive to the potential of children and allow them to develop critical thinking. At the other end of the spectrum, those living in privilege need to learn how to establish relationships based on equality rather than a position of domination.

I take it from both Butler's and Spivak's thoughts that creating "inclusive humanity" is a difficult, never-ending endeavor that builds meaningful connections between all humans. Applied to this book, this perspective means to investigate the potential of the CEDAW Convention to create such connections. I will argue throughout the book that CEDAW indeed "stitches together" the idea of eliminating all forms of discrimination against women with the world's grown norms and traditions, some of them enhancing and some undermining that idea, and that in doing so, it fulfills a crucial function in the translation and realization of gender equality norms.

Strengthening connections that promote gender equality is a multilayered endeavor. I would like to situate this book in that endeavor and stress two meaningful connections to which it contributes. The first is the connection between academics and practitioners, more precisely, between feminist scholars such as myself and women's rights activists. Much of the content of this book is a product of this connection. I have learned a lot from the activists I got to know and interviewed. Their views on global patriarchal and other exploitative structures *as they manifest themselves in real life contexts* has influenced my thinking and writing profoundly. I trust that my work with its focus on analysis rather than action also bears some benefits for them as practitioners, for example, by enhancing processes of reflection and evaluation.

The second connection I aim to make with this book is one between young, comparatively privileged people—such as my students—and ideas of global justice. I have taught students in rural New York and urban Florida. Geopolitically, this is a hegemonic context, and having access to college education provides meaningful opportunities. Nonetheless, many of the students I have worked with have lived lives shaped by deprivation and discrimination, be it in terms of class, race, gender, social status, nationality, or other dimensions. They clearly have something to say in the grand conversation on global justice, but our contemporary hyperconsumerist and militarized Western culture does not give them good tools for critical thinking and seeing injustices, neither the ones they are exposed to nor the ones they partake in producing. Sometimes, for example, when their only idea of connection to "others" is that they "need our help," they seem to lack the kind of education that Spivak envisions for the privileged—they cannot shed that implicit assumption of superiority and see commonalities.

In particular in regard to gender equality, many people in Western countries assume that we are "ahead of the rest." However, there is a lot of ignorance about and tacit acceptance of gender hierarchies. I regularly teach feminist theory to undergraduate students of political science and international relations. The general gist in discussions on feminism, in particular in classes where little time is dedicated to reflecting on gender relations, is that present-day relations between men and women are not problematic anymore. As a consequence, analyses that detect sexism and misogyny are seen as outdated by a majority of students. In one particularly memorable class discussion, a male student said, in passing, "well, we all know a girl that has been beaten up by her boyfriend." This was a purely descriptive statement, uttered in the context of arguing that oppression of women is a thing of the past.

What does this statement mean for the state of gender equality around the world? It indicates that young people in the USA, a country that has made significant strides in confronting sexism, are used to men perpetrating violence against women, in particular against women they love. It proves that gender hierarchies are deeply engrained and hard to unlearn, because their expressions seem so normal. Sexism consists of many layers, the less spectacular of which—like "only" beating up a girlfriend—provide the enabling environment for those that the general public identifies as problems, such as brutal rapes, 'honor killings', sex trafficking, and the like. While the force of sexism varies cross-culturally and to the degree that it is reinforced by other discriminatory structures, it is true that women's work is undervalued everywhere in the world, both in terms of pay and recognition; their reproductive and care work is constructed as a natural instinct and taken for granted; oftentimes, access to their bodies is taken for granted; it seems normal that women are taken less seriously than men; and so forth. Of course, women are not homogeneously discriminated against, and some can build their lives on race or class privileges. What is important is to understand how different layers of discrimination hang together.

This book investigates the contribution CEDAW can make to challenge the multiple forms of marginalization women around the world experience. I have chosen to do this by offering a thorough analysis of the Convention. Since I am interested in the in-depth study of one particular mechanism and the unfolding of its relevance over time, this book follows an interpretive research methodology. I focus on the analysis of concrete connections of and dynamics between contextualized actors as well as their assessments of the processes at hand. I mostly rely on document analysis and expert interviews, the latter conducted between 2000 and 2013 (see appendix 1). Chapter 7 on patterns of States Parties' behavior is the only one that takes a slightly different lens; it presents quantitative—countable—information and offers an interpretation of it.

This book is organized into nine chapters. The first (Chapter 2) lays out the concept of norm translation as framework for the empirical analysis. Norm translation assumes two major "movements" of international norms: one toward international institutions and discourses (global discourse translation); and one away from them, toward domestic contexts where diverse actors engage with these norms by approving, transforming or rejecting ways (impact translation). The concept is an attempt to take the multi-directionality of norm creation and repercussions seriously; it wants to overcome the global-centrism of some of the norm diffusion literature through a de-centering perspective, and it emphasizes the labor-intensity and long duration of normative social change. There is nothing automatic in this process, as images such as "norm cascading" or "boomeranging" suggest. Because norm translation pays close attention to concrete agency aiming at long-term changes, I prefer the image of "stitching together" different pieces (read: discourses and contexts), reminiscent of the intricate and time-consuming work of quilt-making.

Chapters 3, 4, and 5 focus on the process of global discourse translation. Chapter 3 starts with a context description of the broader global discourse on gender equality in which CEDAW was created, identifying three phases of global awareness raising (1945–1975), confrontation of gender hierarchies through intergovernmental institution building and transnational movements (1975–1995), and consolidation of gender equality policies paralleled by persistent and new expressions of gender inequality (1995 to the present). It then presents the drafting dynamics around the Convention as well as its major features, most importantly, a comprehensive understanding of discrimination against women and the notion of substantive equality between men and women.

Chapter 4 traces the development of CEDAW from a treaty that governments have symbolically agreed to into an authoritative international monitoring mechanism for women's rights. The analysis of the Committee's support structures, its international interconnectedness, and its working methods over time reveal a trend of increasing visibility and legitimacy. It also shows that the strengthening of CEDAW on the international level has taken a long time and has been contingent on the persistent "norm work" of Committee experts and advocates within and outside the UN (Chap. 6 reinforces this finding). This process, while successful as a whole, has also been riddled with challenges. The most pertinent among them is that the Committee has to strike a careful balance between creating robust interpretations of women's rights and presenting itself as an authoritative body that is being taken seriously by states.

Chapter 5 is dedicated to the Optional Protocol (OP) to the Convention, which provides for an individual complaint mechanism and an inquiry procedure in cases of women's rights violations. The OP has further contributed to the Committee's work on setting international standards, in particular in the areas of violence against women, gender stereotyping, and reproductive health and rights. Thus, it constitutes a reinforcement of global discourse translation in regard to women's rights. As the Committee's views have, in some cases, helped States Parties correct direct and systemic violations of rights set forth in the Convention, the OP has also become an interesting mechanism of impact translation.

The following three Chapters unpack different dimensions of impact translation, starting with the translation work of non-governmental actors (6), followed by patterns of states' behavior toward the Convention (7) and compliance work within domestic contexts (8). Chapter 6 presents the many ways in which transnational norm translators have added clout to the state-centered character of the CEDAW monitoring procedure. This activism, mostly undertaken by non-governmental organizations (NGOs) but also by UN agencies and the CEDAW experts themselves, has added a new dimension in that it established ties between CEDAW and *societies* rather than states. "Norm translation work" is directed both toward global discourse translation and impact translation, and while most of this work aims at strengthening and supporting the CEDAW framework, some activists also challenge the Convention.

Chapter 7 describes patterns of connectivity between states and the Convention. It departs from the assumption that without significant connectivity, norm translation cannot take place, yet that connectivity is still only a prerequisite for and not equivalent to impact translation. States are first categorized according to their principled affinity to the Convention, represented by commitment to the treaty and its OP expressed in ratification and absence, presence, or withdrawal of reservations. Secondly, States Parties' level of substantive connectivity is described in two related dimensions, namely reporting discipline and dialogue frequency with the CEDAW Committee. In order to provide a kind of "global landscape" of connectivity with CEDAW, the chapter asks if levels of connectivity are influenced by any of the following three characteristics of states: belonging to a certain world region, democratic or non-democratic regime, and level of domestic de facto gender equality. Further, the chapter explores if and how principled and substantive connectivity to CEDAW hang together.

Chapter 8 starts with an overview of CEDAW implementation literature. On the one hand, this literature shows many concrete instances where norm translation based on CEDAW has taken place. One the other hand, it also finds lack of *systematic* implementation, including promising processes that fizzle out and absence of implementation activities altogether. The second part of the chapter looks into two domestic contexts, Chile and Finland, to trace concrete processes of impact translation. They were selected because of their meaningful substantive connectivity to the treaty and the existence of governmental and non-governmental norm translators. Also, they represent different political, social and cultural contexts and thus allow insights into processes of impact translation under varying conditions.

The concluding chapter returns to the initial question of the reach of CEDAW. It discusses two dimensions of this reach. One is the question of sufficient and adequate coverage of the Convention's provisions to work for gender equality. This normative framework is in constant motion—it has been expanded, and it is being contested. The second dimension deals with the transnational connections established—that is, the "stitching together" of the Convention with real-life contexts. Through the empirical chapters, we have seen that CEDAW is created within a broader, in itself evolving, global discourse on gender equality and that a variety of women's rights proponents have used it to influence domestic practices. This kind of translation work is cumbersome and needs to be undertaken over long periods of time. Crucially, the potential of CEDAW depends on the ability of transnational norm translators to connect the Convention meaningfully to domestic discourses and on the authority of women's rights proponents, within and outside of state institutions, in domestic constellations of power. In general terms, the findings of this book support a research agenda that focuses on creating and maintaining connections and takes interest in micro-level processes rather than identifying large-scale causal patterns. This perspective helps to develop a de-centered and de-essentializing vision of global norms.

CHAPTER 2

Theorizing Norm Translation: Women's Rights as Transnational Practice

This chapter lays out the theoretical framework for the book's leading question—that is, how far does CEDAW reach? It brings together two debates: the first one is on the creation, relevance, characteristics, and repercussions of international norms; the second one is on processes of transnationalization. Whereas the first debate is predominantly led among International Relations (IR) scholars, the second is more typically produced by sociologists, anthropologists, and geographers. Accordingly, it unfolds from what the first debate conceptualizes as the "receiving ends" of international norms—that is, real life contexts of different scales. This focus helps de-center the notion of international norms as *causes* of national and local transformations. I draw on these two strands of literature to create a transnational view on what I call "norm translation" in the field of women's rights.

A transnational perspective is, I believe, foundational for a study on the core international instrument to enhance women's enjoyment of their rights. The human rights framework spans the international and the domestic sphere, with an international focus on norm definition and promotion and a domestic focus on norm realization. Accordingly, human rights treaties are less purely international forms of cooperation than, for example, trade agreements that attempt to create rules *between* states. Human rights norms are debated internationally, they are supposed to guide state behavior, but most importantly, they are about far-reaching *societal* change. This is particularly true for women's rights; many phenomena that we now call violations of women's rights are deeply engrained, widespread, and normalized social practices. Such practices were not only long seen as matters

S. Zwingel, *Translating International Women's Rights*,
Gender and Politics, DOI 10.1057/978-1-137-31501-4_2

that should *not* be internationally regulated but also often not even considered to be problematic. The late reframing of "traditions" that discriminate against women into "human rights violations," a term that suggests international responsibility, is indicative of the slowly evolving process of connecting women's experiences with discourses on global justice.[1] Since IR has been, as an academic discipline, a latecomer to recognizing the relevance of gender,[2] I have drawn on other disciplinary traditions not only in order to ground my transnational perspective but also to be adequately attentive to the pervasiveness of gender norms.

The chapter proceeds in three steps. First, it presents three overlapping debates within IR literature on international norms, namely research on concrete mechanisms of international cooperation with the goal to define and promote permissible behavior ("regimes"); research on broader mechanisms of norm creation and diffusion; and research on the consistency and reach of internationally agreed-upon norms. I discuss the first two debates in one section as they both depart from a global-centrist position on international norms and their likelihood to "trickle down." The third debate is qualitatively different as it focuses on the dynamic character and multi-directionality of international norms. The second part of the chapter presents literature on transnationalism with a concern of social relations and situatedness. I discuss general principles of this approach—for example, the reconceptualization of how the global, national, and local relate to each other—and literature that takes a transnational view on human rights practices and women's activism more specifically. The point of departure in these writings is not a cause–effect assumption of international norms. Rather, norm creation and appropriation are considered non-linear processes of negotiation in which various differently contextualized actors are involved. In the final part, I read the two perspectives together to develop the transnational framework that guides my analysis. Thinking of norm translation as "stitching together" disconnected discourses,[3] I highlight two main dynamics involving CEDAW: global discourse translation, which captures the continuous international negotiation of gender equality norms, and impact translation, which brings together transnational and domestic agency that uses international norms to influence domestic gender regimes. This pluri-local agency is often, but not always, in support of international norms and embedded in multiple normative and material settings.

Women's Rights from the Top: Cooperation, Diffusion, De-centering

Within IR, the question of impact of international (women's) human rights norms has interested scholars of regime analysis, norm diffusion, and more recently, approaches that have not yet been labeled but that can be described as sharing a reflexive, de-centered view on international norms. Regime analysis looks at concrete mechanisms of international cooperation; norm diffusion literature explores dynamics of global norm creation and diffusion into domestic contexts with a focus on actor constellations and factors that support or inhibit such processes; and the 'de-centering' literature explores the ongoing dynamics of norm production beyond an international-to-national cause–effect logic. I will present the tenets of these debates in turn and show in which ways they are either useful or insufficient for an understanding of the reach of CEDAW.

International Cooperation and Global Norm Diffusion: Mechanisms of Legitimacy and Trickle-Down Assumptions

Regime analysis emerged as a counter-discourse to the assumption that international cooperation is epiphenomenal to state interests and global power constellations (Krasner 1983). Defined as "social institutions consisting of agreed upon principles, norms, rules, procedures and programs that govern the interactions of actors in specific issue areas" (Levy et al. 1995, p. 274), international regimes have emerged as instruments of joint problem solving in specific global issue areas. Regime analysts usually assume a linear if complex process of regime formation, and, depending on their theoretical convictions, either limited or far-reaching regime effects (Kratochwil and Ruggie 1986; Levy et al. 1995).

International regimes have been created in different fields but figure most prominently in environmental politics. An impressive body of research has indicated the relevance of environmental regimes (Breitmeier et al. 2011), probably because the need for collaboration is evident despite short-term costs and because the knowledge of the global dimensions of environmental degradation is comparatively new, and as a consequence, there is a need for joint and context-specific problem definition and approaches to amelioration. Human rights are another field where international cooperation in form of a "regime" has emerged since the end of WWII (Donnelly 1986). With a look at the evolution of women's rights and norms of sexual non-discrimination specifically, some authors also speak of a women's rights regime (Kardam 2004; Savery 2007). These regimes have been called "promotional" and not "enforcing" (Donnelly 1986, 2013), indicating a rather low likelihood of influence on state behavior. Indeed, the international human rights framework is about *negotiating* the scope of norms acceptable to states and then *monitoring* their norm-abiding domestic behavior. Scholars have argued that the "expressive dimension" of human rights—that is, *rhetorically* committing to eliminate human rights violations by joining international human rights treaties—is in the interest of many states, both norm-abiding and not (Hathaway 2002; Simmons 2009). This argument points to the shortcoming of the regime, that is, the absence of international mechanisms of norm *realization* as such mechanisms are not in the interest of cooperating states.

While this characterization of the human rights regime is still generally accurate, two adjustments seem in order. First, not all dimensions of the human rights framework threaten states' sovereignty to the same degree. A state may see the need to ensure physical integrity and privacy rights as an undue interference in its security policy, but it might perceive the right to health or education as a reinforcement of its welfare policies (Simmons 2009). Accordingly, states may be more likely to commit to the not-so-threatening dimensions of the human rights catalogue. Second, the human rights regime has been strengthened considerably since the 1990s. This is expressed in the expansion of the UN human rights infrastructure, the increasing importance that civil society organizations attribute to human rights, and the emphasis on universal (not only domestic) responsibility for human rights realization, prominently expressed in the "responsibility to protect" (Bellamy 2009) and the increase of foreign and international trials to hold perpetrators of grave human rights violations accountable (Sikkink 2011). While there is no space here to discuss the potential problems in this development, it seems fair to say that in the early twenty-first century, the human rights regime has moved beyond the paper tiger stage, and states have, to varying degrees, constructively engaged with it.

Scholars fall roughly into three categories as to their assessment of the transformative potential of human rights regimes. The *neoliberal* position assumes that there are two groups of states: those that genuinely adhere to human rights and make efforts to implement human rights treaties upon ratification, and those that ratify human rights treaties because they seek a way to increase their international legitimacy without significant costs.

For neither group does the human rights regime produce effects. It does not alter the behavior of the first, as this is not necessary, and it has no means, neither in form of pressure nor incentives, that would produce compliance among the "free riders" (Hafner-Burton et al. 2008; Neumayer 2005; Schwarz 2004).[4] The second, often called *managerial*, position emphasizes the constitutive dimension of human rights regimes. Mechanisms of cooperation potentially strengthen the international community building and contribute to establishing shared values (Henkin 1990; Meyer et al. 1997). Contrary to the assumption that states break treaties whenever this seems to serve their interests, this position observes a strong propensity of states to stick to international agreements and perceive them as opportunities for complex learning (Chayes and Chayes 1995). In this logic, the absence of coercive mechanisms is not a deficit but a precondition for constructive and collaborative problem solving.

The third position covers middle ground—it is optimistic about regime effectiveness *under certain conditions* and aims at teasing out enhancing factors. Given the diversity of states and their interests, compliance has to be conceptualized as "a product of complex causality in which the most significant factors are incentives, institutional design, the rule of law, and the power of legitimacy" (Breitmeier et al. 2011, p. 584). Thus, regimes that combine coercive and managerial elements are better able to provide procedures tailored toward state compliance under widely differing conditions (Smith-Cannoy 2012; Tallberg 2002). Further, several scholars suggest that domestic factors need to be looked at to explain the influence of human rights treaties since these treaties really regulate state–society relations, not state–state relations, as in the case of other forms of international cooperation (Simmons 2009, p. 126). Domestic factors that have been found to be relevant for treaty compliance are: the political predisposition to adhere to human rights (Cortell and Davis 2000; Moravcsik 1995); the attitudes of different domestic constituencies towards human rights, including human rights opponents (Cardenas 2007); characteristics of domestic institutions and their connectivity with international norms (Simmons 2009) [5]; regime stability or transitionality—semi-democratic regimes or those in transition to democracy are found to be most susceptible to treaty compliance (Simmons 2009); the "cultural match" between international and domestic norms (Cortell and Davis 2000); and regional (e.g., Asian or European) patterns in response to an international regime (Cardenas 2007; Moravcsik 1995; Simmons 2009). An additional domestic factor that enhances the compliance with women's rights norms specifically is the absence of a dominant religion and the prevalence of secularism (Simmons 2009; Sweeney 2004).

In light of all these potentially influential factors, Cardenas has pointed to the paradox that many states actually respect and violate human rights at the same time, as conflicting normative positions coexist and create "zones of ambiguity" (Cardenas 2007, p. 129). If we assume such mixed bags of domestic context factors, our expectations in regard to treaty effectiveness should be moderate. Surprisingly, however, a growing body of quantitative research finds significance in international women's rights norms and the CEDAW convention in particular. For example, Gray et al. (2006) extrapolate CEDAW ratification as "the most consistently important factor" in improvements in female life expectancy, female literacy rate, female share in the labor force, and female percentage in parliament in a sample of 180 states (p. 326). According to Simmons (2009), CEDAW ratification has had significant effects on government policies related to girls' education and reproductive rights, even if in the second field, improvements were concentrated in secular states and "muted" in highly religious states. Englehart and Miller (2014) detect robust positive effects of CEDAW on women's political rights, less pronounced effects on social rights, and no effect on economic rights. Finally, Hill (2010) compares the effect of a variety of human rights treaties on state behavior and concludes that CEDAW is the only one that makes a positive difference. However, what these studies do is create a correlation between treaty ratification and societal features that are desirable according to the treaty and that can be quantified. They cannot tell us how these two things hang together and how and by whom they are connected; they can also not say much about non-quantifiable societal changes and how these could be affected by an international regime. Thus, what regime analysis has done is analyze concrete mechanisms of international cooperation, including in the field of (women's) human rights. Depending on theoretical provenience, chances of causal impact of international cooperation have been assumed to be more moderate or more far reaching; the point is, in either case, to show some kind of direct and general causal relationship, not to understand these relationships, or even to find others, perhaps not causal and not quantifiable.

The second field of IR literature, scholarship on global norm diffusion, goes beyond analyzing concrete mechanisms of cooperation. It explores more generally how norms emerge and become meaningful in international arenas and then move toward domestic contexts. A prominent concept of norm diffusion is Finnemore and Sikkink's (1998) "norm life-cycle." It determines three stages a norm—defined as intersubjective "standard of appropriate behavior for actors with a given identity" (p. 891)—passes through to become globally pervasive: norm emergence, norm cascading, and norm internalization. During global *norm emergence*, norm entrepreneurs frame the norm and work to gain support among powerful actors; during *norm cascading*, the norm is embraced by a critical mass of states, becomes internationally institutionalized, and creates "norm followers" who are more convinced by the general approval of the norm rather than by its content. Finally, *norm internalization* is the phase where the norm is implemented in domestic settings, for example, in state bureaucracies. If internalization is far reaching, the norm may no longer be contested. None of these phases is assumed to occur automatically; rather, the sequence is an ideal-type process of norm diffusion.

Another focus of norm diffusion literature is to identify concrete actor constellations that engage in creating and spreading norms. In particular, Risse et al. (1999, 2013) and Keck and Sikkink (1998) have found transnational non-governmental activism in strategic cooperation with governments to be crucial in this process. Keck and Sikkink (1998) have coined the seminal concept "transnational advocacy networks" (TANs); usually, non-governmental organizations (NGOs) play a central role in TANs, yet parts of international organizations and state institutions may also be involved. TANs emerge most likely when civil society claims are blocked by a state and if transnational cooperation seems likely to strengthen these claims and cause what Keck and Sikkink call a "boomerang pattern" (p. 12), that is, a change of state behavior through the joint transnational effort of domestic and foreign actors. The most effective weapon of TANs is to create credible information and to frame it in a way that creates pressure on governments to act. This can most successfully be achieved through campaigns that target concrete, not structural, problems and if it is unequivocal who bears responsibility for the denounced problem.

Norm diffusion literature has made a tremendous difference in theorizing the making of global normative change, and much of the literature showing the increasing international relevance of gender-related norms falls into this framework. It has focused on the "norm entrepreneurship" of gender equality advocates both from the non-governmental sector and from within global governance bureaucracies (Çağlar et al. 2013; Meyer and Prügl 1999) as well as on processes of norm diffusion from global to domestic gender equality policies, enhanced by transnational advocacy networks (True and Mintrom 2001). The literature shows that integration of gender norms has been uneven depending on the policy field—for example, this happened earlier and has been a more transformational process in the areas of development, population policies, and human rights than in macro-economic and security policies (Cohn 2008; Fraser and Tinker 2004; Joachim 2007; Razavi 2013). In general, these findings suggest that gender equality has reached the status of a widely accepted international norm—Chap3, 4 and 5 in this book underline this dynamic in regard to women's rights.

However, norm diffusion literature also has a number of shortcomings. In particular, it assumes a global norm to be fixed and unequivocal once it has been globally agreed upon,[6] ready to be implemented domestically; it takes a perspective that is rather firmly anchored in an international universe and leaves domestic dynamics of norm creation and appropriation underestimated; and it prioritizes certain actor constellations over others and, thus, conceptually reduces context-specific complexities in norm translation processes. I specify these problems in turn.

First, "global norms" are not hammered in stone, and they are not all pointing in the same direction. Rather, they resemble a confusing conversation. If we focus on the human rights framework specifically, it is true that all dimensions of the framework are supposed to form an organic whole with the overarching goal of spelling out conditions for life in dignity. But even this set of norms is not unequivocal. It contains a lot of internal tensions, such as between the right to freedom of speech and the right to non-discrimination (Brehms 2009); it brings about new claims, for example, the right to water (Hiskes 2010); and it is changing over time as ideas are reformulated. One example for such reformulation is how to frame and prevent gender-based discrimination in the field of employment—the notion that female workers need to be protected dominated until the 1960s and was then understood to exacerbate discrimination against women in the workforce (Berkovitch 1999; McKean 1983). This ambiguity is exacerbated by the fact that other powerful international norms may even contradict human rights norms, for example, the norm package of trade liberalization (Abouharb and Cingranelli 2006; Sadasivam 1997). Given this evolutionary character of and competition among global norms, it would be simplistic to assume that a norm that has become internationally accepted (e.g.,. through treaty adoption) will *remain* accepted for the extended future; rather, a lot of work needs to be done to keep it alive and relevant, and even if this work is being done, the continuous authority of the norm is not guaranteed. In the field of gender norms, the rhetorical "victory" of the 1995 Beijing Platform for Action (BPFA) is a good example for this challenge. The rather far-reaching wording of the BPFA was heavily contested all along, but it came under particularly severe attack in the conservative post–9/11 international climate. In this context, insider advocates and non-governmental actors spent a lot of energy just to retain the BPFA's claims; there was no space to advance them, but there was certainly danger that international women's rights standards could be pushed back to less ambitious levels (Hannan 2013).

Secondly, norm diffusion literature leaves domestic dynamics of norm creation and appropriation underestimated. Not only do the "cascading" and "internalization" assumptions suggest relatively isomorphic processes across widely differing contexts, they also do not conceptualize these contexts as norm creators or norm contesters. Epstein (2012) criticizes that this mindset frames out the perspective of the "socializees" in so-called norm socialization processes and infantilizes them as a consequence. As we have seen before, scholars have created classifications of national particularities that help us understand the differences in states' responses to international norms, but the authors' perspectives are still inspired by a global-to-national cause–effect logic. An exception is Savery's work on compliance with international norms of sexual non-discrimination in four states. She claims that norm diffusion crucially depends on and is often inhibited by historically grown domestic gender regimes and "the gender-biased corporate identity of many states" (Savery 2007, p. 225).

Third, norm diffusion literature departs from simplified concepts of actors and actor constellations in the production and spread of global norms. One recurring trope is the assumption of a norm-abiding international community of (liberal) states and a number of deviant (authoritarian) states that need to be socialized into desirable behavior. There are some dimensions of the human rights framework where this vision makes sense, in particular in regard to freedom from arbitrary state interference, which is the foundational idea of liberal states (and is nevertheless often undermined by them). However, when it comes to women's rights, it is more accurate to think of all states as somehow *contributing* to the scope of the framework and all of them *deviating* from this ideal to varying degrees. Another typical actor constellation in global norm diffusion literature is a norm-violating government vis-à-vis a norm-advocating NGO supported by international allies—the constellation in which the "boomerang effect" takes place. This is, however, only *one* possible constellation.

Other possibilities would be a state with an interest in norm adherence and domestic civil society organizations with a fundamentally opposed normative position (Baldez 2013), a context where both international and state actors do not know much about the global normative frameworks they are supposed to diffuse, and a state where the "norm socializers" are domestic NGOs (Jenichen 2013). Many other constellations are possible. The point is to figure out where to situate different actors on a continuum of norm- and interest-driven behavior rather than a priori separating them into norm-adhering and deviating clusters.

Which angle do the debates on international cooperation and norm diffusion provide for an analysis of CEDAW? Literature on the significance of regimes leads us to assume a variety of responses by cooperating actors, spanning the range from meaningful compliance to rejection of women's rights, depending both on regime characteristics and a mix of domestic factors. Attempts to measure treaty effectiveness are likely to find relevance but cannot explain how and by whom this effectiveness was produced. Norm diffusion literature is a useful framework to explain the creation of global gender norms of which CEDAW is an important part. It is also helpful to shed light on the difficult work of "norm entrepreneurs" in terms of framing norms and making them globally legitimate. However, it has neither focused on the evolving character of globally accepted norms nor on their potential of being fundamentally contested and reformulated. Thus, the work that is necessary to keep a norm globally significant is overlooked. Further, norm diffusion literature conceptualizes domestic contexts as receiving ends in the process of norm diffusion, and it promotes a static understanding of actors and the relations between them.

A point that remains under-examined in both debates is the productive power inherent in regimes and norm creation. Neoliberals see absence of power in the Weberian sense, constructivists see forms of collaboration not tainted by coercion, enabling the search for common ground and "good solutions", but there is not much thought given to the ways in which authoritative ideas may constitute hegemonic power (Keeley 1990; Manokha 2009). To the degree that norms are increasingly supported, they unfold disciplining power and create deviant positions. As Chap. 3 shows, gender equality norms have acquired a rather powerfully prescriptive status globally—what are the consequences of this (partial) success of "governance feminism" (Halley et al. 2006)? In the text of CEDAW, for example, we see a "victory" of the construction of women as autonomous individuals over women as defined by their role within the family.

This notion is consistent with the human rights framework, but it was highly contested during the Convention's drafting process (Rehof 1993). The "losing" position, however, has been marginalized within the dominant understanding of women's rights and, at the same time, continued to exist elsewhere. Eventually, it resurfaced globally in more vocal opposition to CEDAW (see Chap. 6) and other dimensions of the global gender equality discourse. In part, this resurrection is a result of being declared deviant from the global consensus.

De-centering International Norms: Constant Evolution and Localized Meanings

Not surprisingly, IR scholarship on norms is in constant evolution itself. A number of ideas have further developed our understanding of international norms along the lines of criticism laid out in the previous section. Two of these are particularly relevant for this study, namely the claims that normative content is *by definition* unsteady and that this unsteadiness has to be studied in movement between different contexts.

As Hofferberth and Weber argue, the meaning of norms is in constant motion due to the intrinsically *interactive* character of norms. In their view, norm diffusion literature has focused too strongly on the regulative effects of norms and lost sight of the fact that norms are constantly negotiated and acted out. Instead, they think of norms as "moral points of orientation that are invoked and re-interpreted in the process of acting" (2012, p. 12). This idea of norms as inter-subjective processes differs radically from the concepts of compliance or norm internalization, and it provides a broader view on the variety of norm-influenced action. One such dynamic is norm re-definition or contestation *after* international norm acceptance. Van Keersbergen and Verbeek (2007) argue that the notorious vagueness of international agreements is not only a *result* of interactive norm creation but also an invitation to *continue* to battle over meaning. They claim that international organizations often provide opportunities for re-discussing agreed-upon norms (e.g., issue-specific world conferences or other periodic meetings), even if such spaces are typically meant to confirm, and perhaps move beyond, the status quo. Thus, international re-packaging of norms is an institutional option.

Various studies exploring international gender equality norms confirm this flexibility of content. Krook and True (2012), for example, explain the changes of meaning of gender equality norms by their exposure to internal and external dynamisms—ongoing definition debates, on the one hand, and transformations in the broader universe of norms-in-process, on the other. Interestingly, even comparatively uncontested norms such as equal participation in political decision making have not remained static over time. The authors show how the norm evolved from an understanding that women should have voting rights in the 1940s to a notion that women's interests could be best represented through an increase in female office holders, often attempted to be achieved by electoral quotas since the 1990s. Verloo and others have studied reasons for the many varieties of meaning attached to the term "gender equality" and the dynamics in policy formation this has triggered (Lombardo et al. 2009; Verloo 2007). In a comparative study of the framing of public policies affecting gender relations within the European Union, the authors find at least three general problem definitions—labeled inclusion (of women), reversal (of androcentrism), and displacement (of existing gender roles)—which result in different problem-solving rationales. While the concept of gender equality is in itself shaped by a set of varying assumptions, public gender policies are, additionally, influenced by other normative frames such as labor market needs or population policies (Verloo and Lombardo 2007). These constraints contribute to changes of meaning. Lombardo et al. (2009) speak of the fixing (limiting and "freezing" by means of authoritative standards), stretching (conceptual broadening), or bending (subordination to other goals) of gender equality. Thus, similar to Krook and True's argument, both internal and external dynamics affect the content-in-motion of a norm. Towns' study on the diffusion processes of three women-related international norms—women's suffrage, the establishment of women's policy agencies, and sex quotas for elected bodies—makes another interesting argument. Rather than creating *similar* conditions (of gender equality) domestically, these diffusion processes have served to reinforce international *distinction* and even hierarchy among states[7] (Towns 2010).

All of the previous arguments make a case against the homogenizing effect of international norms. Another innovative contribution to this discussion is van der Vleuten et al.'s work on the flow of gender equality norms between institutions of *regional* governance. This work introduces a new site of non-domestic norm creation that often carries more legitimacy than the international level because regional organizations are perceived as more authentic to regional interests and traditions. Inter-regional normative influence adds another layer of norm translation that deviates from the problematic global-centrism discussed earlier (van der Vleuten et al. 2014). Similarly, the notion of norm "localization" (Acharya 2004) focuses on the movement of norms from one context to another whereas the key to understanding norm diffusion is to study local agents' ways of reconstructing external norms in a way that they fit in with foundational "cognitive priors and identities" (2004, p. 239). Acharya's point is to see norm localization as a dynamic process in which "the local" is not a passive recipient of norms crafted elsewhere but the crucial space where legitimate and sustainable norm realization can take place. Accordingly, norm localization is framed as sincere if interest-driven effort to deal with the norm. If successful, this process is incremental and contains adaptation (if unsuccessful, the norm will not gain resonance). To illustrate the dynamic, Acharya shows how foundational norms in the Southeast Asian region, in particular the norm of non-interference in domestic affairs, have proven to be standards norm localizers have to deal with when they try to introduce external norms.

For an analysis of the reach of CEDAW, these de-centering approaches stretch the scope of IR literature. They shed light on the moving content of what CEDAW, specifically, and gender equality norms, generally, encompass due to their interactive character. This is relevant to grasp CEDAW as a contested, unfinished concept. The idea of norm localization further stresses the relevance of local agency in bringing international norms to life, even if it applies this focus only to governmental or elite actors as norm localizers, and not yet toward "local communities where the subjects of...rights work and live" (Merry 2006, pp. 2–3). The following section conceptually moves closer to these lived realities.

Transnational Visions of Women's Rights

The approaches presented so far can explain intergovernmental cooperation and norm creation in the field of women's human rights, both in a global-centrist logic and with a view that stretches this logic somewhat. The second part of the chapter offers frameworks developed outside of IR scholarship that make this conceptual stretching more substantial. These frameworks all follow a transnational logic, with different emphases, but with the common denominator to look at context-crossing phenomena in ways that do not a priori think of one context as more fundamental than the other. Rather, the focus is on connecting dynamics and their consequences. I start with laying out a few general principles of literature on transnationalism and then present insights from transnational approaches on (women's) human rights in practice and feminist activism.

Rethinking Container Spaces, Hierarchies and Separations: Transnational Visions of the World

Processes of transnationalization have been scrutinized by sociological, geographical, and anthropological literature for some time (Hannerz 1996; Jackson et al. 2004; Massey 1994; Pries 2004; Vertovec 1999). Pries describes transnationalization as a dynamic of internationalization that stands for "different forms of rearrangements of geographic-social spaces beyond, alongside and above the formerly dominant national society paradigm" (Pries 2004, p. 53). A transnational perspective differs from concepts that take the global or intergovernmental sphere as a starting point; rather, it conceptualizes the global, national, and local as interrelated, it re-reads the alleged homogenizing influence of globalization, and it rejects the local as culturally bounded. I will consider these three ideas in turn.

First, transnationalization creates a new understanding of interrelatedness between global, national, and local spheres. In the discourse of modernity we have come to see these spheres as separate and hierarchical. The global is associated with abstract and powerful concepts such as "space" or "capital," while the local is linked to the concrete, limited, and traditional, with the national somewhere in between. In contrast, geographer Doreen Massey thinks of space as a product of interrelations, as the possibility of the existence of multiplicity and plurality, and as always under construction (Massey 2005, p. 10). Two dimensions of this vision are important: it abandons, on the one hand, the assumption of a qualitative difference between global, national, and local (e.g., abstract–concrete, powerful–victimized) and replaces it with the understanding of situatedness of all action. On the other hand, it thinks of any context as "constructed not by placing boundaries around it and defining its identity through counter-position to the other which lies beyond, but precisely (in part) through the specificity of the mix of links and interconnections *to* that 'beyond'" (Massey 1994, p. 4f). Thus, concreteness and interrelatedness is intrinsic to all local, national, and global processes.

Second, the homogenizing influence of globalization—including global norms—is questioned. Hannerz argues that processes of globalization are always confronted with a powerful local, specified as the site of everyday life, face-to-face interaction, and sensual bodily experience consisting of "diversity, interconnectedness, and innovation, in the context of global center-periphery relationships" (Hannerz 1996, p. 67). The local is not conceptualized as receiving global "trickle downs" but as a site where outside influences are actively integrated and transformed, where they are made sense of, even in the "very local" dimensions of bodies and inner landscapes (Price 1999), and where "trickle ups" are created. Massey reminds us of "thriving globality-producing locales" (2005, p. 102), such as London or Tokyo, to put the notion of the disempowered local in perspective. She also argues against the idea that norms agreed upon elsewhere may take on abstract (universal) legitimacy in a given context. Rather, a locale's dealing with outside influences is a matter of contextualized self-determination with a variety of possible outcomes.

Finally, transnationalization literature also reminds us that the local is not a culturally confined entity but one that has *traditionally* been influenced by transnational dynamics (Sen 1999, p. 242ff). This context-crossing, literally *traveling* notion of culture is often replaced in discourses on international norms by a bipolar vision of backward vs. progressive culture. In respect to women's rights norms specifically, it is common to refer to culture and tradition as the main source of women's rights violations, but this culture is that of the others (Merry 2003), often envisioned as never-changing, provincial, non-cosmopolitan locals. In contrast, participants of international encounters self-identify with a progressive, open-mindedly transnational form of culture that is "largely secular, universalistic, law-governed" (Merry 2006, p. 37). However, as Merry suggests, *all* these norm-guided practices are dynamic and culturally produced positions that overlap to a greater or lesser extent with each other.

Applied to an analysis of CEDAW, a transnational framework suggests, first, that the Convention is one connecting piece in a conglomerate of international women's rights norms, national apparatuses that have made a commitment to these norms, and the everyday life situations in which women's rights are realized. Its intergovernmental nature does not place it on a higher level in an imaginary hierarchy of scales. Second, powerful contextualized agency suggests varying degrees of resonance of international norms depending on the local normative fabric into which the international thread is woven—this makes us expect diverse forms of negotiated implementation of CEDAW. The power of the local further suggests that a norm coming from elsewhere needs to be actively negotiated—rather than implemented—in order to make it legitimate. Accordingly, CEDAW is more accurately understood as a door opener for inclusive domestic debates than as an indisputable international measuring stick. And finally, local cultural contexts constitute dynamic spaces that are principally open to outside influences such as CEDAW. They are not "other" to enlightened international norms but intertwined with them.

The Between-ness of Discourses: Vernacularizing Human Rights

Transnational approaches, often with a background in anthropology, have developed a reading of human rights that focuses on human rights practice far away from but connected to intergovernmental spaces and on the connecting dynamics between the two. Goodale describes a common construction of the universal claim of human rights as inhabiting non-local space, consisting of "certain key locations and artifacts [that] take on added significance as the places where human rights are expressed.... Meetings of human rights activists, international legal forums, headquarters of transnational human rights NGOs, all are semi-sacred places where human rights norms are generated" (2007, p. 12). He considers this an overemphasis associated with the previously mentioned assumptions of the global as abstract and powerful vis-à-vis the local as passive and marginalized. In his view, human rights need to be studied as *practice*, not in the abstract, and such practice is "characterized by contradictions, uncertainties, and a kind of normative incompleteness" (p. 26). He coins the concept of "between-ness" to emphasize the non-universality of human rights practice and its context specific techniques of drawing on the universal discourse that creates diverse combinations between the global and the local. His work on the encounter of a rural indigenous Bolivian community with the human rights discourse during the 1990s provides rich evidence of this between-ness (Goodale 2009). A highlight in this writing is the exploration of one local authority figure who finds a calling in bringing parts of the universal "value package" of human rights (indigenous rights and women's rights specifically) to this marginalized context. Among other strategies, he uses speeches at weddings to disseminate a two-pronged message of human dignity: indigenous people deserve recognition that has been denied to them for so long, and wife abuse is no longer a permissible practice. Together with other strategies, including the opening of a shelter for women, this mediator creates a new "in-between" consciousness in his community that includes acceptance of and resistance to human rights as he understands them.

In a similar vein, Merry (2003) and others have studied ways in which globally produced norms are being translated into "the vernaculars" of ordinary people. "Vernacularization" encompasses a process where:

> chains of actors stretch from the sites of the global production of human rights documents and ideas (in New York, Geneva and Vienna) to localities where ordinary people around the world adopt them. They wrestle with the

> dilemma of presenting transnational ideas in terms that resonate with local justice theories and at the same time are sufficiently different that they will challenge local inequalities. (Levitt and Merry 2009, p. 446/7)

As in the concept of "between-ness" this wrestling process leads to context-dependent variations. In a comparative study of vernacularization processes, the authors find that socialist and collectivist traditions in China, Gandhian social justice ideas and caste-based practices in India, liberation theology and experiences of colonization in Peru, and a civil rights approach to achieving justice in the USA all connect in different ways to global gender equality norms (Liu et al. 2009; Mujica and Meza 2009; Rajaram and Zararia 2009; Rosen and Yoon 2009). The reach of practices of vernacularization differs significantly. In both China and the USA, the authors find adaptation of international impulses into already existing framework rather than significant innovation; the Indian case shows a more transformative strategy of re-invention of local traditions in an international light, in particular the framing of homosexuality as a practice traditionally embraced by Hinduism (Rajaram and Zararia 2009). Transformative vernacularization has to be *culturally* understandable and acceptable; it has to sink in. It might be difficult to integrate external ideas into the familiar, as shown in Merry's analysis of battered women in Hawai'i who are confronted with the idea "to have rights." This idea, while seemingly a rescue anchor in a situation of abuse, was perceived by many women as too dissonant with other norms dominating their lives, in particular being a good mother under all circumstances. Therefore, many women saw it as a confusing rather than helpful idea and integrated it in only scattered ways into their lives (Merry 2006). Thus, the dilemma inherent in vernacularization—that it is necessary to root international norms in local practices and at the same time challenge discriminatory dimensions of these practices—remains. The idea embodied by these works, that is, to study global human rights norms in practice with a focus on compromised dynamics, tensions, and contradictions, is crucial for my notion of norm translation developed in this chapter.

Transnational Feminist Reconfigurations of Agency

As we have seen, feminist IR scholars have thoroughly investigated the multiple dynamics of gendering international politics. In part, these dynamics have been so fascinating because the global "norm entrepreneurs" entered the international scene from the margins, that is, predominantly from the non-governmental sector. Thus, much of the gender in international governance literature has followed the footsteps of women's NGOs as primary actors for global change (Friedman 2003; Joachim 2007; Moghadam 2005; Naples and Desai 2002). Often, the massive efforts of raising global level awareness triggered by increasingly connected women's organizations from many parts of the world has been referred to as "global feminism." This concept, however, has been criticized for its implication that women around the globe share a homogeneous, feministset of interests that in reality is more reflective of Western perspectives than of the many forms of discrimination beyond gender that were foundational for non-Western women's subordinate positions (Mohanty 1984). This confrontation has not only exposed the danger of Western domination within transnational women's networks but also fostered a more understanding cross-cultural dialogue based on respecting heterogeneity (Moghadam 2005).

The importance of heterogeneity among and within women's networks has led many scholars to employ the term "transnational feminism" (Grewal and Kaplan 1994; Mackie 2001), also used in plural, or focus on the relevance of "local feminisms" as globally influential (Basu 1995). In accordance with the previously presented core assumptions of transnationality, transnational feminism challenges the foundations of modernity in "its colonial discourses and hegemonic First World Formations" (Grewal and Kaplan 1994, p. 2) and understands all cultural contexts as hybrids consisting of multiple and overlapping norms and sources of agency. Within global hegemonies and transnational cultural flows, gender relations are shaped by "scattered hegemonies" simultaneously consisting of "global economic structures, patriarchal nationalisms, 'authentic' forms of tradition, local structures of domination, and legal-juridical oppression on multiple levels" (Grewal and Kaplan 1994, p. 17). These hegemonies also reside within struggles for women's rights. Feminist activism may develop alternatives to global processes of marginalization, but it may as well reinforce existing inequalities (Mendoza 2002). Thus, the term "transnational feminism" reflects the understanding that border-crossing activism in the name of women is not automatically empowering for women but rather a form of connectivity that has been filled according to specific (if widely varying) interests. For example, feminist advocacy frames religion predominantly as a source of oppression and, thus, makes it hard for women who see religion as the foundation of their lives to connect to feminist discourses (Grewal 2008).

To use this feminist transnational lens for an analysis of CEDAW repercussions means to de-homogenize, de-essentialize and, basically, *complicate* agency positions and the connections between them in relation to women's rights, in particular in regard to international norms and institutions, states, and civil society organizations. *International institutions* affecting the realization of women's rights have to be understood as evolutionary and sometimes sending contradictory normative signals. As we have seen before, international normative packages are not fixed in meaning but are constantly in motion. In addition, they may collide with other international norms-in-motion. Ewelukwa (2005) shows how two international "value packages"—free trade and human rights—send contradictory messages to African women. The norm of free trade implies economic restructuring to adjust to a global economy, a process that infringes substantially on women's rights, especially their social and economic rights. International human rights norms, however, are not concerned with such "market produced" violations as long as they are not connected to state action. In order to address violations of women's rights comprehensively, Eweluka argues for a "bold reinterpretation of international human rights norms" (2005, p. 83) away from the exclusive focus on the nation-state as human rights violator and toward including other actors in this category (e.g., international, extraterritorial, or transnational).[8] Other examples for such contradictory international messages abound.[9]

Second, *states* are historically contextualized political entities embodying a broad variety of possible attitudes and reactions to international gender norms. States share, by legal definition, the quality of being a sovereign entity, but this is as far as isomorphism goes. Some are "weak" actors that cannot be called sovereign decision makers in a world where powerful nonstate actors—for example, international financial institutions—tell them what to do (Fall 2001). Also, their institutionalized monopoly of power may not reach far internally, in particular not towards the most marginalized sectors in which women are typically overrepresented. Other states *are* comparatively powerful and have the potential to create corporate gender identities (Savery 2007). Their institutional history of long-term exclusion of women from the public sphere often reinforces masculinist norms and practices (Kreisky and Marion 2009). To various degrees, states have become proactive in regulating family relations, reproductive rights, and social welfare. These forms of interference have turned the state into an explicit influence on gender relations, often with the goal (and sometimes with the effect) of creating a more gender equal society (Mazur 2002;

Tickner 2001, p. 120). However, the fact that most states now engage in some form of public gender policy does not tell us yet *in which way* they influence gender relations, only *that* they do it (Moghadam 2005, p. 200). Finally, states are also actors that have to situate themselves in response to diverse (and potentially contradictory) claims in respect to gender relations; these may come from various internal constituencies (e.g., women's movements, religious authorities, or the military) as well as external frameworks (e.g., the European Union) (Kardam 2004; Verloo 2007).

Third, given the heterogeneity of existing NGOs, it is probably accurate to think of this group of actors as exclusively defined by its non-governmental nature and not, in a more narrow sense, as a norm advocate that puts moral pressure on interest-driven state actors. While such an agency constellation is certainly observable, others are too. In developing countries, NGOs are often (perceived to be) part of resource-strong hegemonic coalitions of international organizations, Western governments, and donor organizations that do not connect with local needs and interests (Bagić 2006) and sometimes even weaken the existing infrastructure (Schuller 2012). Reiman speaks in this context of NGOs being the *result* of an international "pro-NGO norm" rather than triggers of norm diffusion, in particular in cases where donors make their financial support for developing states conditional on these states' acceptance of "NGOs as partners and critics" (Reiman 2006, p. 45). The more nationally based NGOs are anchored in international discourses and funding, the more they may cause fragmentation within domestic movements between those with transnational ties and sufficient professional expertise to acquire external funding and those without this cultural capital (Alvarez 2000; Friedman 1999). Also, nationally based NGOs may form precisely to resist international norms and foster a culture of domestic counter-hegemony (Buss 2004; Foley 2004), or they may form independently of such norms and with little motivation to connect to them (Basu 1995; Stachursky 2013).

The re-construction of international institutions as creators of a non-coherent and evolving "web of meaning," states as a group of actors showing a wide variety in terms of level of sovereignty and effects on gender relations, and NGOs as not exclusively ideationally driven norm entrepreneurs helps to better understand the complexities in which border-crossing women's activism is situated. At least four of such transnational actor constellations have been highlighted by feminist scholarship. The first is activism out of different contexts with the aim of making international institutions more gender sensitive and, at the same time, creating transnational space for collaboration. NGO activism advocating for women's rights norms has been dominant in this regard (Antrobus 2004; Joachim 2007; Reilly 2009; Williams 2013), but organizations that promote other models of gender politics have also become increasingly vocal (see Chap. 6; Buss 2004).

The second constellation is agency that makes use of international gender norms to influence domestic gender relations. This broad category contains activism that intends to transplant the international idea of gender equality norms into certain locales, in the sense of the previously presented dynamics of "vernacularization" and "betweenness," that is, always in a form that mixes the norms with lived realities. Promoting actor constellations are diverse. The "classical boomerang" case is that of transnationally connected non-governmental actors pushing a reluctant government, often embedded in societal institutions that favor gender hierarchies of different kinds. Different variations of this pattern can be found, for example, in Japan (Kobayashi 2004; Tanaka-Naji 2009), Ireland (Reilly 2007), Colombia (Simmons 2009), and Nepal (Pradhan Malla 2000). Also, the state could be leading the adoption of international norms, as in the case of Finland (Zwingel 2005b; Chap. 8), or there may be a coalition between non-governmental and governmental norm proponents, as in South Africa (Foster 2000), Brazil (UNIFEM 1998), or Chile (Zwingel 2005b; Chap. 8). In particular in contexts with prevalent patriarchal norms, the state may construct itself as mediator between gender equality norms and resisting constituencies. This may have a balancing (but more often a paralyzing) effect, as in the case of Lebanon (Sabat 2013). And finally, the attempt to bring international norms to local contexts may also be a process not including governmental actors, as in Thayer's study on the transnational and rather reciprocal collaboration between Western donor organizations, Western feminists, an urban Brazilian feminist NGO, and a rural Brazilian women's organization (Thayer 2010), or as in the sub-national work that is being done with CEDAW in the USA in a move to circumvent the national-level blockage of ratification (Lozner 2004).

The third constellation assembles domestic activism that rejects or cannot connect to international gender norms. Weiss' and Jamal's interpretation of the resonance of women's rights norms in Pakistan are a case in point. The state apparatus, conservative societal forces (Weiss 2003), and different women's organizations are suspicious about these norms, given the national context of failed modernist-development, authoritarianism and Islamization (Jamal 2005). Foley (2004) describes for Malaysia that many women's organizations do not consider the international notion of "gender equality" legitimate and have successfully lobbied to integrate the opposing idea of "gender equity" into national legislation. Similarly, Tønnessen (2011) finds that in Sudan, the notion of women's empowerment is linked to a certain interpretation of Islam and not to the women's rights framework, and Stachursky observes for Iran that it *adds* legitimacy to women activists' claims if they refrain from referring to international gender norms (Stachursky 2013).

Finally, there are also actor constellations that do not make reference to international norms, or if such norms play a role, they have merely indirect or unintended consequences. For example, McBride and Mazur (2006) have identified only a low, if generally supportive, level of influence on international gender norms and transnational cooperation between women's organizations in public gender policy formation in post-industrialized democracies. Rather, the widely differing debates on and regulations of issues like abortion, prostitution, and equal employment in post-industrialized democracies suggest that domestic actor constellations were the crucial factors in the domestic framing of policy issues. Also, transnational feminist organizations do often *not* refer to international frameworks (Eschle and Maiguashca 2010; Moghadam 2005). It seems that such decoupling is either an explicit choice, due to disenchantment with the intergovernmental logic, or a more pragmatic result of different proximities. It may also be that connection of different contexts does not always need an intergovernmental mediator; this is the lesson that Davis seems to draw from her study of the transnational travel of *Our Bodies, Ourselves*, the US-initiated and later global bestseller on women's health (Davis 2002). This process has been interactive, transnational, and largely autonomous.

Women's Rights in Motion: Global Discourse Translation and Impact Translation

The debates I have brought together in this chapter provide different insights into the possible repercussions of internationally codified norms. While the first debate develops its analysis from an international point of departure, the second treats global, national, or local contexts as mutually constitutive if shaped by "scattered hegemonies" of diverse power relations. From the international angle, a number of phenomena can be captured, in particular the creation of international norms, state behavior in response to international claims, and cases of concrete and traceable domestic compliance with an international norm. Such a top-down perspective makes it difficult, however, to analyze less unequivocal processes of norm production that are arguably the rule and not the exception. Transnationalization literature sees global norm creation and diffusion as a constant process of negotiating and re-negotiating norms. As strategies for change are produced by situated activism, global norms only resonate in ongoing and collective interpretations and practices. Accordingly, CEDAW is not an international standard but an instrument whose meaning and impact depends on contextualized agency.

For my analysis of CEDAW I would like to read (or "stitch") these two approaches together and focus on two dynamics of gender norms in motion: *global discourse translation* and *impact translation*. I use the term "translation" here instead of "diffusion" because, first, it seems better suited to grasp multi-directionality. Translation functions in many ways and directions, whereas diffusion seems to suggest a one-way movement, in the sense of "spread out from a given starting point." Second, translation is a more active term, the work of "making understand" is more implicit in it than in the idea of diffusion. Translation is also a term critically discussed, in particular in anthropology where the challenges of cross-cultural understanding are at the heart of the discipline. Translation is a complicated endeavor. While there is a genuinely enriching dimension in the encounter with the other, there is also manipulation, both in the sense of willful usurpation as well as in the "faithless appropriation" that creates new meaning in every confrontation and makes it impossible to stay true to the original (Chambers 2006; Tsing 1997). In this sense, I think of norm translation as allowing different avenues of cross-cultural encounters and transmissions of meaning. This notion suggests more variability than norm diffusion traditionally understood, both in terms of directionality and stability of norm content, but translation is nevertheless not a completely open process. Norms change all the time when being translated, but they do so incrementally. Also, my idea of translation emphasizes the work and agency in this process—norms are only being translated if there are translators.

My first constellation—*global discourse translation*—contains activism out of different contexts to influence international institutions and activists' use of such institutions to create transnational links and strategies of action. Cooperation and norm diffusion literature would call this focus global norm emergence and consolidation, but as I have argued, this focus underestimates dynamics of ongoing normative content variations and the "maintenance work" necessary to keep norms productive within inter-governmental settings. I see CEDAW as a piece of global discourse translation, when it was brought to the international agenda by governmental actors with overlapping, but by no means identical, ideas about women's rights (Rehof 1993) and during its more than three decades of existence. During this time, Committee members and other gender experts have worked hard to make the Convention's meaning internationally understood, accepted, and visible and, at the same time, constantly engaged in revisiting the meaning and reach of the Convention's provisions (Zwingel 2005b, 2013a). These processes of international meaning making within the inter-governmental context are elucidated in Chaps. 3, 4, and 5, and the first half of Chap. 6 sheds light on the non-governmental contribution to this global discourse.

The second formation—*impact translation*—includes all agency that connects to international gender norms in order to influence domestic gender regimes. As we have learned from quantitative impact studies on international human rights monitoring mechanisms, international-to-domestic impact is observable, to varying degrees, and altogether on a higher level than a pure interest-driven explanation would expect. In order to follow up on this general finding of impact, it is necessary to trace the actual connecting dimensions to not only show but also explain this impact, including resistances to it. This focus places emphasis on thoroughly characterizing both translating actor constellations and the context relevant for the act of translation. Given the broad variety of potential context factors, it is reasonable to assume that processes of impact translation include widely differing positions on women's rights, including rejecting ones that are typically not articulated in international encounters. However, such positions are harder to trace than affirmative ones as they are less likely to directly connect to CEDAW and the international women's rights framework. Another important dimension of impact translation is, just like for global discourse translation, to see it as a long-term process, with elements of continuity, as expressed in the ongoing scrutiny of states' policies through the CEDAW Committee, and concrete points of change (e.g., a direct reaction to the CEDAW framework). The second half of Chap. 6 and Chaps. 7 and 8 show various dimensions of impact translation, including work of norm translators that aim to create domestic ownership of the Convention, patterns of connectivity that states have established with the instrument, and agency that aims at context-adequate translation of CEDAW.

It is my hope that the "stretched" theoretical vision I have developed here helps expand our understanding of the resonance of internationally codified gender equality norms. The women's human rights framework consists of normative standards that are, within limits, open to interpretation. There are two main dynamics inherent in its translation: one is the continuous re-interpretation of the meaning of CEDAW *in context;* the other is the imperfect realization of this meaning.

Notes

1. For a discussion of the position of women's rights within the human rights framework, their particular nature of straddling the public and the private and their long neglect as less important "traditional" or "development issues," see Binion (1995); Bunch (1990); Charlesworth (1995); United Nations (1996).
2. While feminist approaches in IR are now well established, there is nevertheless a *tradition* of placing gender issues outside of disciplinary boundaries. Martha Finnemore and Kathryn Sikkink summarize this in an article written to celebrate the 50th birthday of *International Organization* (*IO*), one of the most important journals of the discipline. They state that *IO* had hardly ever published work on gender because of "a well-internalized norm…that research on gender and women did not constitute an appropriate topic for international relations scholarship." (Finnemore and Sikkink 1998, p. 894) This norm started to crumble in the late 1980s and early 1990s when works like Cynthia Enloe's *Bananas, Beaches and Bases* (1990) made us re-see so many allegedly gender neutral fields of international politics.
3. I use this term following Spivak's metaphor of "suturing" (2004). It seems fitting in the sense that it suggests cumbersomeness and constant human agency. To my taste, these characteristics are not well embodied in the somewhat effortless images of "norm cascading" or "boomeranging," even if the authors *show* human effort and agency in the processes they label this way (Sikkink 2011, p. 87ff).
4. While there is no doubt that some states comply more with human rights standards than others, it remains methodologically obscure how this position so neatly divides the world into two camps. An underlying "us" vs. "them" logic seems to be at work, as Western liberal democracies are often implicitly equaled with the group of human rights adherents.
5. Federal systems are supposed to be more difficult to connect with international norms than unitary systems because they do not control all areas of

governance on the national level. The same is true for common law systems in comparison to civil law systems because of the far-reaching authority of judges to interpret international treaties (Simmons 2009).

6. The notion of norm emergence is also, as Carpenter notes, under-theorized. As a consequence, processes that do not lead to "successful" global claims are largely ignored (Carpenter 2007).
7. For example, when Western states introduced women's suffrage, they framed this in terms of civilizational leadership. Socialist and post-colonial states introduced suffrage a bit later, and they framed this change in distinction to (and not emulation of) the Western capitalist and colonial legacies and made reference to own traditions of female empowerment.
8. There is a recent tendency within the international human rights framework to address other-than-state actors—for example, multinational corporations—as entities with human rights responsibilities (Pegg 2009), but this has not changed the notion of the state being primarily responsible for the realization of human rights.
9. One blatant example is the intergovernmental *recognition* of female vulnerability in and after armed conflict, especially regarding sexual violence, which has often been combined with an international *practice* of abuse of such vulnerabilities. Members of both international peace-keeping forces and humanitarian aid organizations have been shown to be involved in human trafficking and sexual exploitation (Ndulo 2009).

CHAPTER 3

The Creation of CEDAW within the Global Discourse on Gender Equality

The Convention on the Elimination of all Forms of Discrimination against Women was adopted by the UN General Assembly in 1979 and entered into force in 1981, in the middle of the UN-proclaimed Women's Decade (1976–1985). Due to its comprehensiveness and legally binding character, the Convention has often been called a milestone for the world's women (Pietilä and Vickers 1996). On the occasion of its 30th birthday in December 2009, UN Secretary General Ban Ki-Moon even called CEDAW "one of the most successful human rights treaties ever" (Inter Press Service 2009). This chapter tells the first part of the Convention's international development, or what I call global discourse translation. It lays out the global context of growing gender awareness in which the creation of CEDAW is embedded, starting with the foundation of the UN in 1945. It then portrays the drafting process of the Convention during the 1970s, including major controversies, and presents the main ideas enshrined in the text.

The following chapters—Chap. 4 on the evolution of the CEDAW monitoring committee, Chap. 5 on the new dimension added to the treaty through the Optional Protocol, and Chap. 6 on the work of norm translators to expand the Convention's reach—further contribute to the understanding of global discourse translation around CEDAW. Read together, these chapters reveal that treaty ratification, while a difficult result to achieve, is not the end of international norm creation. Rather, throughout the over three decades of the Convention's existence, there have been

S. Zwingel, *Translating International Women's Rights*,
Gender and Politics, DOI 10.1057/978-1-137-31501-4_3

ongoing and controversial interpretations both in regard to the content covered by the Convention and in regard to the mandate of its monitoring body. I argue that this principally unfinished international deliberation is not special to CEDAW but a crucial component of norm translation processes in general.

Women's Rights in International Context: Increased Awareness, Persisting Inequalities

The origins of international or transnational women's activism is usually dated back to the 1880s when a number of discernible women's organizations with international scope emerged. Studies on international organizing of women up to the mid-twentieth century have stressed four important fields of activism: women's suffrage, anti-war activism, demands for equal labor rights, and claims regarding the legal status of women, in particular in the field of marriage (Garner 2010; Rupp 1997; Stienstra 1994; Tripp 2006). If we define international activism as border-crossing and with a focus on lobbying international organizations, most of this activism had European or North American origins with notable exceptions, such as the Inter-American Commission of Women (Meyer 1999). Cast in a broader sense, women became active in many parts of the world, for example, to promote education for women and girls, end colonialism, and acquire national self-determination (Antrobus and Sen 2005; Jayawardena 1986; Tripp 2006). In the following, I look at women's activism related to the UN because this activism has been most relevant for the emergence of CEDAW. While the literature on UN-related women's activism has been growing steadily,[1] I am not aiming at a full account of these dynamics but provide a summary clustered into three broad phases: international knowledge formation from 1945 to 1975, global transformation from 1975 to 1995, and consolidation and new challenges from 1995 to the present.

International Knowledge Formation on Women's Issues (1945–1975)

According to Berkovitch (1999), the post-World War II situation provided fertile ground for the rise of women's issues as globally relevant for three reasons: first, the UN was founded as an international organization with the mandate to preserve world peace; second, due to decolonization processes, the UN soon became truly inclusive on a global scale; and third, it made the promotion of human rights an international concern for the first time in history. However, it was not within the human rights framework that women's issues became internationally prominent, even if the rights of women (e.g., in the form of non-discrimination clauses) are included in a number of pivotal human rights documents beginning with the Universal Declaration of Human Rights (UDHR) (Morsink 1991). Within the scope of international law, human rights law constitutes a challenge as its construction of the individual as legal *subject*, not *object*, creates a tension with the principle of state sovereignty. Hillary Charlesworth suggests that it might be this "comparatively radical, and vulnerable, nature of human rights law within the international legal order [that] has protected it from internal critique" (Charlesworth 1994, p. 63), that is, in respect to not addressing women's human rights concerns.

World peace, in contrast, was a goal that women's organizations mobilized for from 1945 on. There were both established Western-dominated organizations such as the International Council of Women (ICW), the Women's International League for Peace and Freedom (WILPF), and the newly founded and predominantly socialist Women's International Democratic Federation (WIDF). De Haan (2010a) points to the connections between these organizations, at least before Cold War bipolarity forced them into camps, and to anti-fascism as an important dimension of international women's organizing directly after WWII. Likewise, decolonization was a decisive dynamic for the emergence of global women's issues. The newly independent states took the UN seriously as an agent to support their self-reliance, in particular in socio-economic terms, and the UN aimed at supporting poor states by propagating various development models (Antrobus 2004). In the 1960s, female delegates from newly independent states emphasized the important role Third World women had played in the liberation of their countries, and they argued that the liberation of women was connected to national self-determination, both in political and socio-economic terms (Prashad 2007). This connection had not been made previously.

That the UN became an important global forum for discussing the status of women was not so much because of general institutional awareness but because of the work of committed advocates coming together in the Commission on the Status of Women (CSW). The UN General Assembly created the CSW in 1946 upon the request of the female delegate from the Dominican Republic, Minerva Bernardino (Galey 1995). Its functions were to prepare recommendations for the Economic and Social Council (ECOSOC) on promoting women's rights and on urgent problems requiring immediate action in the field of women's rights (United Nations 1996, p. 13). While it was first a sub-commission of the Commission on Human Rights, it became an independent body in 1947, partly because the Commission on Human Rights did not support its program (Morsink 1991) and partly because women's rights advocates strongly lobbied for a stand-alone body (Stienstra 1994). In the time between 1946 and 1975, the CSW was the most important space within the UN for the articulation of women's issues (Connors 1996a; Galey 1995). It was seen as "a kind of lobby for the women of the world" and as the most "independent body in the UN" (Humphrey 1983, p. 405). It had strong ties with national women's organizations because many members of the CSW headed such organizations in their home countries (Connors 1996a). However, the CSW's official mandate was rather narrow and its resources were limited (Berkovitch 1999). Also, beginning in the 1950s, it could not completely escape the fate of the UN as a whole to serve as a Cold War "battleground" (Baldez 2014; Laville 2002).

The first issues that were raised by the CSW were fact-finding on and strengthening of women's political and legal status. A global survey on the status of women's rights conducted in 1947 "revealed that of 74 sovereign states..., 25 had not granted full political rights to their female citizens, including the right to vote or hold public office" (United Nations 1996, p. 17). Subsequent CSW reports offered further evidence about sex-based discrimination in fields such as literacy and education. In the 1950s, the CSW initiated three legally binding documents: the Convention on the Political Rights of Women, which was adopted by the UN General Assembly in 1952 and came into effect in 1954[2]; the Convention on the Nationality of Married Women (1957/1958); and the Convention on Consent to Marriage, Minimum Age for Marriage and Registration of Marriages (1962/1964).

In the 1960s, the CSW moved from a focus on the legal status of women to one on their socio-economic advancement. It started to discuss ways to grant women equal access to education, employment opportunities and health care, and analyzed the specific needs of women in community and rural development, agricultural work, and family planning. This change of perspective was due to the promotion of economic rights by Eastern European countries and the emphasis that newly independent African and Asian countries placed on the needs of poor women as well as the key role of women in development (Boserup 1970; Galey 1995). A field where the focus on women became a truly transformative factor was population policy. Family planning had long been integrated into development policies with the goal of curbing population growth. However, these policies had never focused on women's needs and their role in family and society—the link had simply not been established. The CSW helped change this when it decided, after some serious contestation, to consider family planning as part of its mandate (Hussein 2004). A 1973 report on the interrelation of the status of women and family planning requested by the ECOSOC and written by Helvi Sipilä from Finland stands for the institutional learning process in this field. It established a strong connection between gender relations and population policies and concluded not only that family planning did benefit women as individuals but also that their improved status had a "decisive influence both on family size and on the success of family planning programmes" (UN Doc. E/CN.6/575/Rev. 1, p. 109f).

By the 1960s, the CSW had developed a comprehensive understanding of the multilayered forms of discrimination women encountered. This knowledge, however, had to be transmitted to a world where gender hierarchies were still idealized rather than seen as "odious or persecutory" (CSW working paper quoted in Cook 1995, p. 441). Thus, upon the request of the UN General Assembly, the CSW prepared a draft Declaration on the Elimination of Discrimination against Women (DEDAW) (GA Resolution 1921, XVIII). This Declaration[3] was to be a comprehensive document following up on the earlier single issue Conventions. The final version of the 1967 DEDAW consisted of 11 articles dealing with the elimination of discriminatory laws and practices (art. 2), the education of public opinion (art. 3), the right to suffrage and to hold public office (art. 4), nationality rights and civil rights on equal terms with men (art. 5 and art. 6), the elimination of discrimination in penal codes (art. 7), the abolition of trafficking in women and exploitation of prostitution (art. 8), equal rights in education (art. 9) and equal rights in economic and social life, especially in gainful employment (art. 10).[4]

DEDAW is representative for the understanding of women's concerns at the time. It contained "the first attempt to define discrimination against women by referring to laws, customs, regulations, practices and prejudice as being responsible for denying and limiting women's equality of rights with men" (Jain 2005, p. 46f), and it figured as an important point of reference during the CEDAW drafting process. Positions were highly controversial in the field of family law. Some delegations saw family laws based on patriarchal traditions as the major constraint to women's equality; others fought for the protection of these traditions and the unit of the family (United Nations 1996). Equal inheritance rights were not acceptable for delegations of some Muslim states. They suggested to add "where suitable," which, in the opinion of other delegations, would have undermined the spirit of the Declaration. In order to prevent *both* exclusion *and* relativization, it was therefore decided to "leave out any straightforward statement about equal inheritance rights" (Interview 1). Another of DEDAW's characteristic is its favoring of protective employment measures. These were based on a broad understanding of the physical differences between men and women, not on a focus on differences in regard to reproduction. Accordingly, the protection (or exclusion) of women from certain types of work "for reasons inherent in their physical nature" (art. 10 (3)) was seen as reasonable (McKean 1983).[5] On November 7, 1967, the UN General Assembly unanimously adopted DEDAW. In the following year, the ECOSOC initiated a voluntary reporting system on implementation of the Declaration (ECOSOC Res. 1325, XLIV), but only a few governments reported.

Devaki Jain describes this first period of knowledge formation as a time when "the tool of language [was used] to jump-start change" within the UN and "when the difference between ... law and practice, became obvious" (Jain 2005, p. 7 and 31). DEDAW can be seen as a symbol for the institutional comprehension of women's subordination, but it did not trigger much change. The CSW as institutional *and* movement-oriented women's space was paramount in this period, but it lost this hybrid character as governments started to send bureaucrats. This turned the CSW into a "more purely political and less of an expert body" (Galey 1995, p. 14) and reduced its mobilizing character.

Global Transformation: "A Feast of Knowledge and Power" (1975–1995)

On the initiative of the women's organization WIDF and after overcoming some governmental resistance,[6] the UN General Assembly declared the year 1975 International Women's Year of the United Nations. The same year, the first World Conference on Women was held in Mexico. It had "repercussions such as the initiators had hardly dared to dream of" (Pietilä and Vickers 1996, p. 76). Following the conference's World Plan of Action, the UN General Assembly proclaimed the years 1976–1985 the UN Decade for Women with a focus on equality, development, and peace. This Decade contained two more conferences, one in Copenhagen (1980) and one in Nairobi (1985). It became a watershed for placing women's concerns on the international agenda (Friedman 1995). While the conferences where technically intergovernmental affairs, they were used from the outset by women's organizations to establish transnational ties and to create an unprecedented global exchange of knowledge. The non-governmental organization (NGO) forum attached to each conference was the crucial venue for this process. Between 1975 and 1995, these encounters evolved visibly both in scope[7] and in the nature of their outcome documents. The Mexico World Plan of Action was a first collective inventory of the problems, and it did, more so than the subsequent conference platforms, follow governmental priorities.[8] The Copenhagen conference of 1980 is famous for the dominance of confrontational viewpoints between women from Western states (called the "First World" at the time) and women from Eastern and Southern states (the "Second" and "Third World") (Ghodsee 2012). However, it also "broke new ground by discussing the root causes of women's inequality" (Antrobus 2004, p. 50) and resulted in the demand of clear commitments from states to integrate women in social and economic development. The 1985 Nairobi Forward-looking Strategies emanated the most complex analysis of gender hierarchies of the Decade. The document identified macroeconomic structures as the most persistent obstacle to the achievement of gender equality and explicitly addressed new issues like violence against women and pornography. The 1995 Beijing Platform for Action reiterated the focus on economic structures and poverty eradication and added a number of new areas of concern (e.g., women's human rights, women in armed conflict, and women and the environment). Thus, the conference series stands for the development of a forceful, transnational public voice, for the acknowledgement of disagreements, and for a multi-vocal critique of a misled socio-economic development model (Antrobus 2004; Friedman 1995; Meyer and Prügl 1999). This fulminant process of articulating a global women's agenda was, however, paralleled by a shift from state-oriented towards market-driven development policies in the 1980s. These policies stressed structural adjustment programs, privatization policies, and self-help approaches to eradicate poverty and had a particularly negative impact on the living situations of poor women (Ewelukwa 2005; Fall 2001). The end of the Cold War exacerbated this trend as state socialism practically ceased to exist (Antrobus 2004, p. 54). Thus, during a phase of high-level sensitization regarding worldwide gender hierarchies, the living conditions of many women actually deteriorated.

Three innovations coming out of the Decade need to be highlighted. First, a set of new institutions working for gender equality was created. At the UN level, the Voluntary Fund for the UN Decade for Women was founded in 1976 and later converted into the UN Development Fund for Women (UNIFEM), a permanent development agency specifically dedicated to women within the UN Development Program (UNDP). The International Research and Training Institute for the Advancement of Women (INSTRAW) was brought into being in 1982. The adoption of CEDAW in 1979 manifested the international momentum in the field of women's rights. In addition to these new institutions with a specific focus on gender equality, already existing UN agencies were tasked with integrating a gender perspective into their respective mandates (Skard 2009). While this institutional representation of gender equality was an important achievement, none of these new entities or focal points received sufficient funding to carry out their mandates, and most of them were confronted with extremely limited channels of influence—some analysts even identify "systemic institutional sabotage" for gender equality work within the UN (Sandler and Rao 2012, p. 12). The result was a rather superficial integration of gender equality principles into the UN bureaucracy (ibid; Skard 2009). However, it should be noted that institution building in this time period went beyond the UN—the women's decade also triggered a trend among states to establish women's policy agencies (Mintrom and True 2001; Towns 2010).

Second, the global dialogue made possible by the conferences enabled a process of complex learning that first acknowledged differences among women and then envisaged joint strategies of action. A crucial factor in this learning was the articulation of women's voices from the Global South (at the time, called "Third World"). While women from East and West were better represented in terms of numbers and resources, women from the South increasingly seized the opportunity of the conferences and their preparatory processes to come together and develop their visions. During the Women's Decade, Southern women often collaborated with women's organizations from Socialist countries as their positions overlapped significantly, for example, in respect to establishing a new international economic order (Ghodsee 2012). This "tripod structure" was crucial for the articulation of differences and for eventually identifying common purposes. Western women were often pitted against a coalition of Second and Third World positions. They criticized women from the South and East for harnessing the conferences for political purposes, while Southern and Eastern women accused "First-World feminists" of imperialism and ignorance of poor women's problems. The controversy between "political issues" and "women's issues" has been described in many writings (e.g., Olcott 2010; West 1999), yet viewed in the long term, the conference encounters started a process of better understanding women in other circumstances and, as a result, enabled collaboration. As much as Western feminists became aware that women's concerns and socioeconomic inequalities were connected to each other, Southern women began to understand feminism "as a politics as relevant to Third World women as it was to women from North America and Europe" (Antrobus 2004, p. 57).[9] The creation of this common ground led to complex analyses and also to the debate of new issues, for example, violence against women in all its forms and reproductive health and rights (Joachim 2007). A process that was also enhanced by the women's decade was the critical assessment of international human rights law from a feminist perspective. Feminist layers criticized the androcentrism inherent in the human rights framework and formulated more gender-sensitive visions. These voices have become transformative for the UN human rights framework, in general, and for the understanding of the CEDAW, in particular (Nash 2002).

As a base for and result of these complex learning processes, the Decade had produced, thirdly, a vibrant, articulate global women's movement whose main nodes are transnational networks (Friedman 1995; Moghadam 2005; Naples and Desai 2002). It has been argued that, since Nairobi, Southern organizations have taken the lead in this transnational networking (Antrobus 2004; Tripp 2006). Western organizations have remained important as well, with Western governments and donors representing the dominant funding sources, while most Socialist women's organizations disappeared from the global landscape with the end of the Cold War. Paradigmatic for this networking culture is the organization Development Alternatives with Women for a New Era (DAWN), a network of women from the South. Since its foundation in 1984, it has delivered groundbreaking analyses on female poverty and alternative development strategies with a focus on women from the Global South. DAWN coined the now widely used term "women's empowerment." Its original meaning was to increase women's ability to act autonomously while at the same time transform oppressive gender relation and economic structures (Sen and Grown 1988). The networks and learning processes of the 1980s made women's movement actors particularly knowledgeable about reframing global justice issues in other fields as well. The UN conference marathon of the 1990s—Environment and Development (1992), Human Rights (1993), Population Policy (1994), Social Development (1994), and Women (1995)—was shaped to a remarkable degree by the input of women's networks. Particularly noteworthy was their influence on the Vienna Human Rights conference. Spectacular events were organized that effectively framed violence against women as a human rights violation and shed light on private, not only state-committed, human rights violations. At the end of 1993 and in clear reaction to the dynamics created at the Human Rights Conference, the UN General Assembly adopted the Declaration on the Elimination of Violence against Women (DEVAW). The Beijing conference in 1995 seems to ride on this wave of success. It became a "feast of knowledge and power" (Jain 2005, p. 143) where women took their complex knowledge a step further to demand participation in formal channels of power. They also demanded that gender should be taken seriously in all national and international decision making. This claim was laid down in the Beijing Platform for Action (BPFA) as "gender mainstreaming".

Consolidation and New Challenges (1995–Present)

The Beijing conference was a climax in terms of global awareness raising and maybe a natural point of decline in terms of UN-focused global activism. Since 1995, the BPFA has constituted an important point of reference; within the UN, its implementation has been evaluated in a series of follow up events—Beijing +5, +10, +15, and +20. However, initial enthusiasm with the conference results has not translated into strong governmental implementation efforts (WEDO 2005). More significantly, the general global context has shifted dramatically and turned the UN into a less significant international arena for gender equality claims. Two dimensions are particularly noteworthy in this regard. First, the macroeconomic conditions have not been supportive for realizing women's rights. After the failure of the purely market-oriented development paradigm dominant in the 1980s, International Financial Institutions (IFIs) adopted a new approach, the so-called post-Washington consensus. The point was to rediscover state institutions as important agents to enhance economic growth. Under the label of "good governance," states were now expected to reduce corruption, ensure the rule of law, and provide basic social services. While this sounds like a move toward more social justice, the new development approach is firmly focused on increasing global competitiveness; ideas such as non-discriminatory working conditions and living wages are subordinated to employability under all circumstances (Razavi 2013). Further, the trend toward deregulation in both developing and developed states has led to a crisis-prone concentration of capital. While the manifold crises since the late 1990s have had devastating effects on large parts of the world's population, the macroeconomic conditions remain virtually unchanged (Young 2013). The second dimension of global normative change is the growth of fundamentalist, often misogynist, ideologies. Economic hardships are known to give rise to fundamentalist doctrines, and they hardly ever envision a gender equal society. In addition to this rise, the post-9/11 shift toward national security and militarization has further contributed to a global climate in which gender equality claims are being de-prioritized at best and attacked at worst (Sen 2005). In other words, the "convergence of militarization, globalization, and conservatism has dealt a blow to the progress that was made at the UN on the social justice front" (Jain 2005, p. 135).

Arguably, the capacities of the UN to address global injustices have decreased in this climate. With the focus on "good governance," IFIs have expanded on their market-focused mandates and exert significant influence on social policies. In many aspects, the UN has taken the role of a follower within the IFIs' neoliberal framework, embodied, for example, in the Millennium Development Goals (MDGs) and the focus on microcredit programs for poor women.[10] Thus, the opening the UN had provided for women's rights claims started to narrow in the mid-1990s. Much of the energy of gender equality advocates within the UN had to be invested in defending rather than expanding on the status quo reached in Beijing, as this status quo was being challenged by anti-feminist positions (Hannan 2013; Sen 2005). These positions typically had religious underpinnings and joined forces in a "transnational conservative counter-network" (Chappel 2006) lead by the Holy See and consisting of states and NGOs alike (Sjorup 1995). Many feminist movement actors have turned away from the UN toward more independent spaces, such as the World Social Forums, to develop visions of global justice, or they have reoriented their work to national, local or "glocal" goals (Eschle and Maiguashca 2010; Wichterich 2007).

However, the collaborative relationships between NGOs and the UN and its several Specialized Agencies are still functional, and despite inimical circumstances, there are a number of issues that have gained new international weight, among them the confrontation of all forms of violence against women; gender-balanced decision making in form of quotas; the continuing realization of gender mainstreaming; the focus on the vulnerability of women in armed conflict and the aftermath as well as their participation in conflict transformation; and, still highly contested, the recognition of discrimination based on gender identity and sexual orientation as a human rights violation. Altogether, the institutionalization of gender equality measures within the UN has continued, even if some of these developments are viewed critically by feminist analysts.[11] In 2011, UN Women—the UN Entity for Gender Equality and the Empowerment of Women—came into being. It has replaced all previous gender-related agencies within the UN, is headed by an Under-Secretary General, and operates on a higher budget than its four predecessors[12] together. While this new entity can be interpreted as an adequate, if belated, institutional representation of the UN commitment to gender equality (Sandler and Rao 2012), it remains to be seen how substantial and transformative its impact will be (see also Chap. 6).

Creating CEDAW: The Drafting Process and Its Results

The drafting of CEDAW falls into the second of these three phases. As we have seen previously, non-discrimination on the grounds of sex was principally recognized within the human rights framework since 1948, but it required the increased level of global awareness that came with the Women's Decade to bring the notion of women's rights to life. According to de Haan (2010b), it was an NGO—the Union of Australian Women—that proposed the creation of a Women's Rights Convention as early as 1972. Around that time, the disappointing repercussions of the 1967 DEDAW and of the previously adopted issue-specific Conventions started to create the urge for a legally binding and comprehensive instrument among many international women's rights advocates. Until the adoption of CEDAW, there was no instrument within the UN human rights framework that systematically looked into female experiences of human rights violations. Feminist lawyers have provided in-depth critiques of this male-centeredness.[13] The crucial bias is the exclusion of the private sphere in human rights law. From this follows that, for example, the right to life is constructed as a right to be protected from arbitrary action of *public* institutions, not from *private* attacks or material circumstances that threaten life. However, women are more at risk to be killed by family members than by state institutions, and they are also more likely than men to die from malnutrition and lack of health care services. Birth-related morbidity and mortality is a threat to the right to life and physical integrity exclusively experienced by women, and hence it was long not seen as a "general" (read: male-experienced) human rights concern (Nash 2002).[14]

With its focus on women, CEDAW has been a crucial impulse for making the UN human rights system and international human rights law as a whole more gender sensitive. The text of the Convention is shaped by the understanding that states are responsible to work for the equality of women with men through eliminating all forms of discrimination against women. This was a tremendous success given the long de facto disregard of women's enjoyment of human rights, but the Convention has also been criticized as not far reaching enough since it "only gives women access to a world already constituted" (Charlesworth 1994, p. 64). In other words, the Convention generally accepts the status quo and assumes that women should enjoy existing rights that were crafted with male humans in mind. It does not transform the human rights framework with a view of fully representing women's experiences (Johnstone 2010a).

Drafting the Convention

The process of creating the CEDAW developed in three stages. First, the CSW worked on a draft from 1974 to 1976. This stage, more so than the others, was shaped by delegates strongly committed to gender equality. When the CEDAW working group of the CSW first met, it anticipated obstacles to the enterprise, both in relation to the content of the Convention and its supervising mechanism (González 2000; Hussein 2004; Shahani 2004). Thus, CSW members who had long worked for a comprehensive Convention were aware that "a cautious negotiation process" (González 2000, p. 5) was necessary. Despite growing tensions in the 1976 session, the CSW managed to approve a draft Convention. Since some issues were not resolved, the document was adopted without a vote and alternative proposals on the controversial issues were included. NGOs did not play an important role in the drafting process, and those that contributed had access only to the CSW negotiations, not to the following stages (Connors 1996a).

The second and third phase of the drafting process took place in Working Groups of the Third Committee[15] to the UN General Assembly (1977–1979), and finally, in December 1979, in the Third Committee as a whole. The agreement reached in the Third Committee was then immediately discussed and adopted by the UN General Assembly. In both stages, governmental concerns were more forcefully represented than in the CSW. Jacobson characterizes the debates in the Third Committee's working group as "long and painful," despite the fact that it began its work with an almost finished draft (1991, p. 446). There were sharp disagreements on content issues and on implementing and monitoring provisions (Burrows 1985; Fraser 1995; Jacobson 1991). Until late 1979 the Working Group had not managed to reach a compromise on all controversial issues and passed the draft, including irreconcilable passages "in brackets," on to the Third Committee. In the last stage of the drafting process, the controversy was ended in four swift sessions because delegations wanted to have the document ready and open for signature at the time of the 1980 World Women's Conference in Copenhagen. The draft Convention was sent to the UN General Assembly for adoption in December 1979. In the debate preceding the adoption, most delegations showed enthusiasm regarding the importance of women's rights, but the document itself was also heavily criticized (UN Doc. A/34/107). For example, the representative of Morocco explained the country's abstention by stating "that delegations failed to understand how vital it is that this Convention strike a fair balance among all existing legal systems. Extremism will never lead to the desired results and goals" (UN Doc. A/34/107, para. 41). Other delegates referred to the incompatibility between the Convention and their national laws and announced that their governments might ratify the document with reservations. The Convention was adopted on December 18, 1979, by a vote of 130 states in favor, 0 against, and 10 abstentions.[16]

The negotiation process was so contentious because the notion of women's rights challenged deeply entrenched social traditions—traditions that were seen as culturally legitimate practices, *not* as human rights violations and certainly not as a realm in which a state's sovereignty should be infringed upon. Simultaneously, the dynamics of the Women's Decade were producing global awareness for the manifold dimensions of women's subordination and for the need to work for gender equality. Five lines of conflict can be identified in the drafting process. The first circled around the strength of the enforcement mechanism. The delegations favoring a weak, non-intrusive mechanism succeeded (Rehof 1993). The other four lines of conflict were content-related. The most antagonistic one ran between two concepts of women, often pitched as secular versus religious visions. The first one saw women as individuals endowed with enforceable rights; the second one perceived them as fulfilling a specific role in family and society and understood the concept of women's rights as linked to that role. Since the first position succeeded more often in the final wording of the Convention, many of the reservations entered to the Convention have aimed to preserve the second notion of women, often with a reference to religious or cultural traditions (see Chap. 7).

The other three lines of conflict were not substantially antagonistic and have increased the Convention's comprehensiveness. One ran between an emphasis on discrimination against women and discrimination based on gender. The first position is dominant in the text, but the proponents of gender-based discrimination were successful in incorporating their point in several articles as well. It should perhaps be noted that the term "gender" as it is understood today was not yet in use and that the drafters understood "sex" to *include* social positions and roles of men and women (Byrnes 2012a).[17] The difference between the two positions lies in the exclusive focus on women versus a focus on transforming the relation between men and women in order to reach equality. The other two lines of conflict were a confrontation between capitalist and socialist views on women's rights—inevitable in the historical context of bipolarity but not detrimental to the content of the Convention—and on some occasions, between the different priorities of industrialized and developing countries.

The Convention's Content

To present the Convention in a nutshell[18]: the *Preamble* enumerates the existing international human rights instruments relevant for the status of women and expresses the need to go beyond them, since discrimination against women continues to exist. It underlines the crucial contribution of women to the well-being of family and society and calls for a change in the traditional role models for men and women, especially concerning the upbringing of children. Further, it makes a connection between the elimination of discrimination against women and the establishment of a new international economic order, the eradication of apartheid, racism, and colonialism and the strengthening of international development, peace, and security. It does not contain binding legal obligations (Chinkin and Rudolf 2012).[19]

The following 30 articles of the Convention are organized into six parts: sections 1–4 enclose the substantive provisions; sections 5 and 6 regulate implementation and ratification of the Convention. Part one conveys the general provisions of the Convention, starting with the broad definition of "discrimination against women" in article 1. Article 2 enumerates "all appropriate measures" the ratifying states (States Parties) should undertake to reach equality between men and women. These measures include: the embodiment of equality in the constitution and legislation; the abolishment of discriminatory laws, regulations, customs, and practices; and the prevention of discriminatory behavior by state and non-state actors. Article 3 guarantees basic human rights and fundamental freedoms for women. Article 4 declares permissible, and in effect, encourages temporary special measures in order to accelerate the achievement of de facto equality between men and women as well as special measures to protect maternity. Article 5 obliges States Parties to modify social and cultural patterns based on the inferiority or superiority of either sex and ensure the common responsibility of men and women in the upbringing of their children. Article 6 calls for the suppression of trafficking of women and exploitation of prostitution.

Parts 2–4 specify these general provisions in substantive fields. Part two covers political rights. It stipulates that women should have the same political rights as men and encourages their political participation on the national (art. 7) and international level (art. 8). Article 9 confers identical nationality rights to women and men, including the same entitlement in terms of passing on one's nationality to natural children. Part three contains the right to equal education (art. 10); equal employment (art. 11); equal health care and access to health care services, including those related to family planning (art. 12); and equal access to financial benefits and cultural activities (art. 13). Article 14 deals with the needs of women living in rural areas, specifically, and the measures required to ensure their equality. Part four regulates matters of civil law. Article 15 grants women equality before the law and in legal proceedings. The comprehensive article 16 decrees that marriage and family relations have to be based on equal rights and responsibilities. This includes that both spouses have the right to enter into marriage with free and full consent and to decide freely on the number and spacing of children, that they have the same rights with respect to ownership, acquisition, and disposal of property during marriage, and that they have equal responsibilities with respect to the guardianship of children. Also, a minimum age for marriage should be specified and child marriage shall have no legal effect.

Part five regulates the implementation procedure of the Convention. According to article 17, an independent monitoring committee of 23 experts has to be installed. Article 18 specifies the reporting obligations of the States Parties. The Committee has the right to adopt its own rules of procedures (art. 19), and its mandate is to report to the UN General Assembly and to make suggestions and general recommendations both to the UN and to the States Parties (art. 21). The time and place of Committee meetings are laid down in article 20. Article 22 allows Specialized Agencies to participate in the reporting procedure. Part six contains modes of ratification and entry into force (articles 25, 27, 30), of revision of the Convention (art. 26), admissible reservations (art. 28), and dispute settlement (art. 29). It also states that no national regulation "more conducive" to achieve gender equality should be affected by the Convention (art. 23) and that states should undertake "all necessary measures" to the full realization of rights recognized in the Convention (art. 24).

Box 3.1: CEDAW in a Nutshell

Art. 1 Definition of discrimination against women
Art. 2 State obligations
Art. 3 Guarantee of fundamental freedoms
Art. 4 Temporary special measures/protection of motherhood
Art. 5 Modification of gender stereotypes
Art. 6 Suppression of trafficking and exploitation of prostitution
Art. 7, 8 Equality in public life, political participation, and international representation of government
Art. 9 Equality in nationality rights
Art. 10 Equality in education
Art. 11 Equality in employment
Art. 12 Equality in access to health care and appropriate services for child bearing
Art. 13 Equality in respect to family benefits, financial credit, sports, and culture
Art. 14 Elimination of discrimination against rural women
Art. 15 Equality before the law
Art. 16 Equality in marriage and family
Art. 17 Set-up of Committee
Art. 18 States Parties' reporting obligations
Art. 19–21 Committee's rules of procedure; election of officers; meeting time and venue; annual report, suggestions and recommendations
Art. 22 Involvement of specialized agencies
Art. 23 More conducive regulations
Art. 24 State Parties' obligation to undertake all necessary measures
Art. 25–27 Signatures, ratifications, and accessions; revisions of the Convention; entry into force
Art. 28 Reservations to the Convention
Art. 29 Dispute settlement
Art. 30 Languages and depository

Major Debates During the Drafting Process

The debates on articles 1, 2, 5, 9, and 16 are particularly interesting in order to grasp controversial assumptions in respect to women's rights during the drafting process.[20] The definition of "discrimination against women" in article 1 represents both the "women only" and the "gender-based" approach to discrimination. It targets women, specifically, but also contains the passage "on a basis of equality of men and women"; the inclusion of the latter was a reaction to the proposal to replace women-specific with sex-based discrimination, generally, which would have included discrimination against men; this idea was discussed in the CSW but did not find a majority (Rehof 1993, p. 44). The wording of article 1 was first emulating the discrimination definition of the Convention on the Elimination of Racial Discrimination (CERD) and included "any distinction, exclusion, restriction or preference on the basis of sex," yet "preference" was deleted in order to enable preferential treatment of women (Burrows 1985; McKean 1983). The wide scope of discrimination shows that the CSW was acutely aware of the importance of the civil or private sphere for the status of women. A first draft listing "the political, economic, social, cultural or any other field of public life" was amended and "public life" was deleted because it did not address the family as sphere of importance (Rehof 1993, p. 49). Further, "civil" was added after "cultural." Also, the definition explicitly includes all women "irrespective of their marital status." The broad scope of discrimination as laid out in this article, in particular the addition of "any other field," makes the Convention a dynamic document—it allows an interpretation of new forms and fields of discrimination (Schöpp-Schilling 2007a, p. 25).

Notably, article 1 contains neither a definition of "women" nor of "gender equality," which was the ultimate goal of eliminating discrimination against women. Chinkin and Freeman (2012) argue that "women" is meant to include girlhood. This scope is confirmed by the focus of a number of articles, most explicitly by article 10 on education. The notion of "gender equality" implicit in the Convention can be characterized as a mix of formal and transformative equality (Byrnes 2012a). Formal equality as the idea that men and women should, in principle, be treated equally in all spheres of life is most often made explicit in the text. Many delegations were opposed to this concept, especially in the field of marriage and family, which they considered to be shaped by complementary male and female roles (McKean 1983). However, the concept of equality as sameness falls short in addressing life experiences of women that cannot be compared with men's because they are different (e.g., violence against women and women's reproductive capacities). Thus, a transformative notion of gender equality aims at changing androcentric structures rather than making women more equal with men *within* such structures. The Convention contains some dimensions of this principle as well. In article 1, this is expressed in the wording "any distinction, exclusion, or restriction made on the basis of sex which has the effect or purpose" to discriminate against women. The term "effect" addresses unintended and, thus, structural forms of discrimination that need to be eliminated (Byrnes 2012a).

Article 2 specifies measures to eliminate discrimination States Parties should undertake "by all appropriate means and without delay." It is a crucial article because it tells states in a concise way what their obligations under the Convention are. It has a strong focus on legal measures—states need to abolish discriminatory laws, integrate the principle of equality in the constitution and other appropriate legislation, legally prohibit discrimination and protect the rights of women. However, it also goes beyond the legal realm and obliges public institutions to refrain from discrimination and to take "appropriate measures" to prevent discrimination against women "by any person, organization or enterprise." Thus, the state has an "obligation of result" in regard to the non-discriminatory behavior of state institutions and an obligation of "due diligence" as to the behavior of private and non-state actors (Byrnes 2012b). In a comprehensive way, article 2 represents both de jure and de facto equality. During the drafting process, it was precisely the comprehensiveness of measures to be included that caused controversy. An early joint draft of the USSR and the Philippines left states' obligations quite vague. It was later replaced by a detailed proposal submitted by Belgium, which became the final version of the article, with three important amendments. First, the original provision that states should insert the principle of non-discrimination into their constitution was widened to include "national constitutions or other appropriate legislation." Second, the paragraph on the elimination of discriminatory laws, regulations, customs, and practices was weakened in replacing the term "nullify" with the more moderate "modify" (Rehof 1993, p. 59). Third, the provision to promote "organizations and movements whose purpose is to advance the status of women" supported in the CSW was later rejected (Gonzalez 2000, p. 6). This would have been the only explicit reference to women's NGOs and their role in realizing the goals of the Convention.

Article 5 calls for measures to overcome social and cultural patterns of discrimination "based on the idea of the inferiority or the superiority of either of the sexes or on stereotyped roles for men and women." In conjunction, it questions fixed parental roles that stereotypically align the child closer to the mother than to the father (Holtmaat 2012). The joint draft of the USSR and the Philippines first contained the legal prohibition of "any advocacy of the superiority of one sex over the other," yet this was considered an infringement of the freedom of speech by Columbia, Finland, and the USA, and therefore the final wording was softened (Rehof 1993, p. 79f). The proponents of a gender equality approach in respect to family responsibilities successfully anchored two ideas into article 5: first, the recognition of motherhood as a social function and the promotion of this idea through "family education"; and second, the "common responsibility of men and women in the upbringing and development of their children" (Rehof 1993, p. 82f). This understanding of maternity and family relations had its opponents. For example, Morocco expressed the conviction that within the family,

> the mother had a privileged role. Therefore, the right which mothers had with regard to their children...could not be sacrificed in the name of equality of the sexes. That right should never be handed over to extremist feminists who rejected motherhood. (UN Doc. A/C.3/34/SR. 70, para. 7)

Probably because of such opposition, article 5 remains extremely vague in terms of implementation. It contains an obligation for states—the modification of social and cultural patterns—yet it does not define *which* patterns need to be modified and neither does it clarify how such modification should be carried out (Burrows 1985). However, article 5 is also the article where ideas of transformative equality are most explicit, as it specifies the need to modify female *and* male social roles for the achievement of women's rights (Nash 2002). In the Committee's practice, the breadth of article 5 has played an important role, in particular in bringing states to look beyond legislative into cultural change in order to achieve substantive equality (Sepper 2008). Also, the Committee has come to understand that implementation of article 5 is a gradual process, yet one that nevertheless requires strong initiative from States Parties (Holtmaat 2012).

In its General Recommendation 25, the Committee declared articles 1 through 5 together with article 24 to be the "general interpretive framework of States Parties' obligations under the Convention." Thus, the content of these articles is supposed to serve as guideline for the implementation of the more specific substantial articles. Further, the open-ended wording of some of these articles—for example, "and any other field" in article 1 and "in all fields" and "exercise and enjoyment of human rights and fundamental freedoms on a basis of equality with men" in article 3—have been used by the Committee as a tool for the "progressive and dynamic interpretation" of the Convention (Chinkin 2012a, p. 122). As Chap. 4 shows in further detail, the Committee has expanded the list of issues it considers to be covered by the Convention, arguing that this is necessary to make it a holistic tool to address women's rights violations, including those that are newly emerging. It has grounded this practice in articles 1 and 3 in particular, arguing that "fundamental freedoms" also include rights that are not explicitly mentioned in the Convention (Byrnes 2012a).

Article 9 contains two parts: first, women should have "equal rights with men to acquire, change or retain their nationality," and these rights should not be affected by marriage to an alien; second, women should have "equal rights with men with respect to the nationality of their children." These two dimensions challenge the legal concept of dependent nationality of women, which at the time of the Convention's drafting was still rather widespread (Goonesekere 2012). According to this concept, a woman did not have a separate personal and legal identity but was under the "wing of protection" of either father or husband; accordingly, she acquired her husband's nationality upon marriage, and children resulting from this union automatically obtained their father's nationality. Some states (e.g., Afghanistan, Argentina, Iraq, and Ethiopia) opposed the first part of article 9 by simply declaring that neither their nationality laws nor their marriage laws were in accordance with it (Rehof 1993, p. 105). The second part faced resistance for similar reasons. Some delegations, for example, Libya and Syria, declared that in their national law, the nationality of a child was automatically that of the father. Other objections were voiced by Denmark, which wanted to give the welfare of the child priority over the right to pass on one's nationality, and Pakistan, which feared that the provision would increase the number of people with dual nationality (Rehof 1993, p. 103f). The final wording of article 9 (2) is rather broad ("with respect to") and does not contain an explicit equal right of parents to *transmit* their nationality to their children. Article 9 represents a comprehensive notion of equal nationality rights: the first part eliminates dependent nationality for adult women, and the second corrects the tradition of exclusive descent of nationality through the father. This second dimension had not been stated in any previous document, and it had to be put to a separate vote in the UN General Assembly. The 92 (in favor), 13 (against), and 28 (abstentions) vote shows the considerable opposition to article 9 (2). States Parties have also entered a comparatively high number of reservations to both article 9 (1) and (2).

Articles 15 and 16 guarantee women equality in civil matters. Civil rights include a broad set of rights, yet CEDAW focuses on five areas that were considered most important to women: equality with men before the law; equal legal capacity with men in all civil matters; the prohibition of any restriction on women's legal capacity; the same right as men in respect to freedom of movement and choice of residence (covered in article 15); and equal rights with men in matters of marriage and the family (covered in article 16).[21] Articles 15 and 16 were built on DEDAW article 6, but other than the 1967 Declaration, they did not link women's civil rights to "safeguarding the unity and harmony of the family." Article 16 covers both equal rights in marriage and prohibits child marriage, a phenomenon that negatively affects many more girls than boys. It was the most controversial article during the negotiation process and has become subject to the highest number of reservations[22] to the Convention (Freeman 2012, p. 441), predominantly because the realm of the family is the field where gender stereotypes and power asymmetries are most deeply entrenched. It is also the social context where the imbalance of male control and female nurturing and subordination has been celebrated as the most adequate gender order in terms of cultural, traditional, and religious values. Article 16, in contrast, embodies an idea of family and marriage in which the spouses are equal in rights and responsibilities and mature enough to take conscientious decisions, starting with the voluntary decision to get married (Freeman 2012). Several specific controversies arose during the drafting process, for example, related to paragraph 1(c) on equal rights during marriage and at its dissolution. Egypt, Indonesia, and Iran found the mentioning of "dissolution" problematic and declared it conflictive with their national laws. The Moroccan delegation argued that the notion of equal rights did not acknowledge the complementary roles of men and women in the family that "had arisen in the deep consciousness of the human race" and that a clear distinction between the two was "necessary for the physic and moral balance of children" (UN Doc. A/C.3/34/SR. 70, para. 11). Article 16 (1c) remained controversial until the end of negotiations and was put to a separate vote in the UN General Assembly (104: 0: 32). Paragraph 1(d) on equal responsibilities of parents was also heatedly debated. First, a version was adopted that stressed the rights of single mothers, yet the implicit acceptance of extramarital relationships was unacceptable for some countries (Rehof 1993, p. 177). In the Third Committee the United Kingdom suggested replacing "whether married or not" with "irrespective of their marital status." This wording included "unmarried," but did not place emphasis on unmarried motherhood as it could also be understood as "divorced" (Burrows 1985, p. 451). Disagreement also arose in regard to gender equal property rights within marriage, to the degree that a mentioning of inheritance on equal grounds was left out entirely (Freeman 2012).

Of the remaining substantial articles, some were largely uncontroversial, especially if preceding legal documents existed. This was the case for article 6, which is basically a reference to the Convention on the Elimination of Trafficking in Persons and Exploitation of Prostitution (1949), and also for articles 7 and 8, which are modeled after the Convention on the Political Rights of Women (1952). Article 7 (c) contains the unique provision for states to ensure that women are not discriminated against participating in "non-governmental organizations and associations concerned with the public and political life of the country." This restricts the principle of freedom of association for organizations such as political parties, trade unions, and religious organizations (Wittkopp 2012). Other articles further developed earlier documents, such as article 10 on education, which was based on the UNESCO Convention against Discrimination in Education (1960) as well as on DEDAW. Article 10 reiterates the two-dimensional responsibility of states to both eliminate discrimination against women in education and facilitate their enjoyment of the right to education, yet it does so in a more comprehensive manner than earlier documents. For example, it states that girls and women should have access to the same educational facilities as boys and men from preschool age to adulthood, encourages co-education as one dimension within the broader attempt to eliminate gender stereotypes and underlines the importance of education in family planning (Banda 2012; Rehof 1993, p. 112f). Similarly, article 11 on equal employment rights expands on several ILO Conventions and the Covenant on Economic, Social and Cultural Rights, yet it does so in a "non-symmetrical,"—that is, women-centered—fashion (Raday 2012b) and with a specific focus on ending discrimination against women in employment on the grounds of marriage or maternity. Among other provisions, it asks states to introduce "maternity leave with pay or with comparable social benefits" and to take appropriate measures "to enable parents to combine family obligations with work responsibilities." The first is a provision that recognizes the need to deal with women's childbearing role in the workplace, and the second aims at transformative equality in conjunction with article 5 (Raday 2012b). In the discussion over article 11, the block confrontation was most prevalent with Western states favoring a concept of equal opportunity and socialist states pushing for protective measures (Rehof 1993, p. 125f).

A significant amount of the procedural provisions in part 5 and 6 of the Convention were controversial during the drafting process. For example, delegations were divided over the nature of the monitoring body for the Convention. The final version of article 17 stipulates it to be an independent advisory body comprised of 23 experts of "high moral standing and competence in the field covered by the Convention" rather than a working group of the CSW, which would have made its membership be comprised of governmental representatives. Thus, the importance to avoid any political motives in the monitoring procedure is recognized, even if the fact that candidates have to be nominated by their governments potentially interferes with their independence (see Chap. 4). It is partly a result of this debate that the Convention is the only human rights treaty that provides for a fixed annual meeting time of only two weeks (art. 20), as this would have been a common construction for a CSW working group (Boerefijn 2012a). Another controversy arose over whether or not States Parties should be allowed to enter reservations to the treaty. Some delegates aimed at limiting this option, but others pointed to the Vienna Convention of the Law of Treaties (VCLT 1969) that explicitly permits states to ratify international treaties with reservations (Rehof 1993).

Article 28 goes along with the VCLT and allows reservations as long as they are not "incompatible with the object and purpose" of the treaty. There was some debate as to how "incompatibility" of reservations with the treaty should be determined,[23] but in the final version of the text, this issue is not addressed. This vagueness has opened the door to a high number of reservations, which have been a major concern throughout the Committee's work (see Chaps 4 and 7). Other procedural issues were non-controversial and largely modeled after already existing human rights treaties, for example, the monitoring process based on periodic reports to be submitted by States Parties in a four-year cycle (art. 18) and the right of the Committee to design its own rules of procedures in order to organize its work, in general, and the constructive dialogue, in particular (art. 19).

Assessing the Instrument

Without doubt, CEDAW represents a big step forward in the promotion of women's rights. It is "the definitive international legal instrument requiring respect for, and observance of, the human rights of women; it is universal in reach, comprehensive in scope and legally binding in character" (Cook 1995, p. 441). Nonetheless, the Convention has also been criticized for both inappropriate substantial (e.g., Charlesworth 1994; Donner 1994; Zearfoss 1991) and overly cautious procedural provisions (e.g., Byrnes 1989; Jacobson 1991; Meron 1990). It contains a tension between a rather comprehensive vision both on discrimination against women and on equality of women with men, on the one hand, and a low-key monitoring mechanism modeled after the interests of states, on the other.

In terms of content, the definition of "discrimination against women" in article 1 responds to the problem of pervasive gender hierarchies in all spheres of life, and the Convention holds states responsible to work against *all* manifestations of it. The concept of equality of women and men enshrined in CEDAW is likewise comprehensive and committed to de facto, not only formal equality. While earlier international documents dealing with the status of women often had a protective character, CEDAW is predominantly based on non-discrimination (Hevener Kaufman 1986). It contains only narrow protective provisions in respect to pregnancy and maternity in articles 4 (2) and 11 (2). Non-discriminatory provisions aim "to revise the legal system in such a way that gender will no longer be a basis for the allocation of benefits and burdens in society" (Hevener Kaufman 1986, p. 78). The content of CEDAW predominantly follows this principle. The general goal is equality of women with men, as set forth in the definition of article 1 and spelled out in articles 2, 3, 7, 8, 9, 10, 11, 13, 15, and 16. Jain (2005) also points to the substantial change CEDAW stipulates in going beyond the elimination of discriminatory laws and including the modification of misogynous customs and stereotypes, and in explicitly making the state responsible to eliminate discriminatory behavior of private actors. Some articles, most specifically article 5, call for a modification of traditional roles and therewith challenge androcentrisms (Byrnes 2002; Nash 2002). There are also omissions in the substantial articles of the treaty. It does not explicitly deal with core dimensions of the human rights framework—such as the right to life, freedom from torture, and freedom of belief and religion—maybe because these rights were not seen as most pressing for the problems women were facing. Other issues cannot be found in the text because they have emerged as powerful global discourses only after the time of drafting, prominently violence against women and discrimination based on sexual orientation and gender identity (Rosenblum 2011). Altogether, it seems fair to say that CEDAW is suitable to enhance the "ongoing transformation of all aspects of sex, gender and sexuality in the name of equal treatment for all individuals" (Nash 2002, p. 421).

In contrast to its substantial strengths, the Convention offers only a low-key mechanism to oversee the implementation of its ambitious goals. Three dimensions seem particularly problematic. According to the text of the treaty, the Committee has no mandate to establish connections to NGOs, it has no way to verify the admissibility of reservations, and its functionality is restricted by an annual meeting time of only two weeks. As the following chapters will show, this extremely unsatisfactory starting point has been widened both formally and informally.

Understanding the Convention in a Changing Global Environment

It took women's rights advocates three decades, from 1945 to 1975, to make their point within UN agencies that women's subordination is a relevant international policy issue. However, this new global awareness remained largely declaratory. The time for more substantial steps came between 1975 and 1995, when the world women's conferences enabled powerful advocacy for women's concerns that resonated worldwide. In this phase falls a good deal of institution building, which is proof that women's issues were taken more seriously by powerful actors than before. Also, there were more holistic articulations of and debates about "women's interests"—these included fierce disagreements, cross-cultural learning and transnational coalition building. The final phase (1995 to present) is shaped by disappointment in light of the fact that global awareness raising, as powerful as it may have been, has not translated into significant change for women. As Jain puts it, "the unpeeling of the layers of equality goes on, and it is a blot on the humanscape that inequality is now on the increase" (2005, p. 160). As it stands, international and transnational struggles for gender equality are ongoing. Table 3.1 summarizes the developments presented.

Table 3.1 Global gender norms in context, 1945 to present

Phase	*Global context*	*Relevant actors, events, and documents*	*Prevalent gender norms*
1945–1975	Foundation of UN; Cold War; human rights framework; decolonization; development as global task (modernization, state-oriented paradigm)	CSW (1952: Convention on the Political Rights of Women; 1957: Convention on the Nationality of Married Women; 1962: Convention on Consent to Marriage; 1967: DEDAW)	Political rights for women Family law based on gender equality Education of women Women and socio-economic development Population policy linked to status of women Protective employment measures
1975–1995	From state-oriented to market-oriented development paradigm; end of block confrontation	World women's conferences 1975–1995; 1990s conferences (environment, human rights, population); UNIFEM (1976); CEDAW (1979), INSTRAW (1982); DEVAW (1993); NGOs and transnational networks (e.g., DAWN)	Comprehensive development framework based on needs and contributions of women Equal employment measures Elimination of violence against women Empowerment of women Women's rights as human rights Reproductive rights and health
1995-present	"Post-Washington consensus"; increased economic disparities and crises; rise of fundamentalisms; new militarization	Dispersion and re-orientation of women's NGOs; rise of anti-feminist networks; UN Women (replacing UNIFEM, INSTRAW, DAW, OSAGI); SC Resolution 1325 and following resolutions	Gender mainstreaming Gender-balanced decision making (quotas) Micro credits for women Elimination of violence against women Women, peace and security Sexual orientation discrimination

CEDAW is embedded in and part of these dynamics. Its content is inspired by legal developments in phase one and was a product of the global rise of gender awareness in phase two. The Convention stands for a comprehensive understanding of discrimination against women and the idea of "equality of outcome." In its historical context, it signifies a big step forward in the promotion of women's rights. Despite controversies regarding the understanding of women's role in society, the document is shaped by a vision of women as autonomous rights holders. The Convention's monitoring mechanism is designed cautiously and is exclusively state-oriented; non-governmental women's rights organizations do not play a part in it. The contrast between strong ideals and halfhearted enforcement mechanisms is indicative of the influence of two types of drafters: women's rights advocates and representatives of states' interests. One may conclude that not even during times of high levels of gender awareness did the drafters succeed (or were interested) in creating effective mechanisms to enhance women's rights realization. The result is also an interesting illustration of the theoretical framework provided in Chap. 2. Treaty drafting and ratification does not conclude the process of global normative consensus formation, in the sense that this global consensus is now ready to be passed on to governments for domestic implementation. Rather, the drafting process is the starting point of global discourse translation, reminiscent of the first round of a boxing match. As the next chapters will show, the participants in this global discourse keep wrestling to make their viewpoints and claims succeed. The international meaning making process around women's rights has just begun.

Notes

1. See, among others, Antrobus (2004), Fraser and Tinker (2004), Garner (2010), Jain (2005), Joachim (2007), Moghadam (2005), Pietilä (2007), Pietilä and Vickers (1996), Quataert and Roth (2012), Winslow (1995).
2. Interestingly, 40 states submitted reservations to this Convention because they did not agree that women should have access to *all* public leadership functions (United Nations 1996).
3. In the process of legal codification of international law, a *declaration* signals more commitment than a *resolution* issued by the UN General Assembly. The final stage is a *convention*, which specifies both the norm and norm-abiding behavior expected from states and is legally binding (Delbrück 1981).
4. The DEDAW is available online at http://www.unhcr.org/refworld/docid/3b00f05938.html.
5. Protective measures in such a broad sense "fell from grace" a few years later when their discriminatory results were understood. This paradigm shift first bore fruit in International Labour Organization (ILO) documents (Berkovitch 1999).
6. Saudi Arabia called the idea of a women's conference "disruptive." Strong words also came from supporters such as Princess Ashraf Pahlavi of Iran who accused "male imperialism…[as having] paralyzed an important part

of society" and called women to stop being "a colony of man" (Antrobus 2004, p. 34).

7. According to Antrobus (2004), approximately 8,000 women (and men) attended the Mexico conference, 10,000 the Copenhagen conference, and 13,500 the one in Nairobi. The Beijing conference is said to have attracted up to 40,000 attendees.
8. Partly, this can be attributed to the strong presence of socialist women's mass organizations. They had close links to their respective governments and saw the establishment of a non-capitalist economic world order as the most important prerequisite for the advancement of women (Ghodsee 2012). Issues addressed were, among others, literacy, education and training, health, nutrition and population, the family, the household and marriage, employment, and political participation. Violence, sexuality and sexual orientation did not appear in the document. It could be that women's organizations working on those issues deliberately chose not to attend the Mexico gathering. At the time, there was considerable resistance toward a government-focused conference among autonomous women's organizations. In 1976, the International Tribunal on Crimes against Women was held as an exclusively non-governmental conference with a focus on violence against women. It was meant to be a counter-event to Mexico (Joachim 2007; Stienstra 1994, p. 126).
9. In much of the literature, the West is pitched against the South while "the East" seems to have disappeared. This is because with the end of the block confrontation, socialist women's organizations disintegrated and indeed lost their voices (Ghodsee 2012). Also, Western historiography has long assumed that socialist women's organizations were only instruments of their governments, but recent scholarship paints a more complex picture of the role of these organizations in the formation of international feminism (de Haan 2010a).
10. For critical discussion of MDG 3 on gender equality and women's empowerment, see Kabeer, 2005; for an overview of feminist assessments of microcredit programs, see Visvanathan and Yoder 2011.
11. The focus of this critique is the de-radicalization of concepts, prominently through the strategy of gender mainstreaming (Braunmühl 2013; True and Parisi 2013; Wichterich 2007). Also, institutionalization of gender knowledge potentially takes away agency from those who are not recognizable as "gender experts" (Prügl 2013).
12. These predecessors were the United Nations Fund for Women (UNIFEM), the Division for the Advancement of Women (DAW), the International Research and Training Institute for the Advancement of Women (INSTRAW) and the Office of the Special Adviser on Gender Issues and Advancement of Women (OSAGI).

13. For example, Binion (1995), Bunch (1990), Charlesworth (1995), Chinkin (1996), Cook (1994a, 1995), O'Hare (1999), Stamatopoulou (1995).
14. While the integration of a gender perspective into international law has progressed in the meantime, it is still not as transformative as feminists would like it to be (Charlesworth 2013).
15. The Third Committee deals with social, humanitarian, and cultural affairs, which includes human rights.
16. The abstaining states were Bangladesh, Brazil, Comoros, Haiti, Mali, Mauritania, Mexico, Morocco, Saudi Arabia, and Senegal. Thirteen more states did not vote (Chinkin and Freeman 2012, p. 7).
17. The Committee has later started to use the term "gender" in its practice and defined it in General Recommendation 28 (Chinkin and Freeman 2012, p. 15).
18. The entire text of the Convention can be accessed via the website of the High Commissioner for Human Rights at: http://www2.ohchr.org/english/law/cedaw.htm.
19. The preamble was heatedly debated because of differing ideas on its appropriate (political) breadth or (legal) conciseness (McKean 1983; Rehof 1993), but it has not influenced the Committee's practice, except in its very early sessions (Evatt 2002).
20. The most exhaustive interpretation of each article of the Convention is Freeman, Chinkin, and Rudolf (2012). Rehof (1993) provides a comprehensive description of the drafting process.
21. In contrast, the Covenant on Civil and Political Rights (CCPR) specifies a broader range of civil rights, among them the right to life and security of the person, the rights of persons in procedures before the courts, the right to privacy, freedom of thought, conscience, and religion, and the right of assembly and to join organizations.
22. Only procedural article 29 (1) on dispute settlement between States Parties involving the International Court of Justice has attracted a higher number of reservations, but these do not affect substantial treaty responsibilities.
23. One proposal was to model it after article 20 of the CERD, which considers a reservation incompatible with the Convention if two thirds of the Convention's States Parties object to it (Clark 1991).

CHAPTER 4

CEDAW as a "Living Document": Over Thirty Years of Committee Work

The Convention entered into force on September 3, 1981, after the ratification of the twentieth state. In the following year, the CEDAW monitoring Committee started to convene to oversee the implementation of the Convention. As of December 2015, it has been ratified by 189 states—the second highest number of ratifications of any human rights treaty only surpassed by the Convention on the Rights of the Child. As this chapter shows, the CEDAW Committee started as a comparatively weak human rights instrument that developed into an effective and authoritative treaty body. In the 1980s, the work of the Committee was impeded by lack of resources, a restricted interpretation of the Committee's mandate, and an administrative set up that isolated the CEDAW Committee from all other human rights treaty bodies (Byrnes 1989; Clark 1991; Jacobson 1991). During the 1990s, the situation improved significantly. the Committee had better service, became more efficient and more self-confident in interpreting its mandate, and attracted more attention from governments and non-governmental organizations (NGOs). The change in institutional recognition is maybe aptly expressed by an anecdote. Ivanka Corti, the Committee's chairperson in the early 1990s recalls that at the opening ceremony of the 1993 Vienna Human Rights Conference, she was not seated among the chairpersons of the other human rights treaty bodies but among the accredited NGOs, a mistake that was an "example of the then-reigning conviction that the Committee was not as important as the other UN human rights treaty bodies" (Corti 2007, p. 40). However,

S. Zwingel, *Translating International Women's Rights*,
Gender and Politics, DOI 10.1057/978-1-137-31501-4_4

in a reflection written 14 years later, Corti finds the Committee being "considered with great respect and…highly appreciated, which is totally justified considering that it is monitoring the human rights of half of the population of the globe" (ibid., p. 49).

This chapter, together with Chap. 5, traces the metamorphosis of CEDAW. It first takes a look at the international embeddedness of the Committee within the UN, in particular in regard to the support structures for its work and its connectivity with other UN entities. Secondly, it presents the development of the main mandate of the Committee, namely to support States Parties in implementing women's rights as specified in the Convention through ongoing and constructive monitoring. The focus here lies on three main features: the composition of the Committee and the repercussions of this composition for the construction of expertise; the Committee's efforts to improve state reporting and make the monitoring procedure more effective; and the Committee's work to assert itself as authoritative interpreter of the Convention, expressed in its position in regard to reservations to the treaty and its General Recommendations (GRs). Chap. 5 features the Committee's work with the Optional Protocol (OP) to the Convention that was added in the year 2000. It is covered separately because the procedures provided for in the OP have added a new dimension to the Convention's international recognition and domestic repercussions.

CEDAW Within the United Nations

Start Low, End High: The Committee's Working Conditions

While all human rights treaty bodies work under conditions of insufficient resources, the CEDAW Committee started its work under particularly catastrophic circumstances. It lacked the resources to carry out even its most basic functions, which made one Committee member refer to CEDAW as "the poor cousin of the human rights Treaty Bodies" (Byrnes 1989, p. 57). Two crucial factors in this respect were meeting time and secretarial support. Contrary to any other human rights treaty, CEDAW limits the annual meeting time of the Committee to two weeks.[1] The Committee soon realized that this time was too short, in particular as the number of States Parties to the Convention was growing fast. In its third session in 1984, the Committee recommended that the ECOSOC provide adequate financial resources and staff to enable its effective functioning

(UN Doc. ST/CSDHA/5, p. 474). This recommendation was the first initiative in a long battle for adequate meeting time. In 1988, the UN General Assembly allowed the Committee, on an exceptional basis, to meet for four additional working days[2] but rejected the same request for the following year due to the costs involved. To circumvent these financial constraints, the Committee established a pre-session working group in 1989 to prepare the examination of periodic reports. This group met for three days and was composed of only five of the 23 members, thus, the costs were low enough to be approved first on an exceptional then on a regular basis. However, as the number of reports awaiting consideration kept piling up, the Committee requested, again, additional meeting time in 1993, but without success (UN Doc. A/47/38, p. 127).

In 1995, five Nordic States Parties to CEDAW proposed to the UN General Assembly to amend article 20 (1) of the Convention, replacing the words "normally meet for a period of not more than two weeks annually" with "meet annually for a period necessary." This amendment would allow for maximum flexibility in terms of meeting time. At the States Parties meeting of that year, a corresponding resolution was adopted (UN Doc. CEDAW/SP/1995/2); however, the amendment would enter into force only after ratification by two thirds of all States Parties. Ratification has been going at a snail's pace; as of December 2015, 70 out of 189 States Parties had ratified—a far cry from a two-thirds majority, which would currently amount to 125 ratifications. In anticipation of such a development, the States Parties meeting also adopted a resolution containing an interim solution. It proposed to grant the Committee two annual three-week sessions plus two one-week pre-session working group meetings until the amendment would enter into force (UN Doc. CEDAW/SP/1996/5). The Committee started to work under these conditions in January 1997. This boost of meeting time reflected the Committee's increased workload and made its working conditions roughly comparable to those of the other treaty bodies (Bayefski 2001).

In order to further reduce its backlog of reports, the Committee asked for even more meeting time and was granted one exceptional meeting of three weeks in the year 2002. In 2005, the Committee requested the UN General Assembly to repeat this exceptional extension of meeting time for the biennium 2006–2007 and to grant permission for the Committee to convene in two chambers for some of these meetings (UN Doc. A/60/38, p. 95). Not only was this request granted but the UN General Assembly also responded favorably to the continuing insistence of the Committee[3] to make the extension of meeting time permanent. UN General Assembly resolution 62/218 allowed the Committee to hold five three-week-sessions with the corresponding pre-session meetings during the biennium 2008–2009, and it granted the Committee three annual three-week-sessions "effective from January 2010, pending the entry into force of the amendment to article 20, paragraph 1" (UN Doc. A/Res/62/218, p. 4).

Taking all costs of conference servicing, documentation, translation, and expenses for the experts together, the Secretariat estimated an extra cost of over US$ 9 million for 2006–2007 and of over US$ 15 million for 2008–2009 to cover the expanded meeting time (UN Doc. A/60/38, p. 242; UN Doc. A/61/38, p. 495). These considerable expenses show that the servicing of CEDAW has become a higher priority on the UN Nations agenda than it was in the 1980s and 1990s. In comparison, a 1993 request of the Committee for extended meeting time was denied because of estimated additional costs of approx. US$ 40,000 to 65,000 (UN Doc. A/47/38, p. 127). As Fig. 4.1 shows, the expansion of meeting time over the last 30 years includes a four-and-a-half-fold increase for meetings of the Committee as a whole (from 10 to 45 days annually), the introduction of a pre-session working group in 1989 and a fivefold increase of its meeting time (from 3 days to 15 annually), and in 2002, the addition of a working group related to the OP whose meeting time expanded from 5 to 10 days per year.

The secretarial support of CEDAW went through a similar process of upgrading. When the Committee started its work, its Secretariat, the Branch for the Advancement of Women, was severely underfunded and under-staffed and did not dispose of knowledge regarding the functioning of human rights treaty bodies (Byrnes 1989). Partly because of the Commission on the Status of Women's (CSW) emphasis in the 1960s, women's issues were perceived within the UN as a matter of socio-economic development, not as a matter of human rights (Stamatopoulou 1995). This perception resulted in an administrative separation. Since 1973, the CSW was not served by the Division of Human Rights anymore but by the Centre for Social Development and Humanitarian Affairs. As the CEDAW Committee dealt with the rights of women, it was grouped with the other women-related UN activities and the corresponding Secretariat. This situation was often criticized because it isolated CEDAW from all other human rights mechanisms and kept gender issues and human rights institutionally apart (Byrnes 1989; UN Doc. HRI/MC/1998/6).

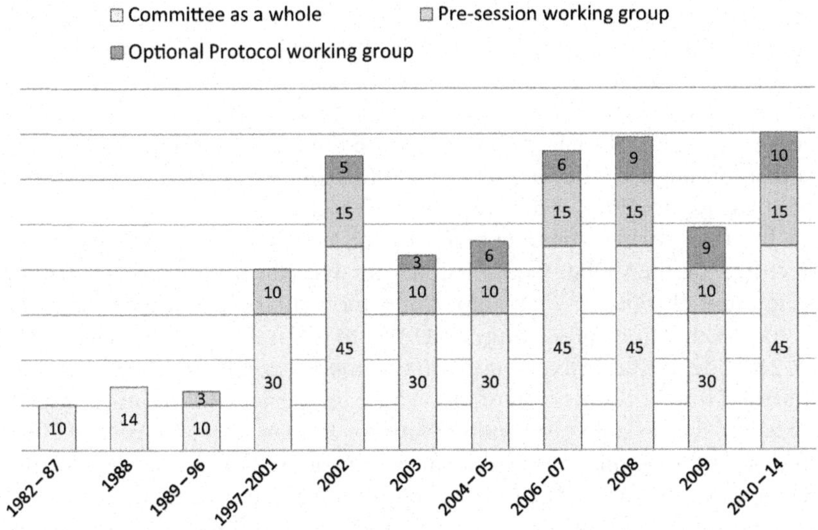

Fig. 4.1 Expansion of annual meeting time (in days), 1982–2014

The servicing for the Committee improved, first by upgrading the "Branch" to a "Division" for the Advancement of Women (DAW) in 1988, then by moving the Division from Vienna, where it was geographically isolated, to New York in 1993 (Pietilä and Vickers 1996). The most significant secretarial change for CEDAW, however, was the creation of a Women's Rights Section within the DAW in 1997. It was founded "in order to respond to the requirements of the Beijing Platform for Action which essentially highlights human rights in a way that hadn't occurred before" (Interview 2). The Women's Rights Section provided invaluable legal expertise to the Committee. The Section's main tasks were to ensure that the sessions of the Committee would run smoothly, to assist the Committee in improving its working methods by supplying background knowledge,[4] and to provide support for States Parties that encountered difficulties in complying with their treaty obligations.[5] The Women's Rights Section also took on a leading role in increasing the gender sensitivity of other UN bodies. Among other things, it prepared a study on gender awareness in all treaty bodies, including recommendations for further action (UN Doc. HRI/MC/1998/6). Thus, the Women's Rights

Section both served as a knowledgeable secretariat for the Committee and strengthened gender awareness in the UN human rights system. This positive development made it less deplorable for some experts that the Committee was still administratively separate from all the other treaty bodies (Interview 3). Others, however, insisted that the Committee's adequate affiliation was with the Geneva-based Office of the High Commissioner for Human Rights (OHCHR) (Interviews 8 and 11).

In 2005, within a broader plan to reform the UN Human Rights architecture, the then High Commissioner for Human Rights, Louise Arbour, suggested that it was "an opportune moment to consider transferring responsibility for supporting CEDAW to OHCHR" (OHCHR 2005, p. 23). She justified this change with the important input of the Committee on the Human Rights system as a whole, in particular its contribution to "respect for diversity and indivisibility of human rights" (Arbour 2007, p. 3). The Commissioner's reform plan proposed far-reaching structural changes, among them the replacement of the existing treaty bodies by one unified treaty body, a proposal that the CEDAW Committee vehemently opposed (UN Doc. A/61/38, p. 2; Schöpp-Schilling 2007b). While those large-scale dimensions of reform have not materialized, the secretarial support for the CEDAW Committee was transferred from the DAW to the OHCHR in January 2008. This included the transfer of some, but not all, staff posts (UN Doc. A/64/342, p. 4; Interview 4). Until 2012, the Committee has held one of its three annual sessions in New York "to facilitate and encourage ongoing cooperation between the Committee and the United Nations gender equality bodies" (UN Doc. A/62/38, p. 226), but this practice ended in 2013 due to budget constraints.[6] The DAW, since 2011 part of UN Women, has continued to support the work of the Committee, for example, by facilitating CEDAW implementation on national levels and providing assistance for the crafting of GRs (UN staff email communication, 2013).

Committee experts viewed the move to Geneva with mixed feelings. On the one hand, they appreciate that the Committee is now treated exactly like all other treaty bodies (Interview 5), and they value having better opportunities to connect to each element of the human rights architecture. On the other hand, they realize that the servicing in Geneva is less specialized in regard to gender issues than in New York (Interview 6). As a UN staff member explains, this has to do with the different administrative structures:

> The Division dealt with the treaty body, a normative body, the CSW, an intergovernmental body, Beijing+5, and there was the opportunity to do substantive research, so they did everything. In Geneva, there is a branch that deals with the Human Rights Council, so only they deal with the political, a branch for the mechanisms, and a branch for research. It is a quite disconnected set up....And the part which deals with the treaty bodies... doesn't have enough staff. (Interview 4)

Thus, while there is the potential to connect to other parts of the human rights system, creating such synergies depends to some degree on a potent Secretariat (Interview 7). Yet OHCHR's resources are quite limited, in particular in the light of ever-increasing responsibilities the Geneva Secretariat has to handle (OHCHR 2011).[7] In the overall picture, secretarial support for CEDAW has consistently improved since the second half of the 1990s and is now on equal levels with the other treaty bodies. Gauging from the Committee's (and other treaty bodies') needs, there is still significant room for improvement, yet the most optimistic prediction for the future is the maintenance of the current level of secretarial support. Given the financial constraints of OHCHR, restructuring of the treaty bodies' functioning and shrinkage of service for them are also possible.

Connectivity with the CSW, Human Rights Architecture, and Specialized Agencies

Because of its unorthodox affiliation somewhere between a human rights and a development instrument, the CEDAW Committee remained rather unknown within the UN in its early years of existence. It took until the 1990s that other UN agencies came to better understand the relevance of the Convention for their work and started to interact with the Committee. Three of such intra-institutional relationships of the Committee are highlighted here: with the CSW; with the human rights treaty bodies and the UN human rights architecture, in general; and with Specialized Agencies (SAs), in particular, the United Nations Fund for Women (UNIFEM, now part of UN Women).[8]

The relationship between the CEDAW Committee and the CSW was virtually non-existent until the early 1990s. This is somewhat surprising given the fact that the mandates of the two bodies strongly overlapped (Byrnes 1989; Clark 1991). In order to confront this lack of interaction, a former CEDAW chairperson requested to take the floor at a CSW meeting and informed the delegates about the Committee's work. She recalls that this was considered unorthodox at the time and she had to overcome some resistance, but eventually her input created a lot of interest among CSW delegates (Interview 8). This early disconnect may have its roots in the fact that the CSW was somewhat sidelined in the set-up of the Convention's monitoring procedure. During the drafting process, there was strong support for the idea that the CSW itself, in form of a working group, should oversee the implementation of the Convention (Boerefijn 2012b). However, the UN General Assembly's Third Committee agreed on an independent committee and included the CSW only to the extent that it should receive the Committee's reports "for its information" (CEDAW art. 21).

Following the efforts of the CEDAW chairperson, the interaction between the two bodies became more regular. CSW delegates routinely received Committee reports, and CEDAW chairpersons attended CSW meetings on a regular basis. The 1995 Beijing conference, in particular, strengthened a collaborative spirit between the two bodies. While the Beijing follow-up process is the task of the CSW, the Committee has repeatedly declared that the Beijing Platform for Action (BPFA) and the Convention mutually reinforce each other and that it is committed to the implementation of the BPFA as well (UN Doc. A/55/38, p. 3; A/65/38, p. 136). Likewise, the CSW refers to the Convention as the legal framework for much of its work. This rapprochement notwithstanding, CEDAW experts have occasionally found the CSW hesitant to rely on the Committee's suggestions, in particular when the CSW first refused to discuss input from the Committee in regard to the OP to the Convention (Interview 8; see also Chap. 5). Such (rare) affronts can be read as concrete expressions of the different "political" versus "independent" mandates of the two bodies.

The second relationship between CEDAW and the UN human rights system can be characterized, in a nutshell, as initial disconnect followed by increasing approximation, even convergence. As we have seen, the CEDAW Committee was first administratively separated from the other human rights treaty bodies. The most obvious disadvantages of this set-up were the Committee's lack of knowledge related to human rights procedures, on the one hand, and the neglect of a women's rights perspective in the rest of the UN human rights system, on the other. The CEDAW Committee greatly benefitted from attempts among the treaty bodies to collaborate in order to harmonize their separately developed working methods. This cooperation was first undertaken in the Meeting of Chairpersons of Human Rights Treaty Bodies. It met for the first time in 1984, and the CEDAW chairperson joined in the second meeting in 1988. The body has convened annually since 1994 to discuss common problems and challenges of the treaty bodies, for example, financial constraints, improvement of working methods, responses to overdue reports and reservations, and use of independent information provided by SAs and NGOs. Between 2002 and 2011, the Chairpersons' meeting was enhanced by an additional body, the Inter-Committee Meeting of the Treaty Bodies. However, since its mandate overlapped with the Chairpersons' meeting and due to OHCHR's financial constraints, it was discontinued (UN Doc. A/66/175, p. 8).

The meetings enabled the CEDAW Committee to learn from the practice of the other treaty bodies and to raise awareness on gender as a crucial dimension of human rights promotion and protection. The 1998 Meeting of Chairpersons agreed to request a study on the integration of gender in the work of the treaty bodies to be prepared by DAW (UN Doc. A/53/38, p. 6). According to this study, gender-sensitivity among the then-existing treaty bodies varied considerably.[9] It concluded that all treaty bodies, not only CEDAW, should integrate a gender perspective, because a "dual strategy—attention to women-specific issues by women-specific machinery, and a gender approach by mainstream mechanisms—reinforces an understanding that gender equality must be addressed as a strategic objective by society as a whole" (UN Doc. HRI/MC/1998/6, p. 6). While CEDAW has certainly had an influence on the other treaty bodies, there has been a broader tendency within the UN human rights framework to take gender institutionally more seriously. Next to general mainstreaming efforts, this is visible in the establishment of additional mandates, such as the Special Rapporteur on violence against women (VAW), its causes and consequences in 1994, or the Human Rights Council's Working Group on the issue of discrimination against women in law and in practice in 2010 (UN Doc. A/HRC/20/28).

This positive trend notwithstanding, various studies and UN reports have documented that the representation of women and gender sensitivity in the work of the treaty bodies and special procedures is improving but not satisfactory (Edwards 2011; Johnstone 2006; UN Docs. E/CN.4/2005/68; A/HRC/4/104). With the exception of the CEDAW and Convention on the Rights of the Child (CRC) Committees, women are still significantly underrepresented within the human rights architecture.[10] This is mostly due to the nomination practice of states, but the Secretariat has also not put much effort into making gender balance a core requirement for the functioning of the treaty bodies (Edwards 2011). The studies also find that while treaty bodies are increasingly more likely to integrate a gender perspective, they do so in an unsystematic fashion (e.g., UN Doc. E/CN.4/2005/68). The newer instruments typically do better because at the time of their drafting in the 1990s and later, gender was better recognized within the human rights context than before. The Convention on the Rights of Persons with Disabilities (CRPD) and the Convention on the Protection of all Persons from Enforced Disappearance (CED), for example, require gender-balanced membership in their monitoring bodies, and the CRC Committee is often lauded in regard to its gender sensitive approach to interpreting the Convention and its equal representation of men and women among Committee experts (Johnstone 2006).

It is a matter of perspective if the engendering of the UN's human rights work has been going far enough. Some identify only superficial changes and no comprehensive integration of gender equality and women's experiences (Charlesworth 2005). Others have seen the long-term influence of gender equality claims bear fruit in the "mainstream" bodies, to the extent that CEDAW, once the symbol of the exclusion of women's rights from the human rights landscape, may at some point become obsolete (Johnstone 2010a). These developments, however, have to be seen in a general environment of urgent need for reform. Since the 1990s, the UN human rights apparatus has expanded to a previously unthinkable degree. While this expansion has strengthened the representation of human rights, it has not always happened in the most efficient ways, and mandates that were newly created not only reinforced but also sometimes overlapped with each other.[11] In response, the High Commissioner suggested to streamline the treaty bodies into one permanent body, but this suggestion was adamantly opposed, also out of the CEDAW Committee, with the argument that each treaty body's specific contribution would be lost (Schöpp-Schilling 2007b; Interview 6). As a consequence the status quo was kept. Thus, while CEDAW has been successfully integrated into the human rights system over time, the system itself is in flux and under scrutiny.

The Committee established a third intra-institutional link toward the UN's Specialized Agencies (SAs). According to article 22 of the Convention, SAs may contribute independent information to the Committee's dialogue, yet it took until about the mid-1990s to activate this possibility in meaningful ways (Byrnes 1989, p. 38; Interview 8). Initially, the Committee did not ask SAs for input that would have been tailored to its monitoring process but rather for general information on agency programs falling within the scope of the Convention (Boerefjn 2012c). Not many SAs responded to this request, and the mutual benefit from this cooperation was not readily apparent. The Committee then made efforts to include the expertise produced by SAs more systematically, for example, it asked for input in regard to GRs, and in 1997, it requested SAs to submit country specific information, which has added depth to the constructive dialogue ever since (ibid). While the Committee still occasionally voices concern about the lack of information and interest coming from particular SAs (UN Doc. A/60/38, p. 165), a good number of SAs have been contributing to the monitoring procedure on a regular basis.[12] At the same time, a range of UN Agencies have gone beyond contributing to the constructive dialogue and used CEDAW as a tool to implement a gender-sensitive human rights approach in their work, a step that has been encouraged by the Secretary General's reform concept known as "the human rights approach to programming" (UNIFEM 2007). Until it became part of UN Women in 2011, UNIFEM was most systematic of all UN agencies in integrating CEDAW into its work. It started to place emphasis on women's human rights after the Vienna Conference on Human Rights in 1993 with a focus on eliminating VAW and not yet with a systematic connection to CEDAW (Interview 9). Starting in the mid-1990s, UNIFEM developed two major strategies to incorporate CEDAW in its work: it directly supported implementation of the Convention on country levels; and it mainstreamed a women's rights perspective into various fields of UN activities by connecting them to the Convention, for example, in the field of HIV/AIDS (UNIFEM 2001), security (UNIFEM 2006), and gender budgeting (UNIFEM 2008).[13] Since the foundation of UN Women, the Committee has repeatedly stressed its interest in a strong relationship with the new entity, and it has underlined and explained the relevance of CEDAW for all aspects of UN Women's work, including the design of the post-2015 development agenda (decision 55/II, UN Doc. A/69/38).

In sum, CEDAW has become more visible and institutionally connected within the UN. Its working conditions and servicing have improved significantly, and contacts between the Committee and other UN entities have developed into mutually beneficial relationships. This has been a positive development for CEDAW itself, but it has also increased gender awareness within various other UN entities. However, considering that international organizations are constantly developing and that the UN as a whole is confronted with budgetary challenges, the upward tendency described here may have reached a plateau.

The Committee at Work

Embedded in this changing international context, how has the Committee developed its ways of monitoring the implementation efforts of States Parties to CEDAW? This section focuses on three important dimensions of the Committee's work: first, its composition, or what it means to be an expert on women's rights suitable to serve on the Committee; second, the Committee's efforts to consistently improve the core tool of its work, the constructive dialogue with States Parties; and third, the experts' work to establish the Committee as authoritative interpreter of the Convention. This last dimension is most visible in the position the Committee has developed in regard to reservations and in its treaty interpretation through GRs.

Who Are the Committee Experts?

According to article 17 of the Convention, the Committee should consist of "twenty-three experts of high moral standing and competence in the field covered by the Convention." The experts should act in their personal capacity, not as representatives of their governments, and they should come from all world regions to represent "different forms of civilization as well as the principal legal systems." The de facto composition of the Committee displays at least four distinct features, namely the broad diversity of professional backgrounds of experts, their relationship to their respective governments, their representation of different regional and cultural backgrounds, and last but not least, their gender.

Typically, human rights treaty bodies are comprised of experts with legal expertise because, in the words of a former expert of the Human Rights Committee, "the application of a human rights treaty is to...a large degree interpretation of the laws" (Interview 10). CEDAW stands out in this regard as its experts have represented a broad diversity of professions and educational backgrounds. A glance at the Committee members serving in the years 2000 and 2010 shows that more than half were or had been employed by their governments, either in the women's policy agency (WPA) or other ministries or as diplomats. About a quarter were practicing jurists holding positions as judges, prosecutors, and attorneys. Another quarter was made up of academics in law, social sciences, literature, or women's studies and other professionals, for example, NGO employees and, in one case, a dental surgeon. About half of the experts have NGO affiliations.[14] Members describe the breadth of professional backgrounds as indispensable for the Committee's work because it enables the experts to shed light on all possible dimensions of discrimination against women. Legal expertise is highly valued, in particular in regard to dealing with the OP to the Convention, but most members would consider a *purely* legal perspective too limited (Boerefijn 2012d; Interview 11).

Given the high number of experts who have held some form of governmental post in their countries, the independence of experts from their governments is questionable in some cases.[15] This was most problematic in the early years of the Committee's work because the Committee had not yet established rules to prevent partiality of experts to interfere with its work. Evatt describes that the high number of government affiliated experts led to some confusion of the Committee's mandate with that of the CSW. Also, it was rather common for experts to intervene in the discussion of their own state's report (2002, p. 523). In line with the practice of other treaty bodies, the Committee later ruled that experts should "refrain from participating in any aspect of the consideration of the reports of the States of which they were nationals" (UN Doc. A/53/38, p. 3).[16] Another often described feature of the Committee's "Cold War years" was the strong partisan spirit displayed by experts from the Socialist block; they tended to praise reports from their peers and lacked objectivity in assessing the situation in Western states (Bernard 2007; Byrnes 1989; Caron 2007; Evatt 2002, 2007). More recently, States Parties have occasionally complained about a particular expert's lack of objective attitude, as did Israel after its constructive dialogue with the Committee in 2005. The Committee has not considered this confrontation problematic, but interpreted the concerned expert's position as an expression of her political independence. (UN Doc. A/61/38, p. 81f).

When it comes to self-assessment, Committee members usually consider themselves completely or sufficiently independent. Those who hold or held governmental positions deem themselves capable of separating their roles, and they often consider it an asset to understand the difficulties governments may face in regard to implementation (Interview 12). However, observers and NGO representatives have suggested that the more experts are empathetic of governmental interests, the less critical and visionary the dialogue becomes (Galey 1984; Merry 2003; Interview 13). Further, as experts are nominated by their governments, candidates who are fundamental critics of their governments' gender policies are not likely to be considered, and likewise, experts whose performance on the Committee is inadequate in the view of their government may jeopardize re-nomination (Bayefsky 2001, p. 102). Experts are elected by the meeting of States Parties to the Convention. In these elections, individual expertise of each candidate is relevant, but another important dimension is vote-bargaining between states. Thus, state A may nominate an expert for the CEDAW Committee and state B one for the CERD Committee, and they may agree on voting for each other's candidate. With the increased recognition of the CEDAW Committee, the voting process has become more competitive, and governmental interests may play an even larger role in getting experts nominated and elected (Acar 2007).

The goal of equitable geographical distribution of experts, aiming at the "representation of different forms of civilization as well as the principal legal systems" is made explicit in CEDAW article 17. It has not always been achieved, even if it is highly important for the Committee to be perceived as culturally balanced. In the early years, Eastern European and Latin American experts were overrepresented partly as a result of ratification patterns (Evatt 2002). However, after the end of the Cold War, Eastern European experts were long absent altogether (Schöpp-Schilling 1999, p. 221). As of the end of 2014, 128 experts had served on the Committee with 26 (20%) coming from *Africa*, 34 (27%) from *Asia*, 25 (19%) from *Latin America and the Caribbean*, and 43 (34%) from the *More Developed Regions*.[17] In relation to States Parties from each region, this distribution means that experts from Africa are somewhat underrepresented and experts from More Developed Regions somewhat overrepresented, with Asian and Latin American experts lying in between.[18] These inequalities originate from the nomination practice, on the one hand, and from the mode of elections, on the other; there are no separate votes or quota systems per region. Art. 17 only states that every two years, 11 out of the 23 members should be elected for a four-year term.

Committee membership *within* each of these regions is also uneven. For example, within the group of More Developed Regions, Western European experts (21) outnumber Eastern European ones (14), and the four CEDAW States Parties in the group of "other" developed countries—Australia, Canada, Japan, and New Zealand—are most strongly represented with eight experts. The 26 African CEDAW experts have come from 16 of the 51 African States Parties, and no country from the sub-region Middle Africa[19] ever sent an expert. This is also true for the five States Parties making up Central Asia,[20] and for the 11 States Parties of Oceania.[21] The Committee has sometimes been accused of being culturally imbalanced, most forcefully in 1987 when a group of Muslim states claimed that it superimposed "foreign cultural values on Islamic precepts"

(UN Doc. A/C.3/42/SR. 27, p.1). However, this controversy fell in the time when the Committee's standing was still rather weak (see in more detail later in this chapter) and has not been repeated. Also, a significant number of experts from predominantly Muslim states have served on the Committee, including more than one from Bangladesh, Egypt, Indonesia, Nigeria, and Turkey.

Committee members themselves think of the Committee as a culturally pluralistic group (Schöpp-Schilling 2007c, p. 250; Sinegiorgis 2007, p. 277; Interview 12). As one expert puts it,

> we speak with 23 voices...but from different cultural, from different legal perspectives....So when we address delegations, we...recognize that each one of us will put different accents, but always from within the parameters of the Convention. (Interview 6)

Committee members deem themselves sufficiently representative of the world's cultural diversity, and they consider their own cultural backgrounds an asset for sound monitoring. This self-assessment is sometimes a bit at odds with another construction of culture that is often employed in the dialogue, both by Committee members and by delegations, namely that of culture as synonymous with traditions that are impediments to the realization of women's rights (Merry 2003).

Finally, out of the 128 experts who have served the Committee until 2014, four have been men, two from Sweden, and one each from the Netherlands and Finland. The almost exclusive female membership has to do with the expertise required for the Committee, yet it becomes striking when juxtaposed with the underrepresentation of women in most of the other treaty bodies. The gender bias in the composition of the Committee has occasionally been discussed among the experts—some wanted to take measures to increase male membership, but others found that the other treaty bodies should first work for higher female membership (Byrnes 1989, p. 9; UN Doc. A/47/38, p. 94). Some experts have suggested that the female-only membership of the Committee has reduced its perceived standing, "because you can still marginalize a Committee comprised of women. If we had this group, with the expertise in this group, and we were male, we would be a very powerful Committee" (Interview 11). Others have interpreted the lack of male candidates for CEDAW as a "misleading perception of the governments. They have not really considered a gender focus, and they don't consider it when nominating candidates"

(Interview 3). Committee members have often described the gender-homogeneity as a positive experience; they talk about the high degree of team spirit, commitment, mutual confidence, and solidarity in the fight against discrimination against women (Schöpp-Schilling and Flinterman 2007; Interviews 8, 14, and 15). To the extent that men join the battle, they are included without reservations, according to the experience of one male expert: "Since I came here…, I have felt accepted, and I think this is because I take the work seriously. Then it does not matter anymore if you are a man or a woman" (Interview 6).

In sum, Committee members comprise a group of women's rights experts with a wide variety of professional backgrounds. Their degree of independence from their respective governments varies as some experts have served in governmental functions prior to or during their membership in the Committee, while others have worked in women's rights NGOs. They have come from all world regions, even if some are more strongly represented than others. CEDAW experts have also been almost exclusively female. In addition to these characteristics, CEDAW membership is also shaped by structures of exclusion. A former Committee member described the experts as "a privileged group: well-educated, articulate, and comparatively wealthy" (Cartwright 1998, p. 181). Becoming a CEDAW member—or a member of any other treaty body, for that matter—is indeed connected to social status; not only is the experts' proficiency closely connected to *academic* education, they also commit to spending a lot of time on their mandate without pay.[22] Thus, women's rights experts with non-academic expertise and limited resources, and those who cannot afford the time investment are unlikely to be part of this group. Also, no expert has been openly lesbian, bisexual, or transgender, a fact that can be attributed to the heteronormative underpinnings of states and inter-governmental contexts.

The Constructive Dialogue as the Backbone of the Committee's Work

The core mandate of the Committee is to support States Parties in fulfilling their treaty obligations. In the Committee's over 30 years of practice, the constructive dialogue with States Parties has been the most important dimension of this mandate, supported by the Committee's overarching interpretation of the Convention through General Recommendations (GRs). The constructive dialogue can be described as a mechanism that "provides ... for a discourse ... of rights which, although not always sufficient alone, at least opens the door to a ... language that the state may be willing to hear." (Johnstone 2006, p. 158). The foundation of the dialogue is state acceptance and respect. When human rights treaty bodies were first created, they were conceived as assistants of states, not as robust monitoring mechanisms. However, especially since the end of the Cold War, all human rights treaty bodies have considerably strengthened their standing and improved their working procedures to the effect that they have become "surprisingly effective tool[s] for human rights protection" (O'Flaherty and Tsai 2011, p. 56). The constructive dialogue embodies a multi-layered set of functions, among others, to comprehensively review national legislation and administrative rules; to monitor state action; to ensure that States Parties understand the provisions of the treaty; to enable States Parties to develop a better understanding of shortcomings in their efforts to realize treaty provisions and to show their achievements; and to facilitate public scrutiny and provide a basis for evaluating progress (UN Doc. E/1989/22, Annex III; O'Flaherty and Tsai 2011, p. 38). State commitment is the most important ingredient to making the procedure effective. A treaty body merely influences states, and it can do this best if it is respected by its States Parties and if it has the ability to interpret the treaty in a consistent manner and apply it to concrete challenges (Evatt 2002). Once this legitimacy of the procedure is created, the treaty body can apply pressure on States Parties, or it can provide the space for other actors to do so. As we will see further in this chapter and in Chap. 6, the space created through the CEDAW constructive dialogue has been effectively used by large numbers of NGOs.

A Dialogue on Equal Terms: Gaining the Respect of States Parties
In its early years, the CEDAW Committee refrained from articulating any assessment of a state's performance, as a majority of experts feared that judging states would interfere with building a relationship of trust (Evatt 2002). Despite this cautious approach, states occasionally complained that the Committee overstepped its mandate.[23] Over time, the Committee has developed a more self-confident approach in advising and assisting States Parties in the fulfillment of their treaty obligations. It strives for a non-adversary atmosphere in order to achieve a dialogue as frank and open as possible (Aouij 2007; Byrnes 2002). One of the Committee experts details this approach as follows:

> As a point of departure, the Committee appreciates that states ratify the Convention and assume the scrutiny of the Committee. It appreciates this decision in the name of the women of that country. The next step is to critically examine what the state is doing. In doing so, it is necessary to consider reservations, since they can undermine the Convention, yet it is important to keep in mind that a state that ratified the Convention is willing to engage in a dialogue. Then, the Committee has to consider what can be expected from a state. That is not to say that states should be released from their duties ... yet it is important to note impeding factors. (Interview 16)

Thus, the Committee aims at encouraging—and by no means damaging—the willingness of States Parties to *accept scrutiny*. From there, it strives to pro-actively support all states—in their widely differing contexts—to achieve the same goal, that is, to implement the Convention's provisions. As the remainder of this chapter shows, the Committee has become increasingly demanding in regard to what it considers treaty obligations of States Parties. The number and density of its GRs, the introduction of a follow-up procedure to its concluding observations, and its views in the context of the OP are proof of this tendency.

It is hard to gauge the degree to which States Parties pay respect to the Committee, in particular because the delegation sent to the constructive dialogue cannot be taken as an adequate representation of the state as a whole (Interviews 5 and 17). However, the way states present themselves in front of the Committee influences the substance of the dialogue which in turn has an effect on what the delegation can bring home and make the government work with. Committee experts have identified a number of elements that reveal a state's attitude toward the monitoring procedure. The first is the composition of the delegation—ideally, a delegation includes high-level politicians, e.g., the head of the WPA, and represents all resorts in which the Convention applies so that all relevant issues can be meaningfully discussed (Interviews 5 and 11). It was rather common in the early years that states only sent a representative of their permanent mission at the UN; this does not allow for an in-depth dialogue as an ambassador is unlikely to be well-informed about the diverse national gender policies. Committee experts have seen a general trend among States Parties to send more competent delegations. This may have to do with a higher interest in women's rights since the 1995 Beijing conference and with states wanting to avoid embarrassing situations which uniformed delegations have sometimes created.[24]

A second indicator for how seriously a state takes the Convention is the quality of its reports. A good report satisfies reporting guidelines, is produced by all relevant governmental institutions, and demonstrates the understanding that the Convention affects a wide range of state policies. While a faulty report may also be an expression of lack of resources rather than of political will, there are elements that are rather unequivocally pointing to lack of state commitment, for example, if a periodic report is not different from the previous one, if it does not take the Committee's last concluding observations into consideration, and if no action in response to the Committee's recommendations are described (Interview 18).

Finally, an indication of (lack of) respect can be found in attitude, for example, if delegations or reports show ignorance about what the Convention stipulates, declare it subordinate to national laws or traditions, or display a certain arrogance vis-à-vis this instrument. The first dimension seems to be phasing out as Committee experts have continuously pointed to the learning curve states have been going through, both in regard to their formal obligations, such as report writing, and in terms of comprehending the Convention in its complexity (Zwingel 2005b, p. 203; Interview 11); as pointed out earlier in this chapter, educating states about their treaty obligations is part of the mandate of treaty bodies. States do sometimes declare the Convention subordinate to sovereign national laws and customs, even if this was a stronger tendency in the Committee's early years.[25] In the experience of experts, arrogance toward the Convention is most often displayed by developed states. They sometimes see CEDAW as a tool that is good for others but largely superfluous for themselves (Interviews 7 and 18).

In sum, CEDAW experts have observed a tendency among States Parties to engage more meaningfully with the monitoring procedure, yet there is still room for improvement. From the perspective of States Parties, respect for a monitoring body increases if the time and resources invested are matched with some meaningful "return" in form of concise concluding observations and recommendations. States Parties do not want to take part in extensive, non-focused debates (Meyer-Ladewig 1998), in particular since their reporting work load rises with the number of human rights treaties they ratify. Much of the recent treaty body reform debate has therefore focused on ensuring sound monitoring while at the same time keeping the workload of state reporting reasonable (Johnstone 2011; O'Flaherty and Tsai 2011).

Consistency and Coherence in Treaty Interpretation

While consistent treaty interpretation is important in and of itself, it also helps to enhance the Committee's acceptance among States Parties if it can be seen as an institution built on a set of reliable standards. The CEDAW Committee has, over time, taken several steps to build coherence, but it also takes pride in a vision of cultural plurality that leads to a multi-vocal interpretation of the Convention (Interview 6). Its beginnings were rather unstructured. The majority of experts were not ready to think of the Committee as a collective voice that should look at state performance objectively, that is, along a certain set of criteria. Rather, the early constructive dialogues resembled a collection of observations of knowledgeable individuals (Evatt 2002). Starting from "non-coherence," the Committee has revised its procedures and worked to reach a collective, if dynamic, understanding of the full scope of the Convention. Maybe the most striking tendency of this development is that the Committee has become more and more comprehensive as to what it considers to be part of States Parties' treaty obligations. While this tendency is a logical reaction to understanding discrimination against women as a deeply engrained and far-reaching global phenomenon, it is sometimes also criticized as an undue and overly demanding interpretation of the Convention. Indeed, the Committee's interpretations create a stretch between CEDAW as a historical versus a living document—and while this stretch helps further the realization of women's rights, it has also created opposing views of what is "right for women" (see in more detail Chap. 6). In the following, I illustrate the Committee's evolving interpretation using four issues that have been prominent in its work, namely its focus on state responsibilities, Violence against Women (VAW), gender stereotypes and related cultural practices, and reproductive health.

The Committee has made it clear that the Convention requires active engagement of States Parties in order to fulfill women's rights. Over time, its understanding of how far-reaching state responsibilities are has expanded and culminated in GR 28 on article 2 (see in more detail later in this chapter). The most basic—and frequent—of the Committee's requests is for states to provide sound documentation ranging from data disaggregated by sex to evaluation of implemented gender equality policies. As States Parties have had a tendency to underline legal changes as their accomplishments to implement the Convention, the Committee has, while urging for non-discriminatory legislation, developed a bolder position in regard to state responsibility for de facto gender equality. For example, it has frequently recommended applying temporary special measures (TSMs) according to article 4 in fields where women have not reached equal levels with men, such as in political decision making, education, and male-dominated sectors of the labor market. The Committee has argued in accordance with its GR 24 on TSMs that the transformation of *systemic* imbalances requires proactive state interference. However, States Parties often remain passive vis-à-vis these recommendations, suggesting that the government does not grasp the meaning of systemic imbalances or does not assume responsibility to change them.[26] Another dimension of state responsibility that the Committee has stressed particularly in the context of VAW is the principle of "due diligence" laid down in CEDAW article 2(e). It stipulates that a state has indirect responsibilities in regard to discriminatory deeds of non-state actors, that is, it has to ensure that these deeds are not silently condoned but actively discouraged and punished and that the victims receive adequate support from the state.

A second feature of treaty interpretation is the Committee's emphasis on VAW. While VAW is not covered in the text of the treaty, the Committee's GR 19 on the topic was not only the first of its GRs that carefully interpreted a specific problem through each relevant article of the Convention; because of its comprehensiveness, GR 19 is also a document that has been crucial in the general international awareness raising process on VAW (Chinkin 2012b). Ever since GR 19 was issued, the Committee has systematically questioned States Parties about their policies in regard to VAW. As one expert puts it, this insistence has contributed to a better comprehension among states of the scope of the problem:

> In my eight years on the Committee [in the 1990s, SZ] the whole issue of violence has become absolutely accepted as a major human rights violation in every state. That doesn't mean to say that they are necessarily doing much about it, but they are finding that it is a serious problem now. Eight years ago, very few states were actually looking for it.... Articulating that, I think, has an impact. (Interview 19)

While it should not be underestimated that states have been learning to take VAW more seriously, this seems to be partly due to the possibility of framing the phenomenon *in line with* the gender stereotype of female victimhood in need of state protection.

The Committee, however, has been keenly aware of stereotypical constructions of gender. As a third important feature of treaty interpretation, it has stressed article 5 on eliminating gender stereotypes based on inferiority or superiority as a core norm of the Convention. It has worked less with this idea in the "public fields" of political participation, employment,[27] and education, where it has mostly focused on women reaching equality with men as a target line. Rather, the Committee has used article 5 repeatedly in order to point to dimensions of private life it deems incompatible with the Convention, such as stereotypical constructions of motherhood, asymmetries in family law, and discriminatory customs. For example, the Committee has at times expressed the view that the elevation and celebration of motherhood is problematic in light of article 5, in particular if it is constructed as a biological trait rather than a social responsibility and if it is not balanced by a construction of responsible fatherhood. Arguably, there is some tension between the notion to foster parental roles based on gender equality (as in article 5) and the protection of motherhood (as in article 4), but the Committee has stressed its understanding of motherhood as a social role and the importance of shared parenting. This position is not always shared by its counterparts in the dialogue who often perceive motherhood as a central function within the family that is beyond comparison (see also Chap. 3).

Further, the Committee has connected gender stereotyping with social and family traditions that subordinate women, for example, it has taken a bold stance against female circumcision, dowry, polygamy, and forced and underage marriage (Freeman 2012). While these traditions are clearly based on gender *in*equality and deserve to be addressed in the framework of the Convention, it has been noted that gender stereotypes that lead to harmful practices prevalent in Western societies have not nearly as often attracted the Committee's criticism (Holtmaat 2012). Thus, while sexist advertising and cosmetic surgery are also addressed in the dialogue, this happens less frequently and with less urgency. This observation suggests that the Committee's self-construction as culturally diverse and globally representative is not without bias (see also Merry 2006). As a privileged, transnational group of experts, the Committee implicitly or explicitly values some traditions as sources of women's empowerment, and it constructs others as an impediment to gender equality that States Parties have to overcome. In a normative context, it is inevitable to distinguish between practices that are "right" or "wrong," but the question remains where the line is drawn and why. It seems that cultures that are far removed from the Committee's self-image of transnational civility are more easily classified as problematic than others. This has sometimes led to somewhat uninformed Committee assessments,[28] but more generally, this tension is an expression of open-ended treaty interpretation.

The fourth crucial treaty interpretation discussed here concerns the Committee's attempt to develop a sound and widely acceptable stance in regard to reproductive health. CEDAW article 12 stipulates that women should enjoy the highest attainable standard of health throughout their lifetime *on equal levels with men*. Contrary to other articles, it envisions a goal that in many aspects requires a women-specific focus rather than one where men figure as comparators, in particular in regard to reproductive health. Article 12 deals with women's health in a general sense, and the Committee has shown that it envisions a wide scope; GR 24 on article 12 sheds light on gender differences in the field of health that include women's lower socio-economic status, and it emphasizes that disadvantaged groups of women—that is, elderly and disabled women—require special state attention.

Due to the ideological battles around reproductive rights specifically, the Committee has been cautious in crafting its position in this field in order to not appear as "too radical." Accordingly, its overarching position is that women's reproductive health includes good coverage of their reproductive needs during pregnancy and as mothers and that women should be able to determine the number and spacing of children they wish to have. This right requires having information about and access to contraceptives, ideally embedded in a public atmosphere that allows discussions of sexuality, contraception, and the implications of parenthood. In the Committee's view, both teenage pregnancies and abortions are an expression of *unwanted* pregnancies, which in turn are a violation of women's reproductive rights (read: women should have the means to prevent unwanted pregnancies). It regularly suggests the introduction of sex education for male and female teenagers and improved access to contraceptives to confront the problem. In the context of the latter, it has often recommended making emergency contraception available, as this seems to be a "gray zone" between contraception and abortion some abortion opponents are willing to accept. In respect to abortion itself, the Committee asks for a regime that does not punish the woman, as punishment does not address root causes, and that ensures that the procedure is not harmful to the woman's health. Contrary to accusations from several critics (e.g., Jacobson 2010) the Committee virtually never promotes abortion per se. Rather, it regularly asks for decriminalization and for the provision of *safe* abortions, in particular in countries where illegally performed abortions cause a high number of maternal deaths. Finally, the Committee also asks states where access to abortion is legal that all women should know about this right and that it should be uniformly available. While many States Parties find the Committee's position on reproductive rights unproblematic, some disagree fundamentally. The contested nature of the issue has made the Committee cautious in its quest for a balanced position. This dynamic has sidelined elements that could make article 12 more transformative, such as the relevance of male partner behavior for women's reproductive health and corresponding state responsibilities.

To summarize, the Committee's treaty interpretation has continuously scrutinized what it needs to realize the Convention. In reaction to pressing issues identified in the constructive dialogues, it has steadily expanded States Parties' responsibilities, for example, in regard to actively working against patriarchal social structures. As we will see later in this chapter, ongoing treaty interpretation also means integrating new issues into the coverage of the treaty. In some fields, the Committee's interpretations have met with resistance or criticism. Cases in point are the Committee's stance on women's reproductive health and rights and its demand to overcome stereotypical roles and functions within the family. Some of the critical voices accuse the Committee of being culturally biased. While this may be the case in some instances, it should also be noted that criticism is often articulated from perspectives that do not favor the notion of gender equality as spelled out in the Convention. All in all, the Committee's treaty interpretation is a mostly accepted, sometimes contested, and principally unfinished undertaking. It is *not* a process with entirely unpredictable outcomes; rather, it solidifies notions of gender equality through establishing standards and reiterating these standards, but this development remains dynamic. This is what it means to think of norms as "content-in-motion" (see Chap. 2).

Creating Efficiency: Technical Improvements of the Constructive Dialogue

Much of the Committee's work has focused on concrete improvements of its constructive dialogue with States Parties. In particular, it has taken measures to support adequate reporting, made efforts to better prepare and carry out the dialogue, and developed a follow-up procedure to enhance implementation. This section addresses these advancements in turn.

The constructive dialogue aims at a continuous assessment of each State Party's progress in regard to treaty implementation. This function depends on reports of meaningful content submitted in a timely fashion, that is, according to CEDAW article 18, one year after ratification for the first report and at least every four years for subsequent reports.[29] The reports, however, have both been of varying quality and have often not been submitted in time (see Chap. 7). The Committee has tried to deal with such shortcomings from its second session on, when it adopted guidelines for the preparation of initial reports (UN Doc. CEDAW/C/7), and later, for second and subsequent reports (UN Doc. A/43/38, Annex IV). It wanted the reports to follow the structure of the Convention and contain not only legal but also de facto information. Periodic reports should further describe steps that had been taken since the previous report. The reporting guidelines were refined several times. In 1995, OHCHR requested that reports to the treaty bodies be separated into two parts: a core document covering information relevant to all human rights treaties ratified by the respective state, and a treaty-specific document. Since 2006, the Common Core Document (CCD) is supposed to cover more ground, including information on "non-discrimination, equality, and effective remedies" (UN Doc. HRI/MC/2006/3). This means that it plays a more prominent part in the constructive dialogue under each single treaty. In 2008, the Committee decided on treaty specific guidelines complementing the ones concerning the CCD. Among other things, states should mention factors and difficulties for implementation of the Convention, they should refer to concluding observations of the Committee, and, if applicable, include responses to communications and inquiries under the OP. Initial reports should be limited to 60, periodic reports to 40 pages (UN Doc. A/63/38, p. 78f). These continuously evolving guidelines together with training workshops for governments on report writing have, in the eyes or Committee members, led to a recognizable improvement of reports. As one expert observes, "governments are now frank in their reports... they are even saying negative things" (Interview 19), which indicates that they understand their treaty obligations better and take them more seriously. However, some commentators have also argued that the reporting requirements for states have not only had clarifying functions but also made reporting unduly demanding (Melander 2007).

Timely submission of reports has been another problem for the Committee's work, as a number of States Parties have been permanently overdue with their periodic reports or have not submitted reports at all. Obviously, such behavior obstructs the idea of a continuous monitoring procedure. In the Committee's early years, this situation was exacerbated by its short annual meeting time, which created an alarming backlog of reports (Zwingel 2005b, p. 147–148). The expansion of the Committee's meeting time, its decision to meet in parallel chambers, and the adoption of several efficiency measures have eased that problem and its backlog is now reasonable. The CEDAW Committee has encouraged timely reporting, partly by "mild pressure," for example, by publishing a list of states with overdue reports in its annual reports, partly by offering assistance. In 1997, the Committee decided to invite the submission of a maximum of two combined reports (UN Doc. A/52/38, p. 1) and later even encouraged States Parties with a high number of overdue reports to combine *all* outstanding reports (UN Doc. A/55/38, p. 49). Since 2002, the Committee has increased its pressure on non-reporting states. It started with sending systematic reminders and offered closed meetings "to discuss challenges to timely reporting" (UN Doc. A/57/38, p. 131f). Since 2005, the Secretariat also has been sending out deadlines to States Parties with long overdue reports, informing them about the session in which their constructive dialogue would take place either with, or, "as a measure of last resort," without their report (UN Doc. A/62/38, p. 119). So far there has been only one case—Dominica—in which a dialogue was held without a report (UN Doc. CEDAW/C/DMA/CO/AR). A few other states—among them, the Central African Republic, Saint Vincent and the Grenadines, Senegal and Solomon Islands—were also targeted for this proceeding, but all of them responded to the announcement with the production of combined reports on the basis of which the dialogue then took place. Apparently, this tactic has been successful in increasing reporting discipline. However, it needs to be noted that States Parties with long overdue initial and periodic reports tend to be small or poor or both; for them, report writing is a significant investment of scarce resources.

Among the Committee's efforts to better carry out the dialogue, three dimensions should be highlighted, namely dialogue preparation, consideration of additional information beyond State Party reports, and the structuring of the dialogue with a view to provide useful assessment for States Parties in the form of concluding observations. In reaction to its limited meeting time in the early years, the Committee initiated a pre-session working group in 1989. It consists of four to five experts in equitable regional representation and came to fruition as a low-budget alternative to the Committee's request for more meeting time, which had been rejected by the Secretariat. The pre-session working group basically establishes a pre-dialogue. It looks into States Parties' reports early and prepares a list of questions in response to the reports. The list is then transmitted to the respective state prior to its constructive dialogue. This practice was thought to save time in the actual dialogue without sacrificing substance. Over time, it went through significant changes, for example, the Committee has invited SAs and NGOs to provide information at this early stage (UN Doc. A/53/38, p.3), and States Parties are now expected to answer the working group's questions *before*, rather than during the constructive dialogue, as this practice had led to the rather tiring dynamic of delegates reading out a list of answers (Byrnes 1989, p. 25; Interview 2). Together with the State Party's report, these responses now form the basis for the dialogue. This practice has clearly added substance to the dialogue, but it has also increased States Parties' reporting work load. In order to keep this additional round of scrutiny manageable, the Committee decided that the pre-session working group should transmit no more than 20 questions to a State Party and asks for a response of no more than 25 pages (UN Doc. A/67/38, p. 4).

Another preparatory measure that the Committee initiated in 1998 is the designation of a "country rapporteur" for each State Party report considered. If possible, the rapporteur should come from the same region as the state concerned in order to ensure context-sensitivity. Her or his tasks include informing the other experts on general patterns and areas of concern in the country, ensuring that all important issues are raised during the dialogue, and preparing a draft of the concluding observations for the Committee to discuss. Over time, the role of the rapporteur has been strengthened, as it has proven to be a useful way of preparing the dialogue and enhancing the production of context adequate concluding observations (UN Doc. A/67/38, p. 37; Boerefijn 2012d).

Another dimension of enhancing the constructive dialogue is the Committee's increasing reliance on additional information provided by SAs, NGOs, and independent National Human Rights Institutions (NHRIs). Despite the general improvement in the quality of state reports, information from independent sources has proven to be urgently necessary to make the dialogue more meaningful. Input from SAs, which is an explicit option according to CEDAW article 22, was first rather sparse but has increased during the 1990s when the Committee started to reserve meeting time for country specific information presented by SAs. NGO interest in CEDAW budded in the second half of the 1980s. While many experts appreciated NGOs' supply of alternative information, it was not right away clear to the Committee how to integrate it into the dialogue. The NGO International Women's Rights Action Watch supplied regular information in the form of so-called shadow reports since 1992 (Evatt

2002). The Committee decided to hold informal meetings with NGO representatives in 1997 (UN Doc. A/52/38, p. 1). The wording of this decision reflects both the hesitation towards and the approval of NGO participation in the Committee's work:

> The Committee was broadly supportive of the involvement of non-governmental organizations in its work, its general view being that non-governmental organizations' material did not compromise the independence of the members....It was stressed that the input of NGOs should not be perceived as clandestine material given to Committee members. (UN Doc. A/52/38, p. 48)

Since 1999, NGOs are assigned one regular meeting per session, including translation service, to present their information. Meanwhile, the Committee has become more unequivocal in recognizing how much it has benefitted from the input of NGOs. It has praised NGOs influence in regard to the constructive dialogue, the drafting of GRs and the proceedings under the OP, and in terms of domestic implementation of the Convention (decision 45/VI, UN Doc. A/65/38, p. 138). Since 2005, NHRIs[30] have become a third group of independent players to contribute to the constructive dialogue, a trend that the Committee has explicitly welcomed (UN Doc. A/63/38, p.84–85). Chap. 6 shows in more detail how crucial the work of NGOs has been in regard to the reach of CEDAW. They have been the most important "norm translators" to bring the Convention not only in contact with governmental policies but also with societal structures and relations.

The third dimension of improvement has affected the dialogue itself. It has been converted from a rather open-ended conversation into a highly structured exchange. This is particularly visible in the introduction of time limits both for the presenting delegations[31] and the Committee members[32] as well as in the practice of clustering questions according to the four substantive parts of the Convention rather than addressing each article in turn.[33] While experts initially refused such limitations (UN Doc. A/41/45, p. 4), they have become more pragmatic on this issue in order to make the most of the limited time at their disposal. In its 58th session in 2014, the Committee decided to follow the practice of other treaty bodies and introduced the simplified reporting procedure based on a "list of issues prior to reporting." This procedure asks States Parties to report on a set of selected and particularly pressing issues rather than on the entire scope of the Convention (O'Flaherty and Tsai 2011). Starting as a pilot in 2015, this option is available for States Parties with overdue periodic reports (UN Doc. CEDAW/C/2014/II/CRP).

One of the Committee's goals in better structuring the dialogue has been to make it more result-oriented. In 1994, it discontinued the practice of publishing a detailed description of each dialogue in its annual report and instead issued concluding observations.[34] The focus of these concluding observations is on providing States Parties with the most relevant observations of the Committee and giving them concrete guidance in their endeavor to implement the Convention. They include sections on difficulties, positive aspects, principal areas of concern, and Committee recommendations for action. Since their introduction, concluding observations have undergone a number of changes, all of them intended to make them more usable for states (Boerefijn 2012d, p.501–504). Despite this general trend of improvement it is also true that the concluding observations have not always been of comparable quality partly because they have to be finalized under considerable time pressure (Byrnes 2002, p. 136).

The most recent innovation in regard to strengthening the outcomes of the constructive dialogue is the introduction of follow-up measures. While the Committee's concluding observations intended to increase treaty implementation, States Parties do not often proactively respond to them. Following the practices of other treaty bodies, the Committee therefore decided in 2008 to expand its concluding observations and identify two recommendations for which it would request a follow-up report on specific implementation steps. The issues picked are the most urgent ones, and States Parties are asked to report back within one or two years (UN Doc. A/63/38, p. 88). The innovation is that the Committee requires a state to develop *concrete* implementation measures on pressing issues *within a short time frame.* NGOs are also invited to submit documentation. In order to assess States Parties' responses, the post of a rapporteur on follow-up reports was created.

In an evaluating report of 2011, the then rapporteur on follow-up characterized the procedure as "achieving its stated goal of acting as a tool of implementation of the Convention." She also stated, however, that its continuation would require adequate time allocation by the Committee and the Secretariat. The Committee agreed to continue the procedure and evaluate it again two years later (UN Doc. A/67/38, p. 43). In its 54th session in 2013, the Committee specified the methodology of the follow-up procedure, introducing categories of assessment (including "full," "partial," and "no implementation" of the recommendation and "not sufficient information to assess") that would correspond with different reactions from the Committee (e.g., no further action required in case of "full implementation"). It also reiterated that States Parties not responding should be systematically reminded (UN Doc. A/68/38, p. 89). The 2013 assessment provides some numerical data about the procedure, for example, that out of the 73 follow-up reports the Committee had requested until its 49th session in 2011, 45 or 62% were received, whereas NGOs had submitted alternative information in 13 of these cases. Only 9 out of these 45 reports were submitted in time. In terms of content, the Committee considered 19% of the reports to represent full implementation of its recommendations, 41% partial implementation, 29% no implementation, and for 11% of the cases, there was not sufficient information for assessment. The assessment comes, again, to the conclusion that the follow-up procedure serves its purpose of enhancing the implementation of the Convention and that it should be continued (UN Doc. A/69/38, p. 55f).

Despite this positive assessment, it remains an open question how much this measure can push treaty implementation. On the one hand, it gives the Committee a tool to "nudge" States Parties and show them what their concrete and prompt responsibilities under the Convention are. The follow-up procedure gives a state the opportunity to present its commitment, and it allows another possibility for NGO scrutiny. On the other hand, it is possible that the procedure develops into yet another layer of reporting rather than a qualitatively different tool to foster issue-specific implementation. Further, many States Parties do not react to follow-up requests in time and need to be periodically reminded. Those who do respond often do not describe concrete measures developed in response to the Committee's recommendation but rather present *any* governmental action broadly relevant to the issue at hand.[35] Finally, NGO participation in the procedure has not been overwhelming even if many of the statements submitted have provided great substance.

As this section has shown, the Committee has worked hard to make the constructive dialogue as comprehensive, efficient, and output-oriented as possible. It remains to be seen if the follow-up procedure, the latest innovation to enhance treaty implementation, primarily, adds another layer of reporting, or if it provides a suitable tool for States Parties and NGOs alike to put the Convention to work. I have argued elsewhere that a sound strategy of treaty implementation has to be based on a division of labor among a wide-cast network of norm advocates (Zwingel 2013b). In this network, an international monitoring body fulfills a crucial function but needs to "pass the ball" to actors more closely rooted within domestic contexts, such as operational UN Agencies, NGOs, and NHRIs, simply because they are better equipped to enhance women's rights as a lived reality.

An Assertive Interpreter of the Convention: Reservations and General Recommendations

Hand in hand with monitoring treaty implementation goes the continuous effort to clarify the meaning and scope of the Convention. As we have seen previously, the Committee has expanded the scope of state responsibilities under the Convention, yet it has also demonstrated increasing assertiveness in the way it positions itself in regard to States Parties' reservations and through its GRs.

CEDAW article 28 allows states to enter reservations upon ratification as long as those reservations are not incompatible with the "object and purpose" of the Convention. This provision can be read as permitting states to become party to the treaty even if they have minor disagreements with it; however, article 28 does not specify who should determine compatibility of reservations, and this leaves the decision to States Parties themselves. Commentators have long lamented that CEDAW has received a particularly high proportion of reservations that contradict its basic tenets (Bayefski 2001; Clark 1991), but there has also been a tendency among States Parties to remove or narrow their reservations over time (Connors 2012a; Chap. 7).

The Committee has been discussing how to deal with reservations from early on, starting with Egypt's first report in 1984 (ibid.). Since the Convention does not assign the Committee any direct function in this regard, experts decided it was their duty to examine how far the implementation of treaty obligations in a State Party was impeded by its reservations. Starting with GR 4, the Committee has consistently urged states to review and withdraw reservations in the light of their self-assumed responsibility for women's rights. In 1987, the Committee took a more forceful step in order to manifest its concern regarding reservations. It had observed that the broadest and, in its view, most damaging reservations had been based on the requirements of Islamic law, yet the meaning of such reservations remained vague as Islamic law is open to different interpretations. As a consequence, the Committee requested that the UN conduct a study on "the status of women under Islamic laws and customs" (UN Doc. A/42/38, p. 80). However, this request was considered by some UN member states as offensive to Islam and the study was never carried out (UN Doc. A/C.3/42/SR. 22, 26–28, 30). The Committee had received a clear signal that it had overstepped its mandate.

This incident notwithstanding, the Committee has continuously addressed reservations in the constructive dialogue, for example, in asking States Parties to clarify meaning and scope of reservations entered and about plans to withdraw them. Its approach has been one of "uncompromising insistence on the universal validity of CEDAW norms" that it sees undermined by reservations based on ethnic or religious diversity (Goonesekere 2007, p. 54). The Committee elaborated its strongest statement on reservations in 1998. It defines its own role in terms of assessing the permissibility of reservations as *complementary* to that of States Parties. Further, the Committee declares reservations to article 2—on the legal and institutional framework to eliminate discrimination against women—and article 16—on equal rights of men and women in marriage and the family—as most dangerous. It ends by urging States Parties to "re-examine... self-imposed limitations to full compliance with all the principles in the Convention by the entry of reservations" (UN Doc. A/53/38, p. 50). The tone of this statement and the built-in scrutiny of reservations in the constructive dialogue show the Committee's firm position in regard to reservations. It also appears that its authority in this matter is not openly questioned anymore.

GRs are another tool through which the Committee clarifies the steps States Parties should take to implement the Convention comprehensively. According to CEDAW article 21, the Committee is entitled to make "suggestions and general recommendations based on the examination of reports and information received from the States Parties." While GRs are not legally binding, they constitute an authoritative interpretation of the treaty and are considered "soft law" (Byrnes 1989). The Committee was initially rather cautious in issuing GRs,[36] mostly because the Eastern bloc members did not consider it appropriate for the Committee to interpret the Convention (Evatt 2002). The early GRs were therefore rather technical and short. In 1986, the UN's legal counsel informed the Committee that adopting GRs was within the scope of its mandate. In reaction, many experts came forward with issues that deserved interpretation. GR 19 on VAW adopted in 1992 is widely recognized as the first substantial interpretation of the Convention and, thus, as a turning point in the Committee's work (Byrnes 2002; Cartwright 2007; Fitzpatrick 1994; Shin 2007). In the words of one Committee expert,

> General recommendation 19 represented the first time that the Committee developed its philosophy and explained itself and produced what I think was a

very influential document. And we followed the same process since then ... it shows a much more in-depth examination than previously. (Interview 11)

In 1997, the Committee laid down guidelines for the preparation of each GR to ensure a qualitative and consensual process (UN Doc. A/52/38, p. 127). Essential elements of this process are that it starts with an open debate on the topic to which the Committee invites input from other bodies and organizations and that the drafting process has to undergo several rounds of consideration within the Committee. Systematically requesting input has become increasingly important for the generation of GRs. For its recently adopted GR 30 on the protection of women in conflict and post-conflict situations, the Committee held one general and five regional consultations[37] in order to increase input of women directly affected by armed conflict. This was the first time a human rights treaty body undertook such broad efforts in the context of compiling a GR (email communication UN Women staff member, 2013).

GRs offer the opportunity to interpret the Convention with a view to expanding its coverage, addressing any newly emerging pattern of women's rights violations, and ultimately, making it a better tool to advance the rights of women (Interview 5). Each human rights treaty has its limitations due to the historical context of its creation. The text of CEDAW does not address the pertinent issue of VAW because this matter was not understood as part of the human rights framework when the Convention was drafted. GR 19, however, incorporated VAW into the Committee's mandate. Also, many GRs discuss state responsibilities in regard to intersectional forms of discrimination against women, a problem that is only implicitly covered by the Convention in article 1 (and explicitly in regard to rural women in article 14). For example, GR 18 addresses state responsibilities in regard to women with disabilities and GR 27 in regard to the rights of older women. GR 25 on temporary special measures attends to the problem of intersectional discrimination most comprehensively (Schöpp-Schilling 2007a).

The Committee has, in general, used GRs to expand the scope of the Convention, yet this is a strategy that bears the potential of conflict. From the perspective of States Parties, "stretching" the Convention should have limits. They do not typically make such disagreement explicit but simply do not follow up on the Committee's interpretation. A case in point is the understanding of temporary special measures. With GR 25, the Committee has clarified that it perceives TSMs as integral part of the effort to achieve de facto equality. Accordingly, TSMs are mandatory tools to correct structural gender hierarchies, not "special treatment" of discriminated groups (Raday 2012a). States Parties, however, have often not followed the Committee's recommendation to introduce TSMs because they consider them optional (Liebowitz and Zwingel 2014; Chap. 8). Another example is GR 26 on women migrant workers adopted in 2008. It spells out a lot of responsibilities in particular for countries of destination of female labor migration, ranging from proper labor codes to non-discriminatory family reunion schemes (UN Doc. A/64/38, p. 15ff). This is an important specification of the women's rights framework as it makes clear the multiple layers of vulnerability female migrant workers experience (Hainsfurther 2009). From the perspective of States Parties, however, CEDAW does not substantially cover issues of migration, and most of them are not prepared to protect the rights of female or male migrants, as the low number of 48 ratifications of the Convention on the Protection of the Rights of All Migrant Workers and Members of their Families indicates (as of December 2015).

One of the most controversial topics of "content stretching" in the Committee's work has been the inclusion of sexual orientation and gender identity into the scope of the Convention. It was particularly disputed within the drafting of GR 28 on article 2 (Interviews 4, 5, 12, 13 and 18). This GR lays out States Parties' obligations in order to ensure gender equality *of outcome*. Consultations for this GR started in 2004 (UN Doc. A/59/38, p. 174) and were concluded in 2010 after an unusually long period of time. Discrimination of LGBTI persons has by now become a concern for human rights activists (Wilkinson and Langlois 2014). The Committee, with its focus on discrimination based on gender roles, has a history of criticizing criminalization of lesbianism in its concluding observations, but it has not been consistent or comprehensive in targeting discrimination based on sexual orientation and gender identity more generally. In 2003, the Committee requested that the Secretariat conduct a study on how other treaty bodies have dealt with sexual orientation.[38] Most but not all experts are of the opinion that sexual orientation is part of the Committee's mandate (Interviews 5, 12, and 18). In addition, NGOs have been active in bringing sexual orientation and gender identity to the table, both in addressing the issue in their shadow reports for the constructive dialogue[39] and in lobbying for its inclusion in the GR on article 2. The supportive position holds that lesbian, bisexual, transgender, and intersex women suffer from intersectional discrimination as women *and* as non-heterosexuals in a heteronormative world. If article 2 is about ensuring equality of outcomes, then states have to take these additional vulnerabilities of women belonging to sexual minorities into account (IWRAW AP 2007b, p. 7). A minority of experts, however, were opposed to integrating sexual orientation into the Committee's mandate. In a consultation regarding GR 28, one expert stated that elimination of discrimination based on sexual orientation was covered neither under CEDAW nor under International Law in general, contrary to the High Commissioner's position (Amnesty International et al. 2008). The Committee adopted GR 28 as a whole by consensus, but it took a separate vote on a number of contentious paragraphs (UN Docs. A/66/38, p. 102; A/67/38, p. 3–4).

Another controversial "stretching initiative" in the work of the treaty bodies addresses extraterritorial responsibilities of states. The Committee has taken a few steps towards the idea of transnational accountability in the constructive dialogue, for example, it has assigned States Parties responsibility to ensure that multinational corporations provide decent working conditions for their female employees, many of whom work outside of the territory of the home state of that corporation in export processing zones (Evatt 2007). It has also started to deal with non-refoulement duties of States Parties in the context of its work with the OP (see chap. 5). However, compared to other treaty bodies, extraterritorial responsibilities have not yet figured central in the work of the CEDAW Committee (Byrnes 2012b; Ruggie 2007).

To sum up the characteristics of the constructive dialogue described: While the Committee has begun its work in a somewhat timid fashion, it has over time come to interpret its mandate as an assertive monitoring body. To effectively support States Parties in implementing their treaty obligations, it needs both the acceptance of states and a consistent way of interpreting the Convention—these two dimensions are intertwined and have been built up over time. As for treaty interpretation, the Committee has developed an increasingly complex vision of all the components necessary to reach de facto gender equality, and accordingly, it has expanded the scope of state responsibilities. In particular, it has stressed the need for systemic transformation, for example, in overcoming hierarchical gender stereotypes. While States Parties have not always followed the Committee's interpretation, its increasingly self-confident position has attracted nongovernmental women's rights proponents to engage with the Committee's work. This engagement has added substance to the global women's rights discourse and strengthened the reach of CEDAW into domestic contexts (see also chap. 6). Further, the Committee has invested a lot of energy in improving the efficiency of its monitoring procedure. This has been demanding for states, as high-quality reports with broad coverage are requested, but it has also been helpful for them as the Committee has focused more and more on clearly articulated assessments and recommendations. Finally, the comprehensive interpretation of what the Convention demands from States Parties is also visible in the Committee's determined approach confronting treaty reservations and developing GRs.

Taking Stock: Where Does the "Women's Bill of Rights" Stand Today?

The three dimensions that this chapter has fleshed out—the Committee's support structures, its international standing, and its working methods—show a process of growing rhetorical and material recognition of CEDAW within the UN. The development and use of the OP to the Convention, detailed in Chap. 5, point in the same direction. This process has led CEDAW to become a strong instrument not only of comparable standing with the other treaty bodies but also of distinct nature due to its double affiliation with the human rights and the gender architecture of the UN. Table 4.1 summarizes the major developments described in the chapter in line with the stages of global gender norm creation presented in Chap. 3.

It is noteworthy that during the 1975–1995 phase—when gender equality norms became widely recognized as globally relevant—the CEDAW Committee was largely invisible and had to fight against normative resistance and resource-related limitations, *in spite of* the fact that it was itself part of that global awareness raising process. Only in the phase of consolidation and decreasing international prominence of gender equality norms (1995–present) did CEDAW unfold its full potential as an expert body interpreting women's rights and monitoring their realization. This time lag shows how much effort it takes to translate a rhetorically accepted idea into a sound and efficient institution. What has been at the heart of the Committee's activities all along is to create the Convention's relevance and the legitimacy of its monitoring body on the inter-governmental stage. In the absence of any other "currency," *to be considered important* is the only way an international instrument may trigger change. Such constant international "norm work" is indispensable—if it is not undertaken,

Table 4.1 CEDAW development as "living document"

Phase	*Working conditions*	*International standing*	*Committee at work*
1975–1995	Lack of resources; Secretariat without human rights expertise; limited meeting time	Almost no connections until Vienna and Beijing Conferences (1993, 1995); start of interaction with other treaty bodies	Modest attempts to structure and prepare dialogue and improve quality of reports; hardly independent information; hesitant position in terms of defining Committee's mandate vis-à-vis States Parties
1995–present	Increase of resources; Secretariat combines human rights and gender expertise; expansion of meeting time	Expanded interaction with other treaty bodies; better knowledge of CEDAW by SAs (UNIFEM in particular); Convention used in their operational work	Structured dialogue; introduction and improvement of concluding observations; significant amount of independent information; clear vision of own mandate (for example, substantial GRs); OP adds new ways to implement Convention

a norm that has become symbolically pervasive may never move into a stage where it attracts inter-governmental commitment. Thus, it is one lesson from this chapter that norm creation on the international level has to be understood as a long and cumbersome process with an open end—and that it does not in itself imply meaningful norm translation toward domestic contexts; this is a different, if related process.

Next to the general international strengthening of CEDAW, this chapter has also shown some challenges on the way. I would like to highlight three. First, the collective of Committee members has to balance the tension between representing strong women's rights advocacy, on the one hand, and the need to create the Committee's legitimacy in an inter-governmental setting, on the other. This tension becomes visible whenever the Committee takes a bold position in terms of treaty interpretation; the more it stretches the scope of the Convention in the interest of women, and it often does so following positions of women's NGOs articulated in the constructive dialogue, the less willing are States Parties to follow. In some fields, such as reproductive rights and sexual orientation, a daring position has also attracted open criticism—a situation that the Committee wants to avoid as it may diminish its international authority. In the view of women's rights advocates, such concerns have sometimes made the Committee's position more cautious, sticking to technicalities more than necessary (Interviews 2 and 13).

A second challenge lies in the complexity of the constructive dialogue. The Committee has continuously worked to improve the process, and while this has lead to a more substantial exchange with States Parties, it has also sometimes resulted in overloading the dialogue and in an undue focus on details. Some experts have therefore stated that they would like to see the dialogue concentrate on central issues (Interviews 3 and 5). On the other hand, it is also important to keep the dialogue's in-depth character, which is why its time limitations continue to be a challenge, in particular when it comes to exceptionally large states and states with federal systems (Interviews 12 and 18).

Finally, there is a crucial dilemma connected to implementation. One the one hand, the Committee wants to trigger implementation of the Convention's provisions; on the other hand, its mandate is to *monitor* implementation undertaken by states, not to engage in implementation itself. The Committee's work on sharpening its concluding observations and adding the follow-up element are reactions to the realization that the monitoring procedure *alone* does often not sway States Parties to proactively implement the Convention. Many experts believe that high-quality concluding observations are the key tool of the Committee to enhance implementation, and they see further room for improvement (Goonesekere 2007). The increased concern of the Committee to facilitate implementation, however, may also weaken its core function. In the words of an NGO representative, this emphasis could lead to a less holistic vision of women's rights, yet it is precisely such a vision that the Committee has the mandate to represent:

> They say ... let's talk about specifics and implementation. Those two things cannot be the things that drive the Committee. They are important, but they are not exclusive. The Committee has to constantly raise the bar on women's rights. That is their first mandate. They don't implement, we implement (Interview 13).

In sum, in an ideal implementation process, the Committee would have the function of a light house; backed by the acceptance of governments, it takes a sufficiently radical approach to detect all forms of discrimination that women in their diversity are exposed to and develops measures to eliminate them. It guides governments on their journey towards elaborating sound and comprehensive gender equality policies in the spirit of the Convention, also drawing on the assessment of non-governmental women's rights advocates. This function makes the Committee the center piece of an ongoing process of global discourse translation, while impact translation work is carried out by various transnational and domestic agents both in the governmental and non-governmental sphere. Chaps. 6–8 shed light on these agents as well as on the enabling and constraining factors under which they operate.

Notes

1. Of the nine presently existing human rights treaties with a monitoring committee attached, the CCPR, CERD, the Convention on Torture and Other Cruel, Inhuman, or Degrading Treatment or Punishment (CAT), the Convention on the Rights of the Child (CRC), the Convention on the Rights of Migrant Workers and their Families (CRMW), the Convention on the Rights of Persons with Disabilities (CRPD), and the Convention on the Protection of all Persons from Enforced Disappearance (CED) either do not specify meeting time at all (e.g., the CERD and CED) or keep it vague (e.g., "shall normally meet annually" in the CRC) or stipulate that meeting time should enable effective performance (e.g., the CCPR and the CAT). The original text of the Covenant on Economic, Social and Cultural Rights (CESCR) does not provide for an independent Committee, but this was changed in 1985 (ECOSOC Resolution 1985/17).
2. The Committee had asked for eight additional days (UN Doc. A/42/38, p. 79).
3. See the Committee's Decisions 36/I, 37/I, and 39/I (UN Docs. A/61/38, p. 164 and A/62/38, p. 2 and 226).
4. For example, it enhanced the Committee's discussion in regard to reservations by providing an analysis of the practices of other treaty bodies (UN Doc. A/56/38, p. 37).
5. The Division conducted various workshops on CEDAW for government representatives, for example, in Benin in 1999 and Bosnia Herzegovina and Kuala Lumpur in 2002 (Ouedraogo 1999; UN Doc. A/57/38, p. 79). Between 2007 and 2009, the DAW assisted Bosnia Herzegovina, Haiti, Liberia, and Sierra Leone in their implementation efforts (UN Doc. A/64/342, p. 12).
6. The Committee subsequently expressed the urge to reinstate the practice of holding one annual meeting in New York in order to have a chance to maintain its relationships with UN Women and the CSW (decision 54/XII, UN Doc. A/68/38, p. 95), but this decision received no positive response.
7. The budget of the OHCHR for servicing the treaty bodies has almost tripled between 2001 and 2010, yet this rise in resources has not matched the increased workload that the rising number of treaty ratifications, treaty

bodies (from 5 to 10 between 2001 and 2010), corresponding experts (from 74 to 172), and treaty body sessions (from 11 to 24 per year) require. In the view of the OHCHR, this situation "causes enormous stress for the Secretariat in its present configuration to substantively and operationally manage" (OHCHR 2011).

8. The Committee has established other links as well, for example it has been present at diverse World Conferences, and it often issues statements on current affairs in which it establishes a connection to the Convention. One example was its comment on the devastating earthquake in Haiti applying a gender perspective to its consequences as well as to disaster relief efforts (UN Doc. A/65/38, p. 132). This rhetorical presence has an additional potential to increase the Committee's visibility.
9. At the time, both the CERD and the CAT Committees had been addressing gender issues only randomly, while the Human Rights Committee (HRC) and the CESCR and CRC Committees had taken a more systematic approach towards gender-based discrimination, visible in the ways women's and girls' related issues were addressed in the constructive dialogue, concluding observations, and GRs. For later assessments with similar findings but increasing scope, see Johnstone (2006), Farha (2008), and UN Doc. A/HRC/4/104.
10. Over the last 30 years, female representation in treaty bodies other than the CEDAW and CRC Committees has increased, but only slowly. It rose from 11% in 1989 to 19% in 2000 and to 27% in 2011 (Byrnes 1989, p. 8; Edwards 2011).
11. For example, the Human Rights Council's Universal Periodic Review has been discussed as a potential threat to the treaty bodies reporting mechanisms due to its similar scope but higher visibility (O'Flaherty and Tsai 2011).
12. Among them have been the ILO, the Food and Agricultural Organization (FAO), the United Nations Development Fund for Women (UNIFEM), the United Nations Population Fund (UNFPA), UNICEF and the United Nations Educational, Scientific and Cultural Organization (UNESCO).
13. UNIFEM's work related to facilitating implementation of CEDAW in domestic contexts is covered in Chap. 6 on transnational activism.
14. Women's mass organizations in socialist countries are included here despite the fact that they are typically closely connected to their governments. Both in 2000 and 2010, two experts were members of such organizations, respectively.
15. It should be noted that, since all treaty bodies have a high percentage of government employees serving on them, this is not a CEDAW-specific phenomenon (Bayefski 2001, p. 102f).
16. The independence of experts has been a continuous concern of the treaty bodies. In 2012, the meeting of Chairpersons issued the so-called Addis

Ababa guidelines to ensure experts' impartiality and to avoid any possible conflict of interest (UN Doc. A/67/222, Annex I). The CEDAW Committee incorporated them into its rules of procedure (UN Doc. A/68/38, p. 88).

17. This regional distribution follows *The World's Women 2010. Trends and Statistics* (United Nations 2010). *More Developed Regions* includes Eastern Europe, Western Europe and Australia, Canada, Japan, New Zealand, and the USA.
18. This is, however, only a general calculation that does not count years of service of each expert—some have served one term or less, others over a decade.
19. Angola, Cameroon, Central African Republic, Chad, Congo, Democratic Republic of Congo, Equatorial Guinea, Gabon, and Sao Tome and Principe.
20. Kazakhstan, Kyrgyzstan, Tajikistan, Turkmenistan, and Uzbekistan.
21. Cook Islands, Fiji, Kiribati, Marshall Islands, Micronesia, Nauru, Papua New Guinea, Samoa, Solomon Islands, Tuvalu, and Vanuatu.
22. Until 2002, experts received a modest honorarium, yet this was reduced to a symbolic payment of $1 per year (Boerefijn 2012d, p. 489).
23. For example, an expert asked the USSR in its first dialogue in 1983 about the participation of women in peaceful conflict settlement in regard to the invasion of Afghanistan, a question that the delegation refused to answer publicly (UN Doc. ST/CSDHA/5, p. 146). Similarly, in its initial dialogue with the Committee in 1986, the delegation from El Salvador did not respond to questions relating to the general human rights situation in the country, stating that it had nothing to do with the situation of women (UN Doc. A/41/45, p. 42). While such complaints have become rare, Belarus has recently complained about the Committee's concerns in regard to the arbitrary arrest, detention, and mistreatment of women in Belarus who had protested the 2010 Presidential election. Belarus considered this assessment of the Committee "false, non-impartial" and "null and void" (Note verbale, 22/2/2011, http://www2.ohchr.org/english/bodies/cedaw/cedaws48.htm).
24. An often cited example of an embarrassing performance is that of the Filipino delegation in 1984. Its head informed the Committee that in the Philippines "women retain their femininity and gentleness because, in such a way, they had obtained many advantages and progress. It was for that reason that no women's liberation movement had existed in the Philippines." (UN Doc. ST/CSDHA/5, p. 244) He was replaced and had to apologize for this statement (UN Doc. ST/CSDHA/5, p. 246).
25. For example, Bangladesh declared in 1993 that the personal status of women was subject to the norms of religious communities (UN Doc. A/48/38, p. 46f); in the same session, Kenya emphasized the need to

preserve cultural practices, even if they went against the rights set forth in the Convention (UN Doc. A/48/38, p. 19f).

26. The in-depth case study of Chile (see Chap. 8) shows one example of such half-hearted reactions to the Committee's recommendation to use temporary special measures in the field of political decision making.
27. Trebilcock (2010) argues that the Committee could make more use of article 5 in the field of employment. Its approach has focused on getting women into standard work and drawing attention to their role as unpaid or underpaid care workers, but it rarely targets the gender-biased ideas of standard work around which the labor market is organized.
28. Merry discusses this shortcoming in regard to the Committee's criticism of the Fijian practice of dealing with rape cases in an extra-judicial way. The Committee could not perceive of this practice as legitimate and sufficiently proactive, but in Merry's view, it missed fundamental contextual parameters (2006). There are other instances where adherence to CEDAW norms without considering context factors may prove to be problematic—the legal abolishment of polygamy is a case in point as it disempowers women who continue to live in polygamous marriages (Wing 2012).
29. The Convention also provides for the possibility to request reports on an exceptional basis, but the Committee has only rarely requested such reports, typically in reaction to a massive outbreak of violence (UN Doc. A/66/38, p. 88–89). I do not consider these reports, because the strength of CEDAW lies, in my view, in ongoing monitoring, not crisis management.
30. NHRIs are independent monitoring institutions to promote and protect human rights within a country. They have to be created in accordance with the so-called Paris Principles adopted by the UN General Assembly in 1993 and require accreditation by the International Coordinating Committee of National Human Rights Institutions.
31. A 1999 rule allowed 45 minutes for initial presentations and 60 minutes for periodic reports (UN Doc. A/54/38, p. 39). Currently, all delegations have 30 minutes for their introductory statement.
32. An expert's statement may be three minutes long and each expert may raise two questions per State Party (UN Doc. A/59/38, p. 261f).
33. This is true for periodic reports. Initial reports are still dealt with on an article-by-article basis, but articles 1 and 2, 7 and 8, and 15, and 16 are considered together (Boerefijn 2012d).
34. Initially, they were called "concluding comments," but the Committee later decided to use the same term as all other treaty bodies (UN Doc. A/63/38, p. 2).
35. Occasionally, they also reject the Committee's recommendations, for example, the United Kingdom (UN Doc. CEDAW/C/UK/CO/6/Add.1).

36. A list of all GRs can be found at OHCHR's website (http://www.ohchr.org/EN/HRBodies/CEDAW/Pages/Recommendations.aspx). CEDAW article 21 also allows the Committee to make suggestions that, according to the Committee's decision, should address UN bodies not States Parties (UN Doc. A/42/38, p. 10).
37. The general consultation took place during the Committee's 49th session in 2011; the regional ones took place in Asia, Europe and Central Asia, Africa, Latin America and the Caribbean, and the Arab region.
38. In a nutshell, this working paper shows that the CESCR Committee and HRC have addressed the issue most regularly in GRs, concluding observations, and views responding to individual complaints. The CRC Committee did so occasionally in concluding observations and the CAT Committee in one concluding observation. The CERD Committee had not dealt with sexual orientation (UN Doc. CEDAW/2003/II/ WP.3).
39. Sexual orientation and gender identity are often addressed as one issue among others in shadow reports, but some organizations write their reports specifically on this dimensions. For the time between 2009 and 2012, this is true for NGOs from Argentina, Chile, Germany, Guatemala, Guyana, Japan, Panama, the Russian Federation, Switzerland, and Uzbekistan.

CHAPTER 5

A New Tool in the Toolbox: The Optional Protocol to the Convention

On December 10, 1999, the Optional Protocol to the CEDAW Convention was opened for signature to CEDAW States Parties. It entered into force one year later and has been ratified by 105 states as of June 2015. The OP provides for two new procedures. The first one allows individuals or groups to submit complaints to the Committee if they see their rights under the Convention violated. The second is an inquiry procedure that allows the Committee to investigate cases of grave or systematic violations of women's rights. The "new tool in the toolbox" expands the means to protect women's rights under CEDAW. It does so in a manner that is conceptually different from the monitoring procedure presented in Chap. 4. This chapter first summarizes the scope of the OP as a result of diverse interests manifested during the drafting process. Secondly, it provides an overview of the Committee's practice in regard to the OP, in particular the evolving character of its jurisdiction. I conclude with some thoughts on the special contribution of the OP to norm translation around the Convention.

In the Victim's or the State's Interest? Main Features of OP to CEDAW

The idea of having an individual complaint procedure had already come up during the drafting process of the Convention but was not seriously pursued (Connors 2012b). It resurfaced in the early 1990s, most prominently in the context of the 1993 Vienna Conference on

S. Zwingel, *Translating International Women's Rights*,
Gender and Politics, DOI 10.1057/978-1-137-31501-4_5

Human Rights. In order to strengthen women's options to claim their rights, the final document of the conference urged both the CSW and the CEDAW Committee to examine the possibility of an OP to the Convention (World Conference on Human Rights 1993, II/40). This encouragement notwithstanding, the process of creating the OP was not initiated by the CSW but by an independent group of experts that met in 1994 in Maastricht to prepare a draft OP. The CEDAW Committee then adopted the outcome document of this meeting as its suggestion no. 7 (UN Doc. A/50/38, p. 2f). According to one CEDAW expert, this was done because the work of the Maastricht group would not have been recognized by governments: "The politics of the UN is such that an NGO initiative like this one, even with three experts from the Committee on the expert group, and some of the world's best experts in the field of human rights and enforcement mechanisms—it would never be adopted as the draft. Never" (Interview 11).

In 1995, the CSW took notice of the Committee's suggestion no. 7 and set up a working group to elaborate a draft OP to the Convention in 1996. Upon the CSW's invitation to submit views on an OP to CEDAW, only 19 NGOs and 18 governments responded with generally supportive comments.[1] The working group adopted a final draft in 1999 after only three years of negotiations. The speed of the process was surprising given that many governments did not consider the OP a pressing concern. Also, during the negotiations, states revealed widely differing positions on the nature of the instrument, with some of them preferring a non-intrusive procedure and others one that took the needs of potential complainants seriously. The later position was reinforced by the continuous and vocal presence of women's rights NGOs. During the course of the negotiations, their expertise became more and more recognized by state delegations.[2] The final text of the OP is a compromise. It retains some but not all elements of the Maastricht draft and strongly focuses on the interests of women, but some concerns of states that make the instrument less accessible to victims are also incorporated.[3] By the end of 1999, the OP was adopted unanimously in the UN General Assembly.

The "new tool in the toolbox" adds two innovations to the CEDAW process: a communications and an inquiry procedure (OP art. 2 and 8, respectively). A communication can be submitted by individuals or groups of individuals who have experienced a violation of rights guaranteed in the Convention or by others acting on the victim's behalf (art. 2). Communications must meet a number of admissibility criteria, most importantly: that the state addressed has ratified the OP (art. 3); that domestic remedies regarding the case have been exhausted "unless the application of such remedies is unreasonably prolonged or unlikely to bring effective relief" (art. 4 (1)); that the matter has not already been considered under another international procedure (art. 4 (2)(a)); that the matter is compatible with the Convention and substantiated information on the incident is provided (art. 4 (2)(b) and (c)); and that the violation referred to has taken place after ratification of the OP (art. 4 (2)(e)). In the case that a communication is considered admissible, it is transmitted confidentially to the State Party concerned, which is given six months to respond (art. 6). In the light of all information received, the Committee takes a view on the communication that may include recommendations addressing the state. The State Party is expected to consider and react to the view and inform the Committee about its corresponding actions. The Committee may request further information from the State Party (art. 7). According to OP art. 8, the Committee is entitled to initiate an inquiry if it receives reliable information indicating "grave or systematic violations by a State Party of rights set forth in the Convention." This procedure is to be carried out confidentially and in cooperation with the state concerned and may include a visit to the territory. The Committee's findings are transmitted to the State Party, which is supposed to respond to them within six months (art. 8). The Committee may ask for follow-up information (art. 9). While reservations to the OP as a whole are not permitted (art. 17), States Parties may opt out of the inquiry procedure (art. 10). Further, the Committee has the right to request interim measures in regard to a communication before its admissibility is verified in order to "avoid irreparable damage" (art. 5), and States parties to the OP commit to ensure that individuals who make use of the communications procedure are not "subjected to ill treatment or intimidation" (art. 11).

Controversies arose over a number of issues, the most important of which were applicability of the OP, standing of petitioners, threshold of admissibility, and the necessity of an inquiry procedure. These will be addressed in turn.

First, delegations disagreed on whether the OP should be applicable to all articles of the Convention or not. Some insisted that not all articles of the Convention were legally enforceable and thus should not be subject of individual complaints (UN Doc. E/CN.6/1996/10, para. 51). Others, however, stressed the importance of maintaining the integrity of the treaty and understanding *all* articles of CEDAW as justifiable (UN Doc. E/1996/26, Annex III, para. 104f). The later position succeeded.

Box 5.1: The OP to CEDAW in a Nutshell

Art. 1: Recognition of Committee competence by OP States Parties

Arts. 2–7: Communications

- 2: Standing of petitioner
- 3: Anonymous and written form; directed to States Parties of the OP
- 4: Communication must be preceded by exhaustion of available domestic remedies; further conditions of inadmissibility
- 5: Committee's right to request interim measures to "avoid irreparable damage"
- 6: Confidential transmission of complaint to State Party; disclosure of petitioner's identity; response within six months
- 7: Consideration of Communications and follow-up procedures

Arts. 8–10: *Inquiry procedure*

- 8: Steps to undertake an inquiry
- 9: Follow-up measures to an inquiry
- 10: Opting out of inquiry procedure permitted

Art. 11 Protection of individuals who make use of the OP

Art. 12: Documentation of Committee's work under OP

Art. 13: Dissemination by States Parties

Art. 14: Committee develops Rules of Procedure

Arts. 15–16: Signature, ratification and accession; entry into force

Art. 17: Reservations are not permitted

Arts. 18–21: Amendments; denunciation; duties of the Secretary General; languages

Second, ideas on standing—that is, who should have the right to submit communications—varied widely. The final version of art. 2 includes *individual* victims and *groups of individual* victims but not groups *per se*, a notion that was proposed to protect women's rights NGOs operating in repressive contexts. Also, the proposal that groups that have "sufficient interest in the matter" should be able to author communications was not included (Connors 2012b, p. 623). However, the wording retains some collectivity and goes beyond the position of some states that *only* individuals should be allowed. A further positive aspect from the point of view of potential petitioners is that communications can be submitted on behalf of the victim(s), typically with their consent, but in cases where the author of the communication can justify it, also without consent.

Third, there were different views in regard to how high or low the threshold for the admissibility of a communication should be. Article 4 stipulates that a complainant must exhaust domestic legal remedies before filing a communication under the OP; this is in line with the basic tenet of international law that a state should always be given the first opportunity to correct a problem within its jurisdiction. However, the formulation "unless the application of such remedies is unreasonably prolonged or unlikely to bring effective relief" allows the Committee to assess if a state's remedies have a realistic potential to "right wrongs" or not. During negotiations, states criticized this qualification arguing that it was unclear how "ineffectiveness" of domestic remedies should be verified, but it remained in the text (Connors 2012b, p. 634). A communication is further deemed inadmissible if it is already considered under another international procedure,[4] if it is not compatible with the Convention or "manifestly ill-founded," and if the facts occurred prior to the entry into force of the OP for the State Party concerned. This last condition has narrowed the scope envisioned in the Maastricht draft and CEDAW suggestion no. 7, which set temporal admissibility at the date of entry into force of the Convention itself.

Fourth, some delegations did not find it necessary to have an extra inquiry procedure in regard to "grave or systematic violations" of rights guaranteed under the Convention. The proponents, who ultimately succeeded, underlined the need for action in cases of systematic violations even without an individual case of grievance. Also, as an inquiry does not require the fulfillment of admissibility criteria, it can be initiated by the Committee any time it has access to "reliable information" on a matter qualifying as a "grave or systematic" violation of women's rights. The scope of this term was debated but not defined during negotiations. Delegations agreed, however, that the phenomenon addressed needs to go beyond single cases of violations. OP article 10 allows states to opt out of the inquiry procedure upon ratifying the OP. This is clearly a reaction to many states' opposition, but in practice, only a small minority of States Parties to the OP has made use of this option.[5]

To name a few other important features of the OP: It does not permit reservations based on the reasoning that states already have the option to enter reservations to the substantial articles of the Convention. The text of the OP does not address the question if its procedures can be used against the violation of a CEDAW article to which the concerned state has entered a reservation, but the Committee has, in its practice, taken a stance on this issue (see endnote 11 this chapter). Further, OP article 5 gives the Committee the right to suggest interim measures to the State Party concerned *before* the merit of a communication has been determined to protect the victim from imminent harm. This is a new element in the development of complaint procedures (Gilchrist 2001), and the Committee has made use of it in several cases. Finally, article 14 gives the Committee full powers to exercise its functions under the OP, but other than CEDAW suggestion no. 7, it does not contain any reference as to what amount of additional resources this task would require. While the vagueness of art. 14 disappointed many, it has thus far not proven to be a practical obstacle for the adequate functioning of the Committee's duties under the OP.

Without doubt, the adoption of an OP to CEDAW signifies international commitment to protect women's rights (Byrnes and Connors 1996). However, it is also clear that the procedure has its pitfalls from the perspective of potential victims. In particular, the admissibility criteria for a complaint are demanding and hamper access to the procedure. Further, the Committee is likely to take rather long to reach an assessment given the procedural demands spelled out in the OP. Once it issues a view, it is not directly enforceable even if the Committee has some means to influence state reaction (Byrnes 2002; Tang and Cheung 2003). Thus, commentators often see the strength of the OP in educating States Parties about their responsibilities under the Convention and solidifying the understanding of women's rights violations in international jurisprudence (Connors 2012b, p. 618; Interviews 4, 20, and 21). They are less optimistic about its direct use for women whose rights are being violated.

Bringing the Instrument to Life: Committee Activism Around the OP

The OP entered into force December 22, 2000, for the first 10 ratifying states and has become, as of June 2015, legally binding for 105 states.[6] Since its entry into force, the Committee, with the support of the Secretariat, has created the working environment necessary to handle its new tasks under the OP, and it has worked on a low number of inquiries (three completed and eight in progress) and an increasing number of communications (34 decided cases as of June, 2014). This section briefly lays out the Committee's work in relation to the OP and shows that this work has gained considerable substance despite many disappointed assessments of "under-usage" of the OP, especially during the first decade of its existence (Connors 2012b, p. 618).[7]

Unlike 20 years earlier when the Committee had to start its work under severe resource constraints, the Committee's additional tasks under the OP have been reasonably funded from the start. The UN General Assembly requested in December 2000 that the Secretariat provide full resources, including staff for the OP to CEDAW (Resolution 55/70, UN Doc. A/56/38). As of 2003, two additional staff positions for the OP were created. Further, the Committee's Working Group on Communications under the OP, which first met in 2002 and was officially set up in 2003, has been able to meet first for six, then for nine, and since 2010, for ten days per year (see Fig. 4.1 and UN Doc. A/62/38, p. 227). The first measure the Committee took in regard to the OP was to formulate rules on how to proceed with communications and inquiries. These rules detail the tasks of the Secretariat in receiving, registering, and transmitting communications to the Committee (rules 56–59), and they call for the establishment of a working group consisting of five experts to deal with communications according to OP art. 2 (rule 62). It is within this working group that the Committee has fleshed out its ways of handling communications. It collaborates closely with the Secretariat and has improved the flow of information,[8] requests background information necessary to deal adequately with each case,[9] and has urged the Secretariat to widely disseminate information on the OP, including all decisions by the Committee. The working group also clarifies issues that emerge during the evaluation of communications, for example, in regard to dissenting opinions[10] and the applicability of reservations in the context of a communication.[11] Once a violation of the Convention is determined, a rapporteur is designated who reports on measures taken by the state to alleviate the violation (rule 73); this rule strengthens the follow-up process and ensures that a case does not simply end with the issuing of the Committee's view. In light of the rising numbers of inquiries the Committee is working on, it requested to expand the mandate of the Working Group on Communications to also evaluate inquiries and rename it Working Group on the OP, to increase the membership from five to seven experts and grant the group additional meeting time of five days per year (Decision 54/9, UN Doc. A/68/38). This request was not granted, but the Committee later decided to establish a separate Working Group on Inquiries under the OP, consisting of five experts, with an additional meeting time of six days (Decision 59/6, UN Doc. CEDAW/C/2014/III/CRP).

Inquiries

To date, the number of inquiries the Committee has dealt with has remained below many activists' and Committee members' hopes. Relatively early after the OP's entry into force, the Committee was concerned with an inquiry on the abduction, rape, and killing of a huge number of young women in Ciudad Juarez and Chihuahua, Mexico. This subject matter clearly qualified as a "grave or systematic violation" of the rights set forth in the Convention. In its final report on the inquiry (UN Doc. A/59/38, p. 161f), the Committee stated that it had first received information of two NGOs and subsequently invited the Mexican government to submit information on the incidents. This information made the Committee decide that an inquiry was in order, and upon the consent of the Mexican government, two Committee experts undertook a country visit in October 2003. The Committee adopted a report that provided a holistic women's rights framework to understand all dimensions of the phenomenon, including the contribution of the state to creating a culture of acceptance for sexist crimes. It also contained a comprehensive set of recommendations (Tavarez da Silva and Ferrer Gomez 2007).[12]

Since 2010, the Committee has become active in eleven more inquiries (2010/1, 2011/1, 2011/2, 2011/3, 2011/4, 2012/1, 2013/1, 2013/2, 2014/1, 2014/2, and 2014/3). Most of them are at a stage where the nature of the violation and the State Party concerned are kept confidential,[13] but two inquiries were recently concluded. In both cases, the provision of independent information coming from NGOs was crucial. Inquiry 2010/1 was concerned with the lack of access to modern contraceptives in Manila, the capital of the Philippines. The "effective ban" on contraceptives other than natural methods was a product of local politics, but the central government did not adequately react to it. The Committee's fact finding delegation notes "pervasive impact" of this policy "on lives and health of women in Manila, in particular….for women from low-income groups." (UN Doc. CEDAW/C/OP.8/PHL/1, p. 5) It finds grave and systematic violations of CEDAW articles 2 (d) and (f) because of discriminatory state action, art. 12 because a state's denial of certain forms of contraception represents discrimination against women in the field of health, and art. 16 (1)(e), because the right of women to decide over the number and spacing of their children was effectively denied. It recommends to the State Party to bring its legal framework regarding reproductive rights in order, withdraw the executive orders that produced the situation in Manila, and work proactively to provide women with information about and access to a broad range of contraceptive measures in accordance with the Convention. The second concluded inquiry (2011/1) concerns the high rate of missing and murdered Aboriginal women and girls in Canada. Since a number or NGOs have raised awareness for this problem over a long period of time, the Canadian government has been responding to it and presented its measures in the context of the inquiry. While the Committee's report acknowledges this governmental action, it also concludes that Canada is still not going far enough to fulfill its due diligence responsibilities under CEDAW article 2 (c) and (e). It also finds that Aboriginal women are exposed to direct discrimination by public institutions, in particular in regard to their right to equality before the law, covered by CEDAW art. 15. The Committee's recommendations provide that Canada should take a more ambitious and comprehensive catalogue of measures within the framework of due diligence than it has done thus far (UN Doc. CEDAW/C/OP.8/CAN/1). As Campbell notes, the Committee's interpretation is so important because of its focus on equality of outcome. It holds that "it is not sufficient for Canada to apply the same standards to Aboriginal women as have been applied to others. Aboriginal women are particularly vulnerable and Canada's response needs to account for their disadvantaged position in society." Hence, the inquiry contributes to "understanding intersectional discrimination and gender inequality" (Campbell 2015).

Despite the recent rise in inquiries, it remains puzzling that the inquiry procedure has been used so rarely, given the fact that it does not have to meet any admissibility criteria and is thus more accessible than the communications procedure. The Committee only needs to receive reliable information on a grave or systematic violation of women's rights to initiate an investigation. It could be that in the eyes of activists it is unclear what constitutes a *grave enough* violation. However, since the scope is on grave *or* systematic violations, *any* systemic form of discrimination, for example a persistent and extreme wage gap, could be subject of an inquiry (Richter 2011). Thus, the breadth of the wording is meant to catch as wide a spectrum of violations as possible, as long as they represent a pattern and not an isolated case. Another factor that has contributed to the underuse of the procedure is that the Committee has not proactively initiated inquiries which it could have, given that it could react to virtually any reliable information it receives, including States Parties' reports (Interview 5). This attitude is unlikely to change, considering the heavy workload of the experts.

Communications

Until June 2014, the Committee has published decisions on 34 communications 18 of which were considered inadmissible,[14] one admissible without merits[15] and 15 admissible with merits[16](OHCHR 2015; see a list of all communications in appendix II). The complaints have been directed at 16 states which represents only 15% of all States Parties to the OP. In addition, the communications have mostly addressed States Parties from *More Developed Regions,* namely 28 out of the 34,[17] a fact that has raised concern as to the global accessibility of the mechanism (Murdoch 2008; Interview 4). It should be noted, however, that the "success rate" of cases is lower in this region, such that the cases with merits are more evenly distributed regionally[18] than the universe of all cases.

The main reason for the Committee's many decisions of inadmissibility—18 out of 34 cases—is the high threshold created by the admissibility criteria laid out in the OP. Particularly three provisions have proven to be hurdles for complainants. The *ratione temporis* rule (stipulating that the violation has to have happened after entry into force of the OP), the need to exhaust domestic legal remedies, and to sufficiently substantiate the case and prove that it affects a right covered by the Convention. The *ratione temporis* rule was most challenging in the early years of the Protocol's existence but the Committee decided, in line with the practice of other treaty bodies, to consider a communication admissible *ratione temporis* not only under the condition that the violation happened after OP ratification, but also if it had happened before *and* was of continuing nature. This approach was applied in regard to communications 4/2004 (A.S. v. Hungary)[19] and 8/2005 (Kayan v. Turkey).[20] Byrnes and Bath (2008) note, however, that the Committee's distinction between a completed and ongoing violation has not always been coherent and could also have been applied to communication 1/2003 (B.J. v. Germany), in which the complainant saw herself affected by structural discrimination because she had, during her marriage, not pursued a career for the sake of caring for the family and as a consequence, suffered from legal and economic disadvantage when she got divorced (UN Doc. A/59/38, p. 244). Experts and observers have expressed hope that "the CEDAW Committee will have another opportunity to address the situation faced by older, divorced women" (Flinterman 2007, p. 291; Sokhi-Bulley 2006).

As for the exhaustion of domestic remedies, the Committee is, on the one hand, very clear that the case must have been brought before domestic jurisdiction *as a case of gender-based discrimination*. In such cases where the victim did not make this argument before domestic courts,[21] the complaint was found inadmissible and referred back to domestic mechanisms. On the other hand, the Committee has been very carefully scrutinizing if the domestic legal processes are "unreasonably prolonged" or if they are "unlikely to bring relief." For example, in regard to communication 18/2008 (Vertido v. Philippines), the Committee considered domestic court proceedings ineffective because of their extreme duration (UN Doc. CEDAW/C/46/D/18/2008). In regard to communications 5/2005 and 6/2005 (Goekce (deceased) v. Austria and Yildirim (deceased) v. Austria) it has taken the view that the victims, especially due to the despair and trauma caused by their experience of domestic violence, were not obliged to be aware and make use of *all* possible domestic legal options available to them, in particular if, from the victim's perspective, they did not appear to bring any relief (UN Docs. CEDAW/C/39/D/5/2005 and CEDAW/C/39/D/6/2005). Thus, the Committee attempts to take the stance of the victim when assessing the exhaustion of domestic remedies. Not surprisingly, this approach stands in contrast to the position of concerned States Parties which overwhelmingly find a reason to declare a complaint inadmissible.[22]

Another reason for denial of admissibility is disagreement among experts on the question if a communication truly affects the rights spelled out in the Convention. This disagreement is typically expressed in dissenting opinions, and six such opinions were formulated in regard to the 18 inadmissible cases. The views on two communications submitted against France, no. 12/2007 and 13/2007 launched by the NGOs *Groupe d'Intérêt pour le Matronyme* and *SOS Sexisme* respectively, show this discrepancy. Both cases were directed against a French law that does not give mothers the same right to pass on their family name as fathers, once brought forward by two women who complained against this law as daughters (no. 12/2007), once by women who complained against it as mothers or women who refused to become mothers because of the law (no. 13/2007). In both cases, the authors saw art. 16 of the Convention violated and particularly art. 16 (1)(g) which obliges States Parties to ensure "the same personal rights as husband and wife, including the right to choose a family name." The French state challenged admissibility because it had entered a reservation against this very subsection of art. 16, but also because it held that in the first case, the daughters did not have victim status as the discrimination affected mothers only, and that in the second case, the complainants also lacked victim status because they either were not mothers or their children had reached maturity (with one exception). In both cases, the Committee reached a decision of inadmissibility, following largely the State Party's interpretation that the authors had no victim status under art. 16 (1)(g), while the dissenting opinion saw a broader case of legal discrimination based on gender stereotypes affecting CEDAW articles 2, 5 and 16(1) (UN Docs. CEDAW/C/44/D/12/2007 and CEDAW/C/44/D/13/2007).[23]

Finally, the Committee had to formulate a position in regard to extraterritorial responsibilities of States Parties under the Convention and admissibility of complaints against such responsibilities under the OP. Thus far, six communications have been brought forward against Canada, Denmark and the Netherlands by nationals of other states who argue that the rejection of their applications for asylum is a violation of CEDAW because deportation to their home countries would directly result in gender-specific and severe human rights violations. All complainants make the case that they cannot expect protection from the respective home state because public institutions are either not willing or not capable to provide such protection. Specifically, the communications claim the exposure to severe spousal violence if deported to Mexico,[24] circumcision if deported to Uganda,[25] gender-based violence and persecution because of political activity if deported to Burundi,[26] sexual slavery and physical abuse if deported to Mongolia,[27] and sexual harassment as a woman belonging to a religious minority if deported to Pakistan.[28] The three concerned States Parties have rejected responsibility based on the following set of arguments. First, none of their institutions actively violated a right under the Convention.[29] Second, as a State Party to CEDAW, they only have responsibilities in regard to their own jurisdiction. Other than the CCPR and CAT, which explicitly contain the duty of non-refoulement under certain and always exceptional conditions, the CEDAW Convention does not spell out any such extraterritorial responsibility. Third, even if there were reasons to apply the principle of non-refoulement,[30] the communication has to establish that there is a clear and strong connection between deportation and exposure to severe human rights violations, a connection that the States Parties claim does not exist.[31] Finally, they claim that it is the home state of the complainants who has violated the Convention and that the communication should be directed against that state. This rejection of responsibility notwithstanding, all three states responded positively to the Committee's requests for interim measures under OP art. 5 and delayed the deportation of the respective author as long as the Committee was considering the communication.[32]

While the Committee has decided inadmissibility in all six cases for diverse reasons, it has made clear that, in principle, States Parties do have extraterritorial responsibilities and that, accordingly, the Committee has jurisdiction over communications of this nature. In its view on case 33/2011, the Committee explained this position for the first time invoking GR 28 where extraterritorial state responsibilities are specified. In short, States Parties are responsible for the effects of all their actions on the rights set forth in the Convention, regardless of whether these effects take place within or outside of their territory.[33] However, the *connection* between the state action and the violation of rights has to be unequivocally established. In line with the position of the States Parties, the Committee has failed to see this connection in most of the present communications (UN Doc. CEDAW/C/55/D/33/2011). Further, the Committee is also aware that all of the home states have ratified the Convention and, thus, made a commitment to protect women's rights. In taking this position, it implicitly goes along with Denmark's statement in regard to communication 40/2012 that States Parties cannot be expected to "return aliens only to countries where conditions were in full compliance with each of the safeguards, rights and freedoms set out in the Convention" (UN Doc. CEDAW/55/D/40/2012, p. 9), and it has carefully examined whether state institutions are indeed unable to protect the victim, as the communication claims, or if the victim has not exhausted all possible domestic support services.[34]

In regard to the communications with merits, the Committee has provided its strongest interpretations in cases on violence, gender stereotypes, and reproductive health. According to Cusack and Pusey (2013), it has applied a less comprehensive gender analysis in other areas, but at least in the field of employment-related gender discrimination, this seems to be changing. Particularly promising is the Committee's view regarding communication 28/2010 (R.K.B. v. Turkey) where it agreed with the author that her dismissal from employment in a hair salon was based on sexist stereotypes and discrimination (her alleged "loose sexual morality") and that the judiciary had failed to recognize these patterns (CEDAW/C/51/D/28/2010).[35]

The Committee's views on domestic violence cases have been praised in terms of their rigor and comprehensive application of the spirit of the Convention (Cusack and Pusey 2013; Johnstone 2010b; Sokhi-Bulley

2006), and they have been ground-breaking in determining the due diligence responsibilities of States Parties in this field. The Committee has dealt with five cases altogether.[36] In three cases, the victims filed the complaints themselves. In A.T. v. Hungary, V.K. v. Bulgaria, and Jallow v. Bulgaria, the Committee made clear that the state violated its duty of providing effective protection of victims of domestic violence. This lack of protection was expressed in the general legal framework,[37] in the lack of availability and accessibility of shelters, and in the ignorance or negligence in regard to domestic violence of both law enforcement officers and judges. Thus, the Committee's views included not only compensation for the authors but also comprehensive legal reforms, capacity building, and allocation of adequate resources (UN Docs. A/60/38, p. 80; CEDAW/C/49/D/20/2008; CEDAW/C/52/D/32/2011).

The two cases brought forward against Austria—Sahide Goekce (deceased) v. Austria and Fatma Yildirim (deceased) v. Austria—concerned two women of Turkish descent who were killed by their legal husbands, in one case after a long history of domestic violence, in the other after a shorter period of assaults and death threats. Both cases were known to the police. In distinction from the first group of cases, the Committee argued that the state's failure to protect the women was not due to insufficient laws and policies but a failure on an operational level—different state organs had not collaborated effectively and in the interest of the victims. While the Austrian government took the position that it had done everything possible, the question arose if in case of imminent threat to life, preventive detention of the perpetrator would have been in order. The State Party argued that it also had to respect the rights of the aggressor, in particular the right to freedom, fair trial, and property, but the Committee nevertheless held that the safety of the victim's life should rank higher in the considerations of state authorities. It recommended comprehensive training of law enforcement officers and better collaboration of authorities with NGOs working in this field (UN Docs. CEDAW/C/39/D/5/2005; CEDAW/C/39/D/6/2005). The Committee's views in all of these cases are milestones in the determination of due diligence responsibilities in regard to domestic violence[38] and have already influenced other judicial organs.[39] The Austria cases in particular make it clear that good laws do not equal sufficient implementation of the Convention; they also need to be applied well (Byrnes and Bath 2008; Zwingel 2013b). However, the Committee was also criticized for not including intersectional dimensions of discrimination in its view. The less-than-optimal dealing of Austrian law enforcement officers was clearly infused by stereotypical assumptions of "different" Turkish family dynamics (Johnstone 2010b, p. 62).

Two communications that were both submitted against the Philippines targeted the reliance of the domestic judicial system on gender stereotypes in rape litigation. In both cases—18/2008, Tayag Vertido v. Philippines and 34/2011, R.P.B. v. Philippines—men accused of rape were acquitted because the female victims did not act as the respective court assumed they should have, that is, they did not physically resist (enough) and did not try to escape. In the first case, the court's position was underpinned by additional gender stereotypes, namely that the perpetrator, a man over 60, could not be a rapist due to his age and that rape was further unlikely because the two individuals knew each other (UN Doc. CEDAW/C/46/D/18/2008; Cusack and Timmer 2011). In the second case, which concerned a deaf mute girl of 17 years who was raped by a neighbor, the court did not deem the physical resistance of the girl sufficient and argued that she could have made her dissent more explicit, irrespective of her inability to express it verbally; as things were, it did not seem unreasonable for the accused to assume consent. The complainant argued that this ruling blatantly disregarded the vulnerability of the victim based on her disability and further detailed the State Party's ignorance of its duties to protect the rights of people with disabilities, in particular of disabled women (UN Doc. CEDAW/C/57/D/34/2011).[40] The Committee held in both cases that the legislation concerning rape needs to be revised and should be based on "lack of consent"—in other words, on the absence of *explicit* consent to sexual intercourse—rather than "lack of physical resistance." It also recommended compensation for both victims and comprehensive training of the judiciary that, in regard to case 34/2011, also entailed attention to intersectional forms of discrimination.

The third strong field of Committee jurisprudence has developed around reproductive health and rights. Its first case in this field, communication 4/2004 (A.S. v. Hungary), dealt with involuntary sterilization. The complainant was a Roma woman who saw her reproductive rights and right to have a family permanently violated by a sterilization that had been performed on her without obtaining her full and informed consent, even if, according to the State Party, it was carried out to save her life. The Committee sided with the author and recommended compensation for her. It also noted in its view that special subgroups of women, among them Romani women, are disproportionally affected by involuntary sterilization, reminded the State Party of its responsibilities toward the reproductive rights of *all* women under its jurisdiction, and recommended training for hospital personnel and other measures to achieve this end (UN Doc. CEDAW/C/36/D/4/2004; Cusack and Pusey 2013, p. 72).

In communication 17/2008 (Pimentel v. Brazil), the mother of Alyne Pimentel held the state accountable for not providing adequate health services for her daughter who encountered complications leading to her death when six months pregnant. The Committee argued with the author that this maternal death was preventable, that Brazil was not complying with its responsibility to reduce the country's high maternal mortality rate, that the lack of adequate reproductive health services violated women's rights, and those of poor and Afro-Brazilian women like the author's daughter in particular (UN Doc. CEDAW/C/49/D/17/2008). Cook (2013) calls this case a historic contribution to human rights law since it is the first treaty body view that frames maternal mortality as a human rights issue. While the phenomenon is routinely deplored, it is often seen as caused by adversarial circumstances beyond a state's reach. The Committee, in turn, argues that *preventable* maternal deaths are due to the lack of women-specific health care services, and that a state, in not providing or under-resourcing such services, violates women's fundamental rights. It further makes clear that intersectional discrimination exacerbates this violation of women's rights, as Afro-Brazilian women are seven times more likely than other Brazilian women to die in childbirth (ibid.).

The last reproductive health case, 22/2009 (T.P. F. v. Peru), concerned a minor girl who had become pregnant from rape and attempted suicide because of the pregnancy by jumping from a roof. At the hospital, where she was supposed to undergo surgery because of the injuries inquired, the surgery was denied to her once it was discovered she was pregnant. Due to illegality, an abortion that would have made the surgery feasible was not considered. The girl later miscarried and the surgery could be carried out, but due to delay of the procedure, the girl was left paralyzed, in need of constant physical care, and psychologically traumatized. Here, the Committee held that the right to health of the girl was violated both because a necessary surgery was denied to her and because she did not have access to therapeutic abortion, as the pregnancy constituted a threat both to her physical health (as it prevented surgery) *and* her mental health (considering she had tried to commit suicide because of it) (UN Doc. CEDAW/C/50/D/22/2009). This view is remarkable because it conceptualizes maternal health to include mental health. Also, it is the first treaty body decision that calls on a state to decriminalize abortion in case of rape and sexual abuse (Cusack and Pusey 2013).

More recent developments of the Committee's views reveal that it is still confronted with asylum-related cases where the complainants use the communications procedure against the country in which they applied for asylum (see earlier in this chapter). All of these cases—No. 49/2013 against Canada and No. 59/2013 and 51/2013 against Denmark—have thus far been considered inadmissible by the Committee, typically because of lack of substance (OP art. 4 (2)(c)), which means that there is no evidence that the targeted state violated the Convention. The Committee also provided a widely recognized decision in a new field, namely discriminatory customary inheritance laws. Two widows had filed a complaint in this matter against Tanzania, also the first case brought forward against an African State Party (No. 48/2013). This case is interesting because the Tanzanian High Court agreed, in domestic proceedings, with the claim of the authors of the communication that customary inheritance laws discriminate against women, and widows specifically, but rather than taking proactive measures, it only recommended that the respective traditional authorities address the problem. The Committee found violations of CEDAW arts. 2 (f) and (c), 5 (a), 13 (b), 15, and 16 (1)(c) and (h). It asked the State Party to compensate the complainants and to initiate structural legal changes (UN Doc. CEDAW/C/60/D/48/2013). However, this case was also a first in that the State Party did not contribute any information to the communications procedure—probably a sign that proactive follow-up measures in response to the Committee's view are unlikely.

How Do States Parties Respond? A Look at Follow-up Measures

The Committee has asked States Parties in 15 cases to take measures to give effect to the Convention; a pattern has emerged in that the Committee's recommendations typically consist of compensation for the author, legal changes if necessary, adequate allocation of resources, and training of those state officials that have been identified as being responsible for or involved in the violation, for example, judges, law enforcement officers, or hospital personnel. The State Party has to respond within six months and describe any action taken. The Committee then examines if it considers this action satisfactory. If it does, it declares the case closed. If it does not, the Committee reiterates its position with an emphasis on those points that it does not see satisfied and invites the state to submit further information.

The responses of States Parties to these recommendations have sometimes been eager and willing and other times reluctant in recognizing the legitimacy of the Committee's position.

Four communications have been declared closed by the Committee, namely 2/2003 A.T. v. Hungary, 4/2004, A.S. v. Hungary, 5/2005 Goekce (deceased) v. Austria, and 6/2005 Yildirim (deceased) v. Austria. In both communications concerning Hungary, the State Party did enact changes on the individual[41] and general[42] level, even if they did not fulfill all of the Committee's recommendations[43] and both authors continued to express dissatisfaction (UN Docs. A/64/38, p. 123f; A/66/38, p.136f). The follow-up measures that Austria described in its response to the Committee were diligent and comprehensive. While the NGOs that authored the two complaints were largely satisfied, they did note that some of the measures were more in the planning than in the realization stage (UN Doc. A/65/38, p. 104ff). Generally, the Committee is of the opinion that a closed communication requires further monitoring, precisely because meaningful institutional change takes time, and addresses this need through the constructive dialogue.

Eleven cases are ongoing, that is, the Committee either awaits a State Party's response, or if it has already received a response, does not yet see its recommendations sufficiently implemented. There is no systematic information available for these pending cases; however, it appears that States Parties directly accused of a violation of the Convention are more reluctant to follow up on the Committee's recommendations than those found to have violated their due diligence duties. For example, the Philippines have thus far been unwilling to compensate the authors of the two rape litigation complaints, and it has been difficult for the Committee to obtain a response from the State Party, as the repeated requests for meeting time indicate (UN Docs. A/67/38, p. 26; A/68/38, p. 103). Also, Belarus has disagreed with the Committee's view in regard to communication 23/2009 (Abramova v. Belarus) that the author was exposed to humiliating and degrading treatment *as a woman* while held in detention (UN Doc. CEDAW/C/49/D/23/2009). On the other hand, the Brazilian government has worked to systematically improve reproductive health facilities and paid compensation to the family of Alyna Pimentel, even if, according to the NGO Dhesca Brazil, which monitors the government's implementation measures, much remains to be done to bring health facilities for poor women up to standard (Cusack and Posey 2013, p. 66; Dhesca Brazil 2014).

What Has the New Tool Added to the Translation of Women's Rights?

Chapter 4 has shown the development of CEDAW from a rhetorically accepted treaty into a sound international monitoring tool. It also described a number of tensions the Committee is confronted with, such as the need to strike a balance between strong women's rights advocacy and the consolidation of its legitimacy in the eyes of States Parties. Overall, however, CEDAW has become an important part of the global discourse on women's rights, and it provides a platform for debating and standard setting that is state-centered, but at the same time, accessible to non-governmental advocates. How has the OP contributed to this development? At least three observations are in order, two in regard to the contribution of the OP to global discourse translation, and one in regard to impact translation.

First, the OP has added new dimensions to the CEDAW monitoring logic. It has, one the one hand, *expanded* the reach of the Convention, since the two new procedures go further than the constructive dialogue in determining when the rights of women are violated by either state action or inaction and what should be done about it. This contains a potential challenge for States Parties, and accordingly, just over half of them (105 or 56%) have accepted scrutiny under the OP. On the other hand, the OP is *more limited* than the monitoring procedure because it does not aim at comprehensively applying the Convention to the entirety of a State Party's action. This new, more targeted function has the potential to develop into a useful complement to the breadth of the constructive dialogue. As the Committee's OP related views and recommendations are applied to concrete cases, they are easier to follow up on than the Committee's concluding observations. Also, they can be used as blueprints for similar cases in different contexts (Johnstone 2010b).

Second, the Committee's work with the OP has added a new layer of interpreting women's rights in the spirit of the Convention. Its views have clarified, in particular, the due diligence responsibilities of States Parties in regard to violence against women and reproductive rights and set standards for state behavior in regard to gender stereotypes, intersectional forms of discrimination, and extraterritorial duties under the Convention. In a number of cases, domestic and international courts have taken notice of the Committee's leadership and followed its argumentation.[44] Such recognition means that the CEDAW Committee's interpretations and understandings translate into other international and domestic contexts, now by new means. It is noteworthy, however, that this new expertise is predominantly legal, and that the Committee took great care to make sure it would be recognized as a competent executor of the OP. This stands a bit in contrast to the Committee's self-construction as a treaty body with broad and beyond-legal expertise it considers necessary to fully cover the scope of women's rights (see Chap. 4). It seems the Committee has been struggling to reconcile these two identities. In regard to early communications, it formulated a couple of overly rule-abiding views,[45] maybe in an attempt to proceed in a legally correct manner, but later views, and in many cases, dissenting opinions, based their interpretation on a broader application of the Convention, foregrounding the *spirit* of the Convention rather than the accurate application of specific articles.[46]

Finally, the OP has the potential to strengthen the ties between the Convention and real-life contexts, and thus, to make a substantial contribution to impact translation. In cases where the Committee finds merits in a communication or inquiry, it sets out concrete steps the State Party has to take. The realization of these steps depends on the State Party's acceptance of the Committee's view and its commitment to comply with that view. While this kind of acceptance cannot be taken for granted, the chapter has described some cases of hands-on improvement, for example, in response to communications against Hungary, Austria, and Brazil. In these cases, governments recognized harm, compensated victims or their families, and addressed structural problems. Victim-oriented treaty interpretation by part of the Committee also raises its recognition and trust among NGOs and potential complainants, which in turn may lead to a higher number of complaints submitted. If women's rights advocates consider the OP a useful tool in their work, the connection between CEDAW and real-life contexts will get stronger. It should be noted that there is room for improvement in this respect, in particular as far as the accessibility and the speed[47] of the procedure are concerned.

Notes

1. Exceptions were Germany, voicing concern about the lack of expertise of CEDAW experts without a legal background (UN Doc. E/CN.6/1996/10, para. 36) and the United Kingdom, fearing that the OP would only be ratified by states already "advanced on equality issues" (UN Doc. E/CN.6/1996/10, Add. 2, para. 8).

2. For example, the Philippines thanked NGOs that had been engaged in the drafting to have given "us both valuable information and inspiration to carry on." A range of delegations expressed understandings of the text that grant NGOs an important role in the use of the OP (UN Doc. E/1999/27, Annex II).
3. For a more detailed account of the drafting process, see Zwingel (2005b, p. 343f) and United Nations/DAW (2000a).
4. This provision has been interpreted in such a way that only the consideration before two *comparable* international mechanisms is inadmissible (Connors 2003).
5. Of the 105 States Parties, these are three: Bangladesh, Belize, and Colombia.
6. This is a high number of ratifications, but it is not evenly distributed across all world regions (see Chap. 7).
7. By the end of 2010, the Committee had made decisions on only 14 cases.
8. In the early years of OP related work, the Secretariat sometimes dismissed a communication because it did not meet prima facie admissibility requirements without informing the Committee. The working group then intervened and requested that the Secretariat provide more information in regard of the correspondence received (UN Docs. A/59/38, p. 89 and A/64/38, p. 106).
9. For example, regarding the question under which circumstances domestic remedies can be considered "unreasonably prolonged" (UN Doc. A/61/38, p. 381), practices of other treaty bodies in relation to their complaint procedures (UN Doc. A/63/38, p. 256), and extraterritorial effects of the Convention (UN Doc. A/68/38, p. 35).
10. Dissenting opinions are considered part of the Committee's dealing with a case and are published together with the Committee's view (UN Doc. A/63/38, p. 260).
11. In this regard, the Committee decided that its mandate to determine the compatibility of reservations with the Convention extends to the procedures under the OP (UN Doc. A/63/38, p. 88). This means that if the Committee considers a reservation incompatible, it will accept communications that target a violation covered by the article against which the reservation is entered. In other words, the fact that a State Party entered a reservation against any of the Convention's provisions does not automatically "protect" it from complaints under the OP.
12. This approach has been recognized internationally and was followed by other international judgments, in particular the Inter-American Court of Human Rights' ruling in González et al. ("Cotton Field") v. Mexico. The Court held the state of Mexico accountable for the torture and murder of three women whose bodies were found in a cotton field close to Ciudad

Juarez. In the ruling, the Court makes explicit reference to the inquiry carried out by the CEDAW Committee. It follows the argument that the murders at hand are based on deeply engrained patterns of discrimination against women perpetuated by the state's inadequate response to the disappearances and insufficient measures to prevent such crimes.

13. Two cases could nevertheless be identified, namely limited access to abortion services in the UK and the extreme level of violence against women in South Africa (National CEDAW Task Team/Masimanyane Women's Support Centre, n. d.).
14. Filed against Canada (2), Denmark (4), France (2), Germany, Italy, the Netherlands (2), Spain (2), Turkey, and the UK (3).
15. Filed against the Netherlands.
16. Filed against Austria (2), Belarus, Brazil, Bulgaria (3), Canada, Hungary (2), the Netherlands, Peru, the Philippines (2), and Turkey.
17. Within this region, 19 communications were filed against countries in Western Europe, six in Eastern Europe, and three in Canada. Further, two communications addressed countries in Latin America and the Caribbean, and four went against countries located in Asia and the Pacific. It was only in 2015 that the first communication submitted against an African state was decided by the Committee (see later in this chapter).
18. Ten of the communications submitted against *More Developed Regions* countries had merits, including all six that were filed against Eastern European states, two (out of two) communications in *Latin America and the Caribbean*, and three (out of four) in *Asia and the Pacific*.
19. This case concerned a sterilization procedure without consent. It was performed before the entry into force of the OP, but the Committee saw the damage for the victim to be ongoing (UN Doc. CEDAW/C/36/D/4/2004).
20. The communication referred to the dismissal of a teacher from a public school for wearing a head scarf. Her dismissal took place *before* the entry into force of the OP, but the Committee argued that the woman's exclusion from public service was an ongoing violation of her right to equal employment according to CEDAW art. 11 (UN Doc. CEDAW/C/34/D/8/2005).
21. Previously mentioned communication 8/2005 (Kayan v. Turkey) did not meet this criterion as the complainant had argued before domestic courts that her right to freedom of religion and expression was violated. Likewise, in communications 10/2005 (N.S.F. v. UK) and 35/2011 (M.E.N. v. Denmark), the Committee found no reference to gender-based discrimination in the two authors' applications for asylum in the respective States Parties (UN Docs. CEDAW/C/38/D/10/2005 and CEDAW/C/55/D/35/2011).
22. There are few exceptions to this rule, namely Hungary, admitting in regard to communication 2/2003 (A.T. v. Hungary) that there were no adequate

domestic remedies in place to protect victims of domestic violence (UN Doc. A/60/38, p. 80), and Bulgaria, which did not contest admissibility of two communications concerning domestic violence and sexual assault of a child (no. 20/2008, V.K. v. Bulgaria, and no. 31/2011, V.P.P. v. Bulgaria).

23. Another case that was controversial within the Committee was 7/2005 (Munoz Vargas v. Spain) in which the victim claimed to be discriminated as a woman (vis-à-vis her younger brother) in acquiring an aristocratic family title. The majority of the Committee decided against admissibility *ratione temporis*, but the two dissenting opinions argued, on the one hand, that the matter was substantially inadmissible because it did not concern a human rights violation and thus was not covered by the Convention, and on the other, that it was admissible because the author was clearly discriminated against by laws and traditions that were based on gender stereotypes (UN Doc. CEDAW/C/39/D/7/2005).
24. No. 25/2010, M.P.M. v. Canada and 26/2010, Herrera Rivera v. Canada (UN Docs. CEDAW/C/51/D/25/2010 and CEDAW/C/50/D/26/2010).
25. No.33/2011,M.N.N.v.Denmark(UNDoc.CEDAW/C/55/D/33/2011).
26. No.35/2011,M.E.Nv.Denmark(UNDoc.CEDAW/C/55/D/35/2011).
27. No.39/2012,N.v.Netherlands(UNDoc.CEDAW/C/57/D/39/2012).
28. No. 40/2012, M.S. v. Denmark (UN Doc. CEDAW/55/D/40/2012).
29. Typically, the complainants do not disagree, but sometimes gender-blind asylum procedures are problematized, such as in regard to communication no. 25/2010 M.P.M v. Canada by the author and in case 35/2011 M.E.N. v. Denmark by the Committee's dissenting opinion (UN Docs. CEDAW/C/51/D/25/2010 and CEDAW/C/55/D/35/2011).
30. According to the CCPR and CAT, this is the case when the rights to life and freedom from torture and degrading treatment are affected. In regard to communication 33/2011, Denmark states that while circumcision would qualify as degrading treatment, it does not see the direct risk of the author to become victim of the procedure (UN Doc. CEDAW/C/55/D/33/2011); in regard to communication 40/2012, Denmark argues that the right affected is the right to freedom of religion, and thus, the violation is not part of the scope that demands extraterritorial protection (UN Doc. CEDAW/55/D/40/2012).
31. States Parties assume safety of the victim upon return because they can settle somewhere far away from the potential abuser or rely on personal safety networks or turn to state authorities for protection. See communications 26/2010 Herrera Rivera v. Canada, 33/2011 M.N.N. v. Denmark, 39/2012 N. v. Netherlands, and 40/2012 M.S. v. Denmark (UN Docs. CEDAW/C/50/D/26/2010, CEDAW/C/55/D/33/2011, CEDAW/C/57/D/39/2012, CEDAW/55/D/40/2012).

32. The Committee requested interim measures for communications no. 26/2010, 33/2011, 35/2011, and 40/2012 (see appendix 2).
33. Both Canada and Denmark have, in later communications, transmitted their position that they do not agree with the Committee's interpretation in this regard. Canada specifically urged the Committee not to "seek to extend the interpretation of the Convention to include a guarantee of non-refoulement" as a "good-faith interpretation... of the text of the Convention... does not support such an implicit obligation" (UN Doc. CEDAW/C/59/D/49/2013, p. 6).
34. This position is particularly noticeable in communication 39/2012, where N., a Mongolian citizen, substantiates severe sexual and physical abuse, but not, in the view of the Committee, that the Mongolian state cannot protect her from such abuse (UN Doc. CEDAW/C/57/D/39/2012, p. 15). It is interesting that Austrian asylum authorities have, at least in one case, taken a more victim-oriented position. They granted a woman from Kyrgyzstan asylum based on her claim that authorities were unable to protect her from severe gender-based violence. One piece of evidence to ascertain this inability was the CEDAW Committee's concluding observations for Kyrgyzstan (Richter 2011, p. 175).
35. Also, in communication 36/2012 (De Blok et al. v. Netherlands), the Committee argued that under art. 11 (2)(b) of the Convention, self-employed women cannot be excluded from access to public maternity leave schemes and recommended compensation for the authors and other women in the same position (UN Doc. CEDAW/C/57/D/36/2012).
36. No. 2/2003 A.T. v. Hungary, 5/2005 Goekce (deceased) v. Austria, 6/2005 Yildirim (deceased) v. Austria, 20/2008 V.K. v. Bulgaria and 32/2011 Jallow v. Bulgaria.
37. For example, a restraining order did not exist in Hungarian law, and the Bulgarian legal framework defined domestic violence with an exclusive focus on physical abuse.
38. A recently decided case, No. 47/2012 Angela González Carreño v. Spain, adds to this legacy. Here, the Committee finds that failing to consider acts of domestic violence in deciding on custody rights by part of Spanish authorities violated the State Party's due diligence responsibilities under the Convention. In the presented case, this resulted in the murder of the daughter of the complainant. The Committee sided with her interpretation that more diligent and coordinated state action, taking manifestations of violence by part of her former husband seriously, could have prevented this tragic development (UN Doc. CEDAW/C/58/D/47/2012).
39. For example, Opuz v. Turkey (ECHR 33401/02, 2009). In this case the European Court of Human Rights applied for the first time the notion of violence against women *as a form of discrimination* as laid out in CEDAW GR 19 (Londono 2009).

40. Among other things, it pointed to the absence of sign language interpretation in police and court proceedings and the extreme risk of abuse deaf women are exposed to, exacerbated by state neglect of their rights and needs.
41. It provided a new apartment and better protection for the author of communication 2/2003 and paid compensation for the author of communication 4/2004.
42. Legal changes and training in regard to communication 2/2003 and training and oversight of sterilizations in communication 4/2004.
43. In regard to communication 4/2004, Hungary did not consider it necessary to amend the public health act as recommended by the Committee.
44. One prominent case is the European Court of Human Rights' decision in Opuz v. Turkey (ECHR 33401/02). Another is González et al. ("Cotton Field") v. Mexico before the Inter-American Court of Human Rights. It is not clear to me why endnotes cannot reference each other, but I erased that reference.
45. For example, communications no. 1/2003 (B.J. v. Germany), 12/2007 and 13/2007 (*Groupe d'Intérêt pour le Matronyme* and *SOS Sexisme* v. France, respectively).
46. This is true for dissenting opinions regarding communications no. 12/2007, 13/2007 (*Groupe d'Intérêt pour le Matronyme* and *SOS Sexisme* v. France, respectively), 7/2005 (Munoz-Vargas v. Spain), and 15/2007 (Zheng v. Netherlands).
47. The average time between submission of a complaint and the Committee issuing a view is 26 months (see appendix 2).

CHAPTER 6

Creating "Thick Connections": Translating Activism in the CEDAW Process

While the Convention's international authority has been growing, its exclusively state-centered notion of rights enforcement has limits. CEDAW shares this limitation with all human rights treaties. They are based on two components, namely governmental commitment to implement treaty provisions, expressed in ratification, and an independent monitoring mechanism to support this process; only the more recently drafted treaties contain additional features to foster domestic resonance.[1] In reality, it is a minority of governments that is strongly enough committed to women's rights to engage in serious implementation efforts simply because they ratified CEDAW. In most cases, activism of NGOs has been crucial to build a "thick connection" between the treaty and domestic institutions, discourses, and practices.

This chapter describes this "translation work," as I call it; it has become a pivotal component both for global discourse translation and impact translation of the Convention. The chapter first traces translating activism that is geared toward the global discourse. Most of it is about strengthening CEDAW as an international procedure and the women's rights framework more generally speaking, but there is also a growth of anti-feminist voices that criticize and challenge this framework (Buss 2004; Reilly 2009). The second part of the chapter presents activism that increases the visibility of CEDAW in domestic contexts and supports domestic implementation efforts. For both dynamics, NGOs are the most relevant agents, but for impact translation, operational UN agencies have also played an important role.

S. Zwingel, *Translating International Women's Rights*,
Gender and Politics, DOI 10.1057/978-1-137-31501-4_6

Transnational Activism in Global Discourse Translation: Supporting CEDAW Versus Promoting Anti-feminism

Despite the UN's traditional reluctance to grant NGOs a formal role within its intergovernmental set up, most sectors of the UN, including the human rights mechanisms, have gradually opened its doors to NGOs since the early 1990s. While the pre-1990 human rights treaties, including CEDAW, do not mention NGOs, the later Conventions specify a role for non-state actors in their respective monitoring procedures.[2] In practice, all treaty bodies have become aware of the crucial role NGOs can play in the constructive dialogue and have taken measures to allow NGO involvement (Bayefsky 2001).

In the early years of CEDAW, there was virtually no contact between the Committee and NGOs. Partly, this was because the Committee was geographically difficult to access for NGOs. Until 1993, it held its meetings alternately in Vienna and New York, and since not many international bodies met in Vienna, it was not attractive for NGOs to have a presence there (Freeman 2010). Also, many women's organizations had been created recently, and most of them were more interested in community activism and raising public awareness than in engaging with a rather unknown international procedure (Smith et al. 1998). Finally, there was also reluctance within the Committee as some experts feared that NGO involvement might deter States Parties from engaging in the monitoring procedure (Jacobson 1991; Chap. 4).

Over the more than 30 years of the Committee's existence, this relationship has fundamentally changed. CEDAW meetings are now attended by higher numbers of NGOs than those of other treaty bodies (Connors 2010). What has also changed is the growing recognition of NGO contributions within the Committee and within the Secretariat (Byrnes 2002). Committee experts see NGO input as vital for their work and have repeatedly acknowledged their active role in the constructive dialogue (Interviews 5, 7, 12; Chap. 4), even if they are aware of the different roles NGOs and the Committee play in the struggle for gender equality. Since 2008, NGO reports have been posted on the OHCHR's website together with the reports of States Parties and all other documents related to the constructive dialogue. This measure reflects the institutional acknowledgement of NGO contributions as an integral part of the monitoring procedure.

The Door Opener: International Women's Rights Action Watch

The first NGO to connect with the CEDAW Committee was the International Women's Rights Action Watch (IWRAW). It was founded in 1986 and is based in Minneapolis, USA. IWRAW wanted to maintain the momentum created by the Nairobi conference in "hooking onto the CEDAW treaty as an instrument that belongs to women" (Interview 22), yet the founders did not want to employ the "naming and shaming" strategies typically used by human rights NGOs as they thought these would not work in the field of women's rights. Instead, they developed an approach "that would enlist enough people in the activity to make a difference without it being totally confrontational with governments and totally focused on violations instead of positive change" (ibid.). IWRAW became active in three fields: making CEDAW known among women's NGOs, providing independent information for the CEDAW monitoring procedure, and treaty interpretation.

Shortly after its foundation, IWRAW created an information and facilitation network around CEDAW. The network was open to any organization, scholar, or individual interested in engaging in the CEDAW process and in the rights of women more generally. The center piece of the network was its newsletter, *The Women's Watch*. It was first launched in 1987 and served for making contacts, distributing news and information, identifying national NGOs when their government was up for the constructive dialogue, and discussing strategies, often related to concrete events such as the 1995 Beijing conference. *The Women's Watch* was produced and mailed around the world by IWRAW until the year 2000. While much of the information published in this newsletter is now available via various Internet sources, in pre-Internet times, *The Women's Watch* was a groundbreaking connecting tool. In its peak time, it reached over 5,000 organizations and individuals (Freeman 2010)[3].

IWRAW was aware how instrumental independent information would be for the functionality of the constructive dialogue. Through its network, it encouraged women's organizations to provide such information to the Committee, but as not many groups reacted, IWRAW itself started to write alternative reports in 1992 and made them available to Committee members (Freeman 2010). IWRAW wrote reports mostly about countries from the Global South, typically in consultation with domestic women's organizations.[4] As NGO interest in shadow report writing increased, IWRAW shifted its emphasis towards facilitating national NGOs in writing their own reports and presenting them at the Committee's sessions. IWRAW also produced shadow reports for the Committee on Economic, Social and Cultural Rights, as it found this treaty body's scope to be most relevant for women's empowerment. IWRAW stopped writing reports for CEDAW by 2003 partly because of lack of funding but also because the organization had "accomplished what IWRAW was established to accomplish, i.e. make CEDAW known to NGOs globally" (email-correspondence, January 2004).

Finally, IWRAW has been engaged in "develop[ing] and generat[ing] ideas about how to use the Convention and what the Convention means more in depth" (Interview 22). To provide space for this, IWRAW organized annual workshops on specific topics in the field of women's rights. Those workshops took place in New York during the January sessions of CEDAW and brought Committee members and other experts together. In January 2000, for example, the debate focused on the synergies between CEDAW and the Beijing Platform for Action (BPFA) as a "double commitment of states" (Timothy and Freeman 2000, p. 1). IWRAW has provided other forms of expertise in the global discourse on women's rights, for example, by contributing to the CEDAW Committee's drafting of General Recommendations. While the organization is less active today, it played a crucial role in making the constructive dialogue accessible to NGOs.

Making Global-Local Connections and Expanding Women's Rights: International Women's Rights Action Watch Asia Pacific

The second crucial NGO directly engaging with CEDAW is International Women's Rights Action Watch Asia Pacific (IWRAW AP). While the name of the organization was derived from the US-based IWRAW, the two organizations function independently from each other (Dairiam 2007). IWRAW AP was founded in 1993 and has its base in Kuala Lumpur, Malaysia. It presents itself as a regional organization grounded in the experience of Asian women. IWRAW AP describes its mission as contributing "to the progressive interpretation, universalisation, implementation and realisation of women's human rights through the lens of CEDAW and other international human rights treaties" (IWRAW AP 2015a). Thus, in the terminology of this book, IWRAW AP's mission is both about global discourse translation and impact translation. As implementation may face a number of barriers, for example a "hostile culture or tradition [or] a gender bias in the administration of justice" (IWRAW AP 2015b), the realization of rights depends on well-trained, strategically savvy activists and their ability to influence state institutions and society more broadly speaking. IWRAW AP's two most important contributions to global discourse translation are the links it has established between domestic NGOs and the CEDAW Committee and its analytical contributions to global debates concerning women's rights.

Establishing Global-Local Connections

The first strategy—bringing women's voices into the CEDAW dialogue—started from the bottom up. IWRAW AP first reached out to women's organizations from South and South East Asia to alert them about the international human rights framework and its value for their struggles. It conducted training seminars to clarify core concepts such as substantive equality and the functioning of international mechanisms. The seminars also support the trainees to use international standards in their own work, for example, by presenting and discussing best practices of using CEDAW (IWRAW AP 2002; Interview 23). Following this initial focus on awareness raising IWRAW AP initiated the Global to Local program in 1997. It was developed in cooperation with experts from other NGOs and with the support of UNIFEM. To date, the program has been unique in facilitating the direct participation of women's groups in the CEDAW monitoring procedure, and NGO representatives from most States Parties have benefitted from it.

The program consists of a pre-session, in-session, and post-session phase. Before the CEDAW session, IWRAW AP gets in touch with groups and individuals from states that are coming up for the constructive dialogue and encourages them to write a shadow report. Once it has identified groups to volunteer for this task, IWRAW AP assists NGOs in preparing the report and makes sure it is distributed to the CEDAW experts in a timely manner. The assistance provided in this stage is quite extensive—"we will go through the report and give them detailed comments, section per section" (Interview 13). When choosing suitable organizations for the program, IWRAW AP looks for groups that are willing to prepare a shadow report, lobby CEDAW experts during the session, and carry out follow-up activities after their return home. The in-session part of the program starts with an on-site training preceding the CEDAW session. Trainers advise NGO representatives how to craft and present their statements before the Committee and how to lobby the experts. Depending on the time frame, NGOs are also instructed on fundamental CEDAW principles. According to one IWRAW AP trainer, this is always a useful learning experience for NGOs, because some realize that they hadn't really understood the Convention and that IWRAW AP has a lot of expertise to offer (Interview 13). The next step is the NGOs' presentation of their statements to the Committee. One goal that IWRAW AP has pursued through the Global to Local program is to make the complexities of gender-based discrimination within each State party visible. Thus, IWRAW AP has facilitated the representation of minority groups within domestic NGO delegations, such as indigenous or immigrant women's groups and NGOs working on issues of sexual orientation and gender identity. In regard to the latter, IWRAW AP sees a particular need because the Committee has not been proactive in addressing the issue by itself:

> If there are groups on LGBT rights, we ... insist that they ... be integrated in the NGO delegation and will get the floor to speak. ... We were very tired of listening to the Committee not raising the issue. ... Our strategy is to consistently raise it in every single NGO report. (Interview 13)

The on-site part ends with a one-day meeting dedicated to developing follow-up activities for each organization. In the post-session phase, NGOs return home, disseminate the Committee's concluding observations, and work to influence the government's implementation activities. IWRAW AP continues to offer assistance, for example, by running a mailing list for participating organizations that offers a forum to share and discuss implementation strategies.

The Global to Local program has helped many women's organizations apply CEDAW as a framework for national action. Some NGOs report that government officials take them more seriously after their international intervention (Interview 26). Also, coming together with NGOs from other countries shows them the global relevance of their work (Interview 13). IWRAW AP itself is aware of its position of power based on accumulated expertise. It is one of the organization's principles to not abuse this position and to build partnerships

> based on mutual respect and trust. ... we play a supporting role in their CEDAW-related work ... and aim to "add value" to local activism by providing the much needed link to the "disconnect" that traditionally exists between ... human rights monitoring at the international level and those grassroots organizations demanding accountability from their governments. (Interview 23)

While IWRAW AP has done a lot to build that bridge, occasionally the gap between local realities and international standards becomes visible. One telling example for such a mismatch was related to me by a Global to Local trainer. An NGO from Sierra Leone that partook in the program demanded in its oral statement to the Committee that the government should only allow the practice of female genital mutilation (FGM) from age 18 on and not earlier. The Committee, in turn, was outraged about this statement because it considers FGM a harmful practice under all circumstances. In the interpretation of IWRAW AP's Global to Local trainer, the NGO "wanted a strategic comment that would forward their work. In Sierra Leone, 90% of women are affected, so they can't erase it, the government has no political will. [And their idea was that] ... at the age of 18, women will not consent. If they don't consent, there will be no FGM" (Interview 13). This episode represents an interesting "translation gap"; while the ultimate goal of the NGO and the Committee are reconcilable—end FGM—the strategy as framed by the NGO deviated too much from what the Committee considers the universal standard of women's rights. The NGO for its part developed a strategy according to context constraints and was not aware that an uncompromising international statement could have added strength to their claim at home. While such normative clashes between NGOs and the Committee are the exception to the rule, they show that there is a great deal of difficulty in the attempt to connect local claims with global standards, even among like-minded advocates. In navigating these difficulties, IWRAW AP has helped to make NGO concerns and the Committee's ways fit together. This has contributed to creating a mutually beneficial dynamic between the Committee and hundreds of women's organizations from almost all of its States Parties.

Clarifying the Meaning and Scope of Women's Rights

IWRAW AP's other important contribution to norm translation is its continuous effort to clarify and further develop core concepts of women's rights, both CEDAW specific and beyond. I showcase just two examples of this interpretive work, namely IWRAW AP's positions on intersectional discrimination and sexuality rights.[5] IWRAW AP's stance regarding these issues is based on the idea of substantive equality or equality of outcome in a context of manifold structures of discrimination (IWRAW AP 2009). In IWRAW AP's founder's words,

> there is a tendency to look at these manifestations [of discrimination, S.Z.] and deal with them separately. Yet the problem has to be dealt with holistically. We must address several institutions at the same time—family, market, community and the state. These institutions interact and reinforce this web of discrimination, facilitating a denial of responsibility. (Dairiam 2002, p. 3)

The commitment towards equality of outcome made IWRAW AP elaborate on the intersection of discrimination based on gender, race, class, ethnicity, nationality, and more recently, sexual orientation. If substantive equality is the main goal of CEDAW, then the Committee has to understand and address the particularly harmful situation of women affected by multiple dimensions of inequality. The text of the Convention makes some, but not extensive, reference to intersectional discrimination, for example, in the comprehensive definition of discrimination in article 1 and in article 14 on the special situation of rural women. The issue of intersectionality has moved into the center of the Committee's attention during the drafting of GR 25 on article 4(1) (on temporary special measures), partly due to the input from NGOs like IWRAW AP. The NGOs argued that temporary special measures did not constitute a state's preferential treatment of certain groups; instead, they were "aimed at leveling the playing field since the field is tilted in favor of groups that have historically benefitted from preference and privilege" (IWRAW AP 2006, p. 4). Accordingly, CEDAW experts should be aware of the state's special responsibility regarding women suffering from multiple forms of oppression and temporary special measures should be designed to benefit all women, including the most marginalized. The final wording of CEDAW GR 25 reflects this perspective.[6]

More recently, IWRAW AP has used the framework of intersectional discrimination to underline that sexuality rights are covered by the Convention. In a paper geared towards NGOs, IWRAW AP noted that the CEDAW Committee has been more hesitant to comment on sexuality as a dimension of discrimination in its concluding observations than the HRC and the CESCR Committee, but that its framework is actually better suited than that of other treaties to address sexuality rights of women. The HRC, for example, has supported decriminalization of non-heterosexual partnerships based on consenting adults' right to privacy, but it has not called for sexuality rights per se. Within the framework of CEDAW, sexuality rights could take on the broader meaning of sexual autonomy of women, including the right to live a non-heterosexual identity without discrimination. However, this "package" of rights—self-determination in matters of sexuality, reproductive health, and sexual identity—is heavily opposed by many (see further in this chapter). As a consequence, the CEDAW Committee has been more fervently attacked than other treaty bodies when it has addressed sexual identity issues. To create a counterbalance in this respect and support the Committee in taking up sexuality rights in its concluding observations, IWRAW AP urges NGOs to integrate sexual identity issues into their shadow reports and presentations (IWRAW AP 2007a).[7] IWRAW AP has also directly contributed to the drafting process of the Committee's GR 28 on article 2 (on state obligations under the Convention). This GR covers a broad range of issues, yet its adoption was delayed because of reluctance within the Committee to include sexual identity in the concept of intersectional discrimination. IWRAW AP, together with other NGOs, lobbied strongly for the inclusion of state responsibilities in regard to intersectional discrimination, explicitly targeting discrimination based on sexual identity (IWRAW AP 2007b).

As these interventions indicate, IWRAW AP has sought to systematically bring non-governmental voices and ideas into the CEDAW Committee's constructive dialogue. In doing so, it has pushed to expand the meaning of international women's rights with the intention to include *all* forms of discrimination women may experience. While I have focused on the organization's influence on CEDAW, IWRAW AP has been outspoken in regard to other international processes as well; for example, it lobbied for an Optional Protocol to CESCR; together with other NGOs, it has tried to integrate a women's rights perspective into the Association of Southeast Asian Nation's newly developed human rights infrastructure, and it has been involved in the process of designing the UN's post-2015 development agenda, insisting on integrating (rather than sidelining) the concept of women's rights and substantive equality.[8] Thus, IWRAW AP has been making enormous efforts to enrich global discourses on women's rights by connecting them to domestic activists' views.

Re-writing the Women's Rights Framework: "Pro Women/ Anti-feminist" Interventions

The growing global recognition of the women's rights framework has not only attracted support but also triggered the articulation of dissenting positions that self-identify as "pro women" or "anti-feminist." In particular, since the Beijing conference in 1995, such voices have tried to influence international debates on women's rights within several UN bodies, most notably the CSW (Buss 2004; Druelle 2000; Goodenough 2010; Reilly 2009; Interview 24). CEDAW sessions have thus far not been their target because CEDAW embodies the women's rights framework and interaction with its monitoring Committee would imply acceptance of the framework. The anti-feminist organization REAL Women of Canada, for example, disagrees both with the Convention's content and what it considers a biased feminist interpretation of that content through the CEDAW Committee—hence, in the view of the organization, attending the monitoring process would be "a waste of time" (Interview 24).

"Pro women/ anti-feminist" positions are taken by governments, intergovernmental organizations and non-governmental organizations from different parts of the world. They do not necessarily share the same agenda but agree that feminist perspectives are misled and have a Western bias, and at the same time, unduly dominate international discourses. This is seen as problematic and in need of correction (Interview 24). The core package of anti-feminist ideas can be summarized as follows: while women are individuals and human beings with rights, they are also parts of societies and communities where they perform crucial social functions complementary to those of men. Of particular importance is the role women play as mothers and within the family, both for their self-fulfillment and for society as a whole. To guarantee rights to women means to support and give them choices *within* these roles. This understanding of women as role players has accompanied the global discourse on women's rights since its inception. It was also prominent during the drafting process of the Convention, even if the idea of women as autonomous individuals superseded and is dominant in the text (Rehof 1993; Chap. 3).

With CEDAW gaining increasing international authority, the Convention, and even more the Committee, has become the target of criticism for anti-feminist organizations. In their views, both the treaty and the Committee experts misread the needs of women around the world, and this misreading results from a feminist bias infused by Western individualism. For anti-feminist organizations, it is important to *recognize* societal structures as grown traditions with broad legitimacy—women's rights are to be realized in harmony with them. This idea is diametrically opposed to the work of feminist organizations such as IWRAW AP and the Committee itself. Their aim is to *transform* societal structures that discriminate against women.

How does this position translate into concrete claims? For example, the anti-feminist organization REAL Women of Canada rejects the demand of Canadian feminists to establish a national day care program because it would not take care of the needs of those mothers (or fathers) who decide to raise their children at home. As a representative of the organization puts it, "REAL Women of Canada believes that government support for child care should go directly to the family so that they can decide how the child should be raised and under what circumstances" (Interview 24). This argument assumes a context where free choice is possible—raise kids at home or have them attend day care centers—but this choice requires affordable institutions of child care. The assumption that there is no need for structural transformation comes across in other positions of the organization as well, for example, in its rejection of the claim of equal pay for work of comparable value (Interview 24). Another and probably the most heatedly contested area between feminist and anti-feminist voices is that of reproductive and sexuality rights. These rights are considered a fundamental dimension of women's self-determination by women's rights activists. "Pro women/anti-feminist" voices reject them because they interpret reproductive rights either as free access to abortion, which would be antithetical to the role of motherhood and the institution of the "natural family" (Buss 2004) or as a Western tool to impose population control over the rest of the world (Interview 24). Reproductive rights are also a field where "prowomen/anti-feminist" voices see an undue isolation of women's interests from their context since most women rather care for rights that enable the wellbeing of their families, such as maternal and child health care, access to food, water, and education (ibid.).

One representative of the "pro women/anti-feminist" position is the Organization of Islamic Cooperation (OIC), an international organization with 57 member states. It has repeatedly taken a stance on gender issues in different UN forums, for example, in the Human Rights Council, and its predecessor, the Commission on Human Rights; together with the Vatican, OIC blocked a resolution in the Commission that would have recognized sexual orientation as a possible source of discrimination (Reilly 2009, p. 156). It also tried (unsuccessfully) to undermine the Human Rights Council's resolution 15/23 on the elimination of discrimination against women by proposing to insert wording that would have allowed states with effective discriminatory laws to maintain that status quo (Goodenough 2010). The OIC has also developed its own agenda on women's issues, mainly through biannual ministerial conferences on

Women's Role in the Development of OIC Member States (OIC 2015). These conferences have produced programmatic statements all of which underline the important role of women in OIC states, in particular within the family. Women's high poverty levels and violence against women are acknowledged as problems. Measures in several fields, for instance, in employment, political decision-making, and education are considered necessary for their empowerment. Improving women's health figures prominently, but the terms "reproductive health" or "reproductive rights" are not used. While this agenda overlaps with core international women's rights documents (if without referencing them), its goal is to enable women to fulfill their role as mothers, educators, employees, and decent members of society—under dignified and healthy conditions.

Another example of "pro women/ anti-feminist" voices is a set of US- and Canada-based organizations that focus either on national-cultural tradition (e.g., the Heritage Foundation), religious and family values (e.g., the Catholic Family and Human Rights Institute), or on both, yet from a decidedly female standpoint (e.g., Concerned Women for America and REAL Women of Canada). All of these organizations have been attending CSW sessions in the last decades, and they also have been outspoken against CEDAW accusing it of promoting a radical feminist agenda worldwide (Interview 24). The issues most frequently held against the Committee are its alleged defamation of motherhood, its pro-abortion stance, its criticism regarding discrimination against lesbian women, and its interference in the domestic affairs of sovereign nations in general (Catholic Family and Human Rights Institute 2007; Concerned Women for America 2002; Heritage Foundation 2009). Lesbianism and feminism are often portrayed as wrong, mutually reinforcing, and antithetical to the empowerment of "real women." Thus, one claim that "pro women/ anti-feminist" organizations make is that homosexuality as a possible dimension of discrimination needs to be kept out of the women's rights picture. In other words, homosexual women deserve non-discriminatory treatment as women but not as lesbians.

While these accusations deserve respect as particular value statements, they nevertheless misunderstand the rationale employed by the Committee when it interprets the Convention. For example, the Committee has been harshly and repeatedly criticized for its alleged defamation of motherhood; the base for this accusation is the Committee's concluding observation for Belarus in 2000, where it expresses concern regarding "the continuing prevalence of sex-role stereotypes and…the reintroduction of such symbols as a Mothers' Day and a Mothers' Award, which it sees as encouraging women's traditional roles" (UN Doc. A/55/38, p. 37). Read in context, this position elaborates on CEDAW art. 5, which requires States Parties to overcome gender stereotypes and work toward "the recognition of the common responsibility of men and women in the upbringing and development of their children". Accordingly, the elevation of motherhood *alone*—read: not of fatherhood, and also not of any other fields of female achievement—reinforces stereotypes the Convention seeks to overcome. As for the Committee's pro-abortion stance, a careful examination of its recommendations shows that it typically urges States Parties to provide *safe* abortion services and decriminalize abortion only when it is concerned about the detrimental health effects of *unsafe* abortions, including high maternal mortality (Jacobson 2010; Chap. 4). Concerned Women for America lists a number of other areas where the Committee unduly "injects itself into domestic social and political affairs of sovereign nations," such as "indoctrination of children," which mainly targets the elimination of sexist stereotypes from school curricula and textbooks (addressed in CEDAW art. 10 (c)), or "mandatory sex education and contraception," which translates into the access to education, "including information and advice on family planning" (according to CEDAW art. 10 (h)) (Concerned Women for America 2002). These incompatibilities notwithstanding, a check of the general agenda of an organization like REAL women of Canada also reveals overlap with the women's rights framework: recognizing the diversity of women and their preferences, the organization works for a broadening of women's career options, equal pay for equal work, and different forms of child care facilities so that both working and stay-at-home mothers are enabled to live their choice (REAL Women of Canada 2015).

"Pro women/anti-feminist" voices have impacted the Committee, if mostly indirectly; they have made clear that they do not acknowledge CEDAW as a legitimate document.[9] More vehemently, they refuse to accept the CEDAW Committee as an authoritative interpreter of the meaning of women's rights. In the view of REAL Women of Canada, the experts' statements "reflect only the views of the individuals on the Committee and the feminist ideologies which they promote" (Interview 24). Considering that the CEDAW Committee long had to fight for intergovernmental recognition (see Chap. 4), it is not surprising that Committee experts want to avoid being seen as a group of "radical feminists" and, once labeled this way, risk marginalization within the UN context and beyond. This legitimacy pressure might explain why Committee experts are relatively shy in addressing women's discrimination based on homosexuality and hardly pick up the issue if it is not mentioned by NGOs (IGLHRC 2009; Interview 13).

In sum, if we look at the contributions non-governmental women's organizations made to the global discourse translation of CEDAW, we see two trends. One the one hand, there is a strong and continuous network of organizations that support CEDAW. These organizations have contributed to a more radical (in the sense of transformational) understanding of women's rights globally. IWRAW and IWRAW AP specifically have also enabled many other women's NGOs to directly contribute to the CEDAW dialogue. Their input has made the monitoring procedure more substantial. On the other hand, global discourses on women's rights have become broader and more contested due to the presence of "pro women/anti-feminist" voices. While some goals of these organizations overlap with the CEDAW framework, they often distance themselves from the work of the CEDAW Committee as too "radically feminist." Thus, the authority of the Committee as legitimate interpreter of women's rights is put into question.

The Bridge to Impact Translation: Making CEDAW Visible in Domestic Contexts

In conjunction with making the Convention known internationally, activists in support of women's rights have also worked to raise awareness on CEDAW within domestic contexts—the process called "impact translation" in this book. Three groups of actors that stand out in this regard are the Committee members themselves, women's NGOs such as IWRAW AP, and, as the most active operational UN agency with a focus on the dissemination of women's rights, UNIFEM and UN Women, respectively (UNIFEM became part of UN Women in 2011).

Spreading the Word: The CEDAW Experts

Over time, CEDAW experts have established a tradition of promoting the Convention in countries of their home region and often times beyond. They often attend regional and national conferences on CEDAW, visit countries upon invitation from governments and NGOs, conduct training workshops for government institutions, the judiciary, or Parliamentarians on the use of CEDAW, and speak at events that inform the general public about the Convention. For example, a CEDAW chairperson from the Latin America and Caribbean region visited Chile and Costa Rica upon invitation from NGOs and female lawyers associations to inform about the Convention (UN Doc. A/56/38, p. 6f). In the context of a UN program to help post-conflict states implement the Convention, a CEDAW expert from Africa advised the governments of Sierra Leone and Liberia in the process of writing their first reports. It was her impression that her input helped the governments understand their responsibility for the report rather than delegating the writing to the women's ministry alone or to consultants (Interview 18). Another Committee member from Africa trained Parliamentarians in francophone African states on the Convention and worked with the Inter-Parliamentary Union (IPU)[10] to enhance the involvement of Parliamentarians both in the reporting and implementation process (Interview 5). She also undertook country visits to Turkmenistan and Pakistan where she helped integrate the Convention into national policies. Also, experts often contribute to implementation activities in their own countries, for example, by contributing to the drafting of national gender equality plans, revising gender-discriminatory laws in the light of the Convention, influencing judicial reforms, or using the Convention as practicing lawyers (Interviews 5, 17, 18, 25). While this kind of translating activism is unsystematic and dependent on each expert's professional networks and personal enthusiasm, it has become significant simply by accumulation.

Systematically Connecting the Dots: IWRAW AP

While many women's NGOs are involved in bringing international women's rights "to the ground," this section focuses on the work of one organization that has already been introduced—IWRAW AP. This is mainly because of the comprehensive strategies it has developed to connect the Convention with regional and national contexts. As Shanti Dairiam, founder of IWRAW AP, puts it:

> IWRAW Asia Pacific was built on the premise that, without a politically aware and active constituency of women at the national level, the normative gains made in relation to women's rights at the international level could not be sustained.... The contribution that IWRAW Asia Pacific has made

> is a bridge … between national and international activism. (Dairiam 2007, p. 313f)

IWRAW AP is a relatively small organization with currently 13 staff members. Its work is funded by a mix of donor agencies, including the Ford Foundation, the Global Fund for Women, HIVOS Netherlands, Oxfam Novib, the Open Society Institute, and UN Women (IWRAW AP, 2015c). Since its creation, the organization has had to develop its work under precarious circumstances as funding sources are volatile.

Three of IWRAW AP major translation strategies are capacity building on women's rights for various constituencies, facilitation and coordination of domestic efforts to increase the impact of CEDAW, and the establishment of regular regional meetings to reflect on past and future strategies. The first strategy, capacity building, aims at enabling domestic women's rights groups to embed their activism within the human rights framework. IWRAW AP has provided countless workshops to clarify core concepts of the human rights framework, in particular, the principles of substantive equality and non-discrimination, as well as their meaning in contextualized settings. It first undertook trainings with domestic NGOs in several South East and South Asian countries.[11] Based on growing training experience, it developed a training package consisting of several modules and created a network of resource persons who are able to conduct training workshops in their respective states. Thus, IWRAW AP has passed on its knowledge to a number of multipliers in the region. In addition, IWRAW AP has identified the need to sensitize new constituencies, in particular lawyers and governments, and it has expanded the regional focus of its training workshops to Pacific, Central Asian, and Central European states. The Global to Local program presented earlier also contains a strong emphasis on clarifying the concepts inherent in the Convention and how they can be applied in domestic settings.

Second, and as a logical consequence of domestic capacity building, IWRAW AP has worked closely with women's organizations to create impact of the Convention in their countries. One comprehensive project in this regard was a program called Facilitating the Fulfillment of State Obligation to Women's Equality launched in 1997 in 12 countries in South and South East Asia.[12] This project helped to establish national networks of NGOs to monitor state action in regard to CEDAW implementation. As a starting point, the coordinating group of each national network produced a baseline report on the status of women, including suggestions for further action to be taken by the state.[13] Each network then developed strategies of advocacy and established relationships with government agencies to enable implementation on different levels. In some countries, the Facilitating Project yielded remarkable results, for example, it contributed to the reform of discriminatory inheritance laws in Nepal[14] and helped to dramatically increase the number of women elected into local government positions in Pakistan.[15]

The third dimension of IWRAW AP's work has been to convene regional meetings in South and South East Asia where resource persons, NGOs, and depending on the subject, government officials, UN agencies, and lawyers from different countries come together to reflect on past and future strategies. These meetings either have a specific thematic focus or reflect more broadly on the lessons learned from the work with CEDAW. In some instances, meetings are dedicated to discuss new dimensions of or challenges for women's rights, for example, the relevance of trade liberalization for the human rights of women, sexuality rights, or women's rights in conflict and post-conflict settings. Regional meetings also bring together experts to discuss various dimensions of CEDAW implementation. For example, a 2008 meeting in New Delhi focused on the opportunities and challenges of promoting implementation based on the Committee's concluding observations. A special concern of the regional meetings organized by IWRAW AP has been to expand ratification and use of the Convention's OP. In 2005, a global consultation on strategies to use the OP attended by participants from over 50 states was held in Malaysia; other regional meetings on the matter followed, for example, the "Africa NGO Meeting on Realising the Potential of CEDAW and the OP to CEDAW as a Tool for the Protection and Promotion of Women's Human Rights" in 2008. It was the first regional meeting that IWRAW AP co-organized on the African continent together with Women in Development West Africa (WILDAF) and Women in Politics, Zimbabwe (WIPSU) (IWRAW AP, 2015d).

All in all, IWRAW AP's widespread activities show that it not only brings the voices and concerns of domestic women's rights activists to the international level but also translates in the opposite direction by creating awareness regarding international women's rights among domestic constituencies, enhancing implementation efforts, and providing regional spaces of reflection and strategic planning. Most organizations bundle their scarce resources to focus on one or two of these dimensions; IWRAW

AP is, despite its small size, an exceptional "norm translator" connecting *all* the dots.

UN Agencies and the Dissemination of Women's Rights

The final group of norm translators that have connected CEDAW with domestic contexts are UN specialized agencies with operational mandates. UNIFEM was the "key driver" in this regard as it started to integrate CEDAW in its work by the early 1990s (Hintjens 2008). In 2011, the four UN entities dedicated to women's issues—UNIFEM, the Division for the Advancement of Women (DAW), the International Research and Training Institute for the Advancement of Women (INSTRAW) and the Office of the Special Adviser on Gender Issues and Advancement of Women (OSAGI)—were merged into UN Women, a better funded and more visible representation of UN activities related to women's empowerment and gender equality (UN Women 2015a). The organizational structure of UN Women expresses the agency's commitment to women's rights—CEDAW is explicitly mentioned as a guiding document—but the areas on which it concentrates its work do not list women's rights explicitly.[16] There have been mixed assessments as to UN Women's role in regard to the advancement of women's rights. Some see a continuation of previous work, within existing normative frameworks but based on a better infrastructure both for global norm development and for country-specific implementation (UN Women staff, email communication 2013). Others have observed a process of re-invention, where UN Women, in order to gain recognition within the UN, has distanced itself from the predecessor institutions and their (real or perceived) weaknesses (Mackay 2014). Another position argues that UN Women has so strongly focused on overcoming the fragmentation of the predecessor institutions that it has detached itself from the more substantial work of norm development (Charlesworth and Chinkin 2013). In particular, UN Women has thus far missed the opportunity to strengthen the concepts of women's rights and substantive equality for the entire UN system. Should this absence of leadership in normative questions continue, UN Women would resemble only "a renovated room with no substantive view" (ibid., p. 36).

While UN Women's role in regard to women's rights is still developing, UNIFEM's CEDAW-related work is a particularly far-reaching example of gender norm translation. Unfortunately, it has become difficult to find a trace of UNIFEM's work online, as the websites of UN Women's predecessor organizations have disappeared from the web shortly after the merger. UNIFEM was created as a temporary trust fund for women in 1976 and transformed into a regular UN Institution in 1985. Before becoming part of UN Women in 2011, it was affiliated with the United Nations Development Programme (UNDP) and focused on reducing women's poverty and exclusion, ending violence against women, reversing the spread of HIV/AIDS among women and girls, and advancing gender justice in democratic governance.[17] Following the Vienna Conference on Human Rights in 1993, UNIFEM started a women's human rights program with an emphasis on eliminating violence against women. In the second half of the 1990s, it started to systematically incorporate CEDAW. UNIFEM expanded its women's human rights work, appointed a full-time CEDAW advisor and provided assistance for effective implementation of CEDAW, for example, in the form of training seminars on CEDAW on regional and country levels for NGOs, governments, and members of the judiciary. Also, UNIFEM supported the Global to Local program initiated by IWRAW AP, had CEDAW translated into local languages, produced radio spots to make it more widely known, and published a collection of best cases of CEDAW implementation (UNIFEM 1998). Subsequently, UNIFEM shifted its approach and sought opportunities to meaningfully integrate the Convention into its areas of work and, in particular, into the struggles that its collaborating partners engaged in. Thus, rather than thinking of implementation of the Convention as a good in itself, this approach asked, "what can women doing work on HIV/AIDS with a specific gender dimension on the pandemic... gain from using CEDAW as a tool? What can women doing work on land rights gain from using CEDAW?" (Interview 9).

Throughout the 2000s, UNIFEM expanded on this two-pronged approach of integrating CEDAW in its areas of work, on the one hand, and carrying out programs with a specific focus on the Convention, on the other (UNIFEM 2007). For example, it developed ways in which the Convention could be used to make state budgets gender sensitive (UNIFEM 2008)[18]. Also, UNIFEM used the UN-wide "human rights based approach to programming" to make the advancement of women's rights the guiding principle of all its programs from the planning stage to the implementation stage. This approach has proven to be quite transformative; one example of its impact is UNIFEM's land rights analysis in the Commonwealth of Independent States that supported legal changes in several countries of the region to better secure women's land ownership (UNIFEM 2007, p. 24).

At the same time, UNIFEM continued to carry out CEDAW specific programs. The most impressive of these because of its comprehensiveness and funding level was the CEDAW Southeast Asia Program (CEDAW SEAP). With a budget of US$ 8.43 million provided by the Canadian International Development Agency (CIDA), it was designed to support the implementation of CEDAW in seven countries of the region—Cambodia, Indonesia, Lao Peoples' Democratic Republic, Philippines, Thailand, Timor-Leste, and Vietnam—over a four-year period (2004–2009). It targeted three levels of change—increase public awareness of women's human rights, repeal discriminatory laws, and make institutional structures and processes of government more gender sensitive—within three thematic areas, namely political participation of women, poverty eradication, and combatting domestic violence. Project participants in each state set their own context-specific priorities within the program's framework. According to an independent evaluation (UNIFEM/Universalia Management Group 2008), CEDAW SEAP had a range of positive outcomes. NGOs in all seven countries benefitted from the program: it strengthened ties of collaboration (or established new ones), which also led to more comprehensive and inclusive shadow reports (e.g., Vietnam, Philippines), it helped NGOs make use of the OP to the Convention (Philippines) and to situate their work, for example, on violence against women, in the broader framework of women's rights. On the level of governmental sensitization, the program worked to increase the "ownership" of the reporting procedure, which means that the periodic reports were written with broad involvement of governmental institutions, and to prepare delegations for the constructive dialogue. The program also helped push for stronger gender equality provisions in new Constitutions (Thailand and Timor-Leste), influenced a variety of gender equality legislation (e.g., the law on domestic violence in the Philippines), and worked for increased gender awareness of members of the judiciary through trainings and studies. Another dimension of the program was that capacity building on CEDAW often focused on "displaying its meaning" to people. Here, innovative means such as radio clips and dramatization of the Convention's content were used (UNIFEM/Universalia Management Group 2008; UN Women 2015c). CEDAW SEAP was evaluated positively, in particular because of its context-sensitive multi-stakeholder approach. Project participants valued the neutral, yet knowledgeable role that UNIFEM played and found that it provided a suitable framework to foster collaboration between governments and NGOs.[19]

UNIFEM undertook CEDAW specific work in other world regions as well. For example, its office for Central and South Eastern Europe carried out a four-year program (2006–2009) called Accountability for Protection of Women's Human Rights in the four post-Yugoslav countries of Serbia, Kosovo, Bosnia-Herzegovina, and Montenegro. This program focused on capacity building of government institutions in the light of CEDAW with the goal to make constitutional reform processes gender sensitive and enhance the realization of women's economic rights. In addition, UNIFEM continuously organized regional workshops on CEDAW geared toward NGOs, facilitated shadow report writing (e.g., in Bosnia and Herzegovina and Macedonia—here for Roma women specifically), and worked with courts to improve their application of CEDAW (Albania).[20] While UNIFEM as an operational UN agency was most active in regard to CEDAW impact translation, DAW also provided support for CEDAW implementation, mostly through technical support for States Parties and regional training workshops for governments on reporting to the Committee (UN Women 2015d). After the merger into UN Women in 2011, many of the technical assistance and training programs have continued, and through its net of country offices, UN Women also keeps working with governments to support CEDAW implementation on-site (UN Women staff member, email communication 2013).

Other UN agencies have also used CEDAW as a guiding framework for their work, among them, UNICEF and FAO. UNICEF strongly draws on CRC and CEDAW to emphasize the rights of boys and girls (UNICEF 2003). The connection of UNICEF's work to CEDAW is established in two ways: first, it helps promote the rights of girls, and many of UNICEF's initiatives focus on girls, in particular in the field of education. Second, the promotion of women's rights indirectly fosters children's rights because women who enjoy their rights are considered to be the strongest promoters of the rights of their children. A joint publication by UNICEF and UNFPA reiterates the point that women's and children's rights reinforce each other and explains this in regard to both organizations' efforts to promote the rights of adolescent girls and prevent maternal mortality, child marriage, and the spread of HIV/AIDS (UNFPA/ UNICEF 2011). The FAO has, in the context of its general mandate of achieving global food security and improving the living conditions of rural populations, made direct use of information on the situation of rural women provided by States Parties to CEDAW to design its programs (FAO/IFAD/ILC 2004). Some of these programs target discriminatory legislation or customs pertinent to land ownership because "secure access to land by women is a basic factor in food security" (ibid, p. 16).

Looking at these examples of translation work undertaken by operational UN agencies, it seems fair to say that some transformation has taken place. After a phase of institutional indifference toward CEDAW (see Chap. 4), UNIFEM was the first to comprehensively integrate the Convention into its operational work, and UN Women has continued some of this tradition. UN agencies without an explicit focus on gender issues also work with the Convention's principles if they see it as an enhancement of their general mandate. However, the principled integration of a women's rights perspective into operational work of UN agencies is less pronounced today than it used to be. This has to be seen in the context of broader developments, in particular the diminished relevance of a human rights perspective in development policies.

Creating Missing Links Through Translating Activism

"Translation work" aims at connecting international frameworks with contextualized practices. Such a connection was not envisioned by the designers of CEDAW nor does it play a role in international law generally speaking. The Convention does not dispose of any implementation mechanism other than the willingness of governments, enhanced by Committee advice. CEDAW-related translating activism builds a bridge between the Convention and *societies* rather than only governments; it connects what was previously not connected. Such activism makes a tremendous difference for global discourses on women's rights because it brings principally excluded voices and concerns into the intergovernmental system. In terms of impact translation, it paves the way for meaningful use of international frameworks domestically. Thus, it is fair to say that the work described in this chapter is the cornerstone of norm translation processes. It is work that is often less visible than phenomena that can be more neatly placed into a specific context, such as the intergovernmental adoption of a treaty or the domestic amendment of a law. Yet I argue that it is this bridge-building work that brings international agreements to life.

Translating activism toward the global level has both supported and criticized CEDAW. The supporters have worked to bring domestic activists and their input to the Committee's constructive dialogue and to other global debates on gender norms. As IWRAW AP's Global to Local program shows, it requires a lot of effort to bring excluded voices into international discourses. Thus, the program includes contacting, selecting, and preparing NGOs, teaching them effective ways of intervention in the UN context without patronizing them, and helping them use the added value of their international engagement for their future work. Supporters have further contributed to the ongoing international debates on the scope and meaning of women's rights—often, they have pushed the intergovernmental standards and made them more inclusive, as the debate on intersectionality has shown. Voices critical of CEDAW and its understanding of women's rights also influence the global discourse. While they factually go along with a significant part of the women's rights framework, they stress those areas where they fundamentally disagree with the interpretation of the Committee and challenge its legitimacy. This criticism has broadened the global discourse on gender equality but also added antagonism. Translating activism toward domestic contexts focuses on enabling actors to use the Convention in their own work, or in other words, to create "local ownership" of CEDAW. IWRAW AP and UNIFEM/UN Women have developed the most far-reaching translation strategies in this regard. These strategies include capacity building and awareness raising regarding CEDAW, and, crucially, provide women's rights advocates with a powerful international framework that adds legitimacy to their claims.

While translation activism related to CEDAW has been successful in concretely contributing to societal treaty implementation, it is confronted with a problem. It is dependent on funding priorities of donors, which means that continuity cannot be guaranteed. For example, the CEDAW SEAP program funded by CIDA clearly enhanced the process of implementing the Convention into societal and institutional structures, yet it ended after four years. Processes of social transformation, however, take much longer. Several organizations, among them IWRAW AP, have continuously attracted funding for their activism. However, it is becoming more and more difficult because the human rights framework plays a diminished role in development policies (see Chap. 3), because donor priorities have shifted towards funding short-term and output oriented projects (AWID 2013), and because other types of gender-related activism, for example related to security, now compete with women's rights work for funding. Thus, translation work is both part of and dependent on global and domestic discourses-in-motion.

Notes

1. The Convention of the Rights of Persons with Disabilities, for example, requires States Parties to establish focal points within governmental institutions and independent mechanisms to enhance and monitor implementation of the Convention (CRPD, art. 33).
2. For example, article 45 of the CRC states that "the Committee may invite the specialized agencies, the United Nations Children's Fund and *other competent bodies*... to provide expert advice on the implementation of the Convention" (emphasis added). Similar formulations can be found in article 74 of the CRMW and in article 38 of the CRPD.
3. *The Women's Watch* is archived on IWRAW's website under publications (IWRAW 2009).
4. For IWRAW reports written between 1993 and 2002, see IWRAW's website, Reporting to UN Bodies, IWRAW Shadow Reports (IWRAW 2009).
5. For other international debates IWRAW AP has been active in, see http://www.iwraw-ap.org/.
6. All GRs are available at http://www.ohchr.org/EN/HRBodies/CEDAW/Pages/Recommendations.aspx.
7. Other NGOs have also become vocal in this aspect; for example, the International Gay and Lesbian Human Rights Commission publishes shadow reports and supports shadow report writing of other NGOs on discrimination based on sexual orientation and gender identity, mainly for CEDAW, but also for other treaty bodies and the Human Rights Council's Universal Periodic Review process. A few years ago, it has also publicly criticized the Committee for not mentioning discrimination based on sexual identity in its concluding observations in cases where this was urgently necessary (IGLHRC 2009, 2015).
8. More comprehensive information of IWRAW AP's manifold activities can be found at its website (http://www.iwraw-ap.org/), in particular under Activities, IWRAW Asia Pacific Reports, and Our Publications, Media, Newsletter.
9. For example, REAL Women of Canada finds that the treaty does not sufficiently cover the needs of women who are not gainfully employed and criticizes the absence of religious rights for women (Interview 24).
10. The IPU itself has been an active sensitizer for Parliamentarians in regard to CEDAW. In collaboration with the UN, it produced a handbook on CEDAW for Parliamentarians (Inter-Parliamentary Union/ United Nations 2003). Subsequently, IPU has also conducted annual information seminars on different aspects of "Parliaments and CEDAW" in collaboration with DAW/ UN Women and OHCHR.

11. IWRAW AP has regularly worked with constituencies in South Asia (Bangladesh, India, Nepal, Pakistan, Sri Lanka) and Southeast Asia (Burma, Cambodia, Laos, Indonesia, Malaysia, Philippines, Singapore, Thailand, Timor Leste, Vietnam) as well as in Mongolia and Hong Kong (IWRAW AP 2015a).
12. Bangladesh, India, Indonesia, Lao PDR, Malaysia, Mongolia, Nepal, Pakistan, Philippines, Sri Lanka, Thailand, and Vietnam.
13. For example, the baseline report of Bangladesh focused on diverse forms of violence against women. It stated that legal provisions confronting violence were often not enforced and many laws were not suited to address violence against women; one particular concern was that marital rape was not a legal category. The report recommended that the state become more proactive in regard to violence against women (IWRAW Asia Pacific 2015d).
14. The core NGO Forum on Women, Law and Development (FWLD) focused its baseline report on inheritance rights. Its work crucially influenced the Parliament to pass the Country Code (Eleventh Amendment) Bill in 2002, which reversed several existing discriminatory laws, including inheritance laws. A conference FWLD organized with testimonies of women who had suffered from the discriminatory inheritance laws brought many of the attending Parliamentarians to vote in favor of the bill (IWRAW AP 2005, p. 72f).
15. In Pakistan, the *Aurat Foundation* prepared a baseline report on women's political participation. This report suggested a 33% allocation of seats for women, a measure that was granted in the 2000 local elections, accompanied by broader measures to address the obstacles female candidates would be facing. A broad coalition of women's organizations campaigned in support of women running for elections, provided capacity building programs for potential candidates, initiated a public debate on women's leadership capabilities, and eventually helped a stunning 36,000 women be elected into local government institutions. Further, the monitoring network held consultations with women councilors after they were elected to identify problems in their work and to formulate future strategies (IWRAW AP, 2004, p. 19f).
16. UN Women's focus areas are: Leadership and Political Participation; Economic Empowerment; Ending Violence Against Women; Peace and Security; Governance and National Planning; the Post-2015 Development Agenda; and HIV and AIDS (UN Women 2015b). For all of these areas, UN Women spells out the normative framework that typically includes CEDAW.
17. These areas of work were listed on UNIFEM's last website (http://www.unifem.org/about/) which is not anymore available online.

18. Key ideas of this CEDAW-based framework include appropriate budget allocation for laws or other measures created to achieve gender equality, the absence of gender-based discrimination in public spending or revenue creation, and women's participation in budget decision making (UNIFEM 2008).
19. While CEDAW SEAP was not continued after 2009, a program of similar scope called Regional Mechanisms to Protect the Human Rights of Women and Girls in Southeast Asia followed. It aimed at enhancing CEDAW implementation through the newly created ASEAN human rights mechanisms and disposed of a budget of US$ 2,810,476 (UNIFEM 2010, p. 21).
20. As the original UNIFEM website documenting these projects has disappeared from the Internet, a source specifying this work cannot anymore be provided.

CHAPTER 7

Auditing the Contract Partners: States Parties' Connectivity with CEDAW

As we have seen in the previous chapter, norm translation work is instrumental in thickening the relationship between the international women's rights framework and domestic contexts because the CEDAW Convention itself provides only a thin link to treaty norm implementation. It assumes state responsibility on the basis of ratification and monitors state action. This chapter takes a closer look at states as the contract partners to CEDAW and investigates their relationship to the treaty further. How seriously do states take their commitment to the Convention, and how is that commitment expressed? I will look at two dimensions. First, how do states connect to CEDAW *in principle*? Do they position themselves as close adherents to the treaty, or do they partly or entirely reject it? This type of *principled connectivity* is measured in three dimensions, namely ratification of the treaty itself, reservations, and ratification of the OP. Secondly, I ask how States Parties connect to CEDAW beyond principled commitment; this type of *substantive connectivity* is measured in reporting discipline and frequency of dialogues with the CEDAW Committee. For both questions, I take all States Parties (and partly non-States Parties) into account. I juxtapose the results with three potentially explanatory dimensions: world region; regime type (democratic or non-democratic); and de facto situation of gender equality, as measured by the United Nations Development Program's (UNDP) Gender Inequality Index (GII). The aim of this chapter is to show patterns of connectivity between states and CEDAW, assuming that

S. Zwingel, *Translating International Women's Rights*, Gender and Politics, DOI 10.1057/978-1-137-31501-4_7

the reach of CEDAW depends on the degree to which a state connects to it. Concrete processes of impact translation are presented in Chap. 8.

Before delving into these two dimensions of connectivity, a clarification is in order as to which entities are entitled to express their adherence to CEDAW. According to CEDAW article 25 (1), "all States" can become parties[1] to the Convention. Thus, in line with basic principles of international law, statehood is a prerequisite for ratification. While some treaties such as the CRPD also allow for ratification by international organizations, CEDAW does not.[2] Further, entities whose statuses as sovereign states are unclear or contested are also excluded from becoming a party to the treaty. Under this category fall de facto sovereign states that lack international recognition, such as Taiwan or Kosovo. However, these entities can declare unilateral adherence to an international treaty and engage in implementation, a step that Taiwan has taken in regard to CEDAW (Kroworsch 2012; Foundation for Women's Rights Promotion and Development 2015). Other forms of insufficient statehood are territories for which it is not clear by whom they are "effectively controlled." One example is the Turkish Republic of Northern Cyprus, which is neither under the control of the Cypriot government nor internationally recognized as a sovereign state, except by Turkey, or the West Sahara, which is partly controlled by Morocco, but Moroccan sovereignty over the territory is not internationally recognized. Another example are the Palestinian Territories, which have long been controlled partly by the Palestinian National Authority and partly by Israel, through de facto military control. Israel took the position that it had no responsibility to report to the Committee on the Occupied Territories because it lacked effective control; the Committee, on the other hand, assumed Israel's control and thus expected coverage from the Israeli delegation (Byrnes 2012b, p. 95). The Palestinian case also shows that statehood is a fluid construct; after a long process of being a state-in-becoming, the State of Palestine was recognized in 2012 by the United Nations (UN) General Assembly resolution 67/19 as a "non-member observer state." In 2014, the State of Palestine submitted its official request for accession to CEDAW, which was subsequently approved by the UN Secretary-General (Hatuqa 2014). Apparently, Palestine is now "state enough" to ratify treaties.[3]

To summarize, only sovereign and internationally recognized states can formally connect to the Convention. This rule means that the rights of a significant number of women who do not live in such unambiguous constructs of statehood cannot be monitored and protected through the treaty, such as the rights of Taiwanese, Kosovar, Northern Cypriot, Sahrawi, and many more women. Being aware of these exclusions helps avoid the simplistic assumption that an international human rights treaty could ever have "full global coverage." Such awareness is also in order regarding other dimensions of exclusion. For example, many women who live in sovereign states whose governments effectively control only parts of the territory can also not benefit from governmental commitment to CEDAW. On the other hand, there is the possibility of voluntary adherence to international human rights treaties that can be exercised by international organizations, not fully sovereign states (as in the case of Taiwan), and by subnational entities such as cities or municipalities. The latter form of voluntary adherence has been a particularly useful tool in non-States Parties—a prominent example is San Francisco in the USA (The Women's Institute for Leadership Development for Human Rights 2008; Lozner 2004)—but they also take place in States Parties to CEDAW such as in the case of São Paulo, Brazil (Kroworsch 2012). Thus, formal membership to CEDAW is clearly defined but de facto norm translation may extend beyond these boundaries.

Principled Connectivity with CEDAW

The concept of principled connectivity with CEDAW developed here is a composite of three components. First, did a state ratify the treaty, and if so, how long did it take to express its commitment? Second, has the state committed to the entire treaty, or has it entered moderate or even far reaching reservations to it? And third, did it ratify the OP, which represents an additional commitment to the principles enshrined in CEDAW? I call this principled connectivity because all of these dimensions say something about the *affinity* of a given state to the Convention; however, they do not yet entail any concrete *action* by the state in the spirit of the Convention.[4] To identify patterns of principled connectivity, each of the three dimensions is represented by a numerical score that together can reach a maximum of seven points.

CEDAW Ratification Patterns

As of June 2015, 189 sovereign states have ratified the Convention, with only a small group—Holy See, Iran, Niue, Palau, Somalia, Sudan, Tonga, and USA—remaining non-States Parties. This makes CEDAW the second-most ratified human rights treaty after the CRC. Experts have offered different explanations for the reasons of treaty ratification; for example, Landman (2005) and Smith-Cannoy (2012) find that democracies are more likely than authoritarian regimes to ratify human rights treaties, and among them, newly formed democracies are more likely to do so than established ones. I follow Simmons' view that governments take this step seriously and that "ratification decisions reveal governments' best guess about the political and legal costs and consequences of explicit commitment to the international human rights regime" (2009, p. 59). This process may be informed by a genuine attempt to implement the provisions of the treaty or by a rather strategic approach to gain international prestige without having much to do to earn it. Simmons calls these positions "true positives" versus "false positives." The decision-making process may also result in refusal of ratification if there is significant domestic resistance to the content of the treaty—these would be "true negatives."[5] In the case of CEDAW, the high ratification numbers indicate that there is very little rejection of women's rights norms in general. However, in states where some dimensions of the women's rights framework are contested, ratification processes may be complicated and take a long time; for example, Pakistan had a rather cumbersome ratification process (Weiss 2003). In addition, domestic contestation may lead to "partial" ratification expressed in reservations. There is also the possibility of "false negatives"—states that do not ratify even if they seem to be in general agreement with a treaty. In the case of CEDAW, the USA fits this description as its domestic legal and cultural framework is much closer to the Convention's provisions than that of many States Parties. Indeed, the reasons that keep the USA from ratifying CEDAW lie only partially in disagreement with the treaty, even if there are some substantive incompatibilities[6] (Baldez 2014; Ernst 1995). More importantly, the USA has a legacy of rejecting international guidance, let alone scrutiny, derived from its self-construction of "American exceptionalism" (Cohn 2004; Ignatieff 2005), and it has a process of ratifying international treaties in place that allows a one-third minority in the Senate to veto the process. Since there has always been a sufficient number of Senators who oppose CEDAW, ratification was never brought to the Senate floor.

The Convention entered into force[7] for 30 States Parties in 1981, one year after it was opened for signature. From then on, we see a steady rise in treaty membership of an average of eight to nine states per year (see Fig. 7.1). The two World Women's Conferences in 1985 and 1995 provided an increased incentive to ratify the Convention—18 states

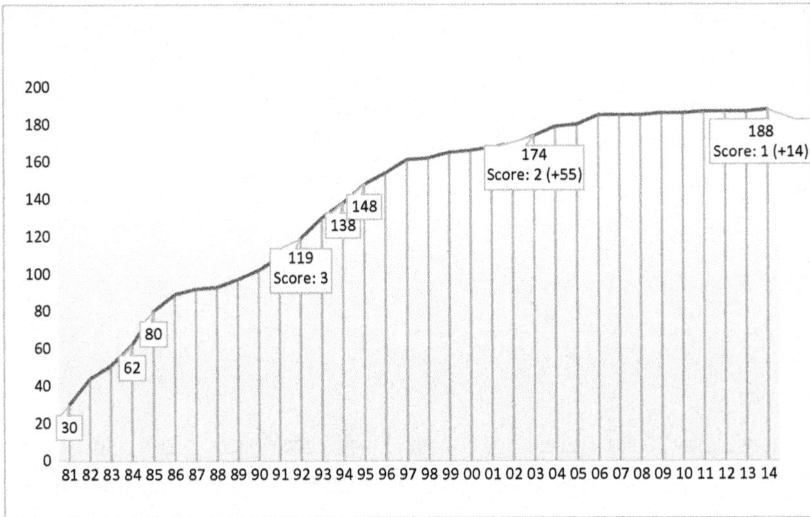

Fig. 7.1 States Parties to CEDAW, 1981–2014

became CEDAW States Parties in 1985, and 10 in 1995. Since about 1998, membership growth has slowed down to between one and two new States Parties per year.[8] According to the assumption that faster ratification signifies bolder commitment to the treaty,[9] States Parties are divided into three groups: states that became parties to CEDAW early (1981–1992) received a score of 3; states that took a medium amount of time and ratified between 1993 and 2003 received a score of 2; and states that took a long time to make the decision to ratify (2004–2014[10]) received a score of 1. Non-States Parties received a 0. Figure 7.1 shows that the early ratifying states are by far the largest group (119), followed by a group of 55 states that ratified between 1993 and 2003, and a small group of 14 states that ratified by 2004 or later.

There are significant differences across world regions in terms of CEDAW ratification (see Fig. 7.2). Following the regional classification of the UN,[11] *Latin America and the Caribbean* has the most unanimous and swift ratification record of CEDAW; in 1993, all states from the region were States Parties. *More Developed Regions* has the second best regional record. Eastern European states (including the former Soviet Union) were the fastest in ratifying CEDAW in the early

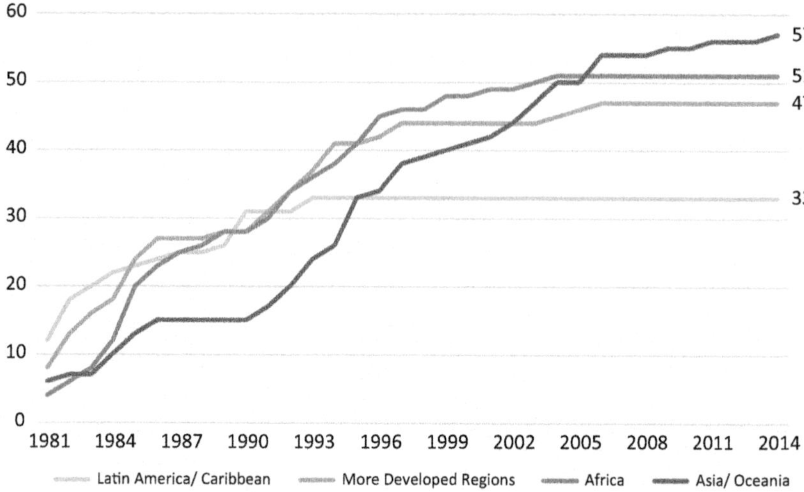

Fig. 7.2 States Parties to CEDAW per world region, 1981–2014

1980s, but most of the other states in that group did not ratify until the mid-1990s. There are only three states—Monaco, Montenegro, and San Marino—that became parties to CEDAW in the interval of 2004–2014. Two states belonging to the region, Holy See and the USA, remain non-States Parties. States from *Africa* were a bit more hesitant in ratifying CEDAW from early on, but with the 1985 World Women's conference in Nairobi as a regional incentive, most of the African CEDAW States Parties (34) ratified by 1992, a good number (16) by 2003, and only one after that. Until 2004, 51 out of 54 African states had joined CEDAW. South Sudan ratified in 2015, and Somalia and Sudan remain non-States Parties. Finally, *Asia and the Pacific* has been the world region with the most prolonged process of ratification. Until 1992, 21 states of the region had become States Parties to CEDAW. In the medium time period (1993–2003), the number of Asian States Parties to CEDAW rose to 47; again, the 1995 World Women's conference in Beijing added regional visibility to the Convention. Between 2004 and 2014, 10 more states from Asia and the Pacific states acquired CEDAW membership. Four of the region's 61 states—Iran, Niue, Palau, and Tonga—remain non-States Parties.

In terms of regime type, CEDAW ratification patterns confirm the expectation that democracies are more prone to ratify human rights treaties. By 2014, 117 (62%) of the 188 States Parties were de-facto democracies and 71 (38%) were not.[12] Of the non-States Parties, three are democratic and six are not. While these numbers tell us that *both* regime types have ratified, there is a significant difference in pace. Democracies have had a tendency to commit earlier to the treaty than non-democracies. Seventy-two percent of democracies ratified early, 22% in the medium and 6% in the late interval. The sequence for non-democracies is 49% in the early, 41% in the medium, and 10% in the late period.

Patterns of Reservations

A reservation is defined in the Vienna Convention on the Law of Treaties of 1969, article 2 (1)(d) as a "unilateral statement … made by a state, when signing, ratifying, accepting, approving or acceding to a treaty whereby it purports to exclude or to modify the legal effects of certain provisions of the treaty in their application to that State." The function of reservations in international law is to make it easier for states to become party to a treaty; Cook (1990) notes that, especially in the field of human rights where entering a treaty does not offer a state any direct advantage, reservations have become tolerated on pragmatic grounds. However, reservations have the potential to undermine the integrity of a treaty and are thus a highly controversial subject (Lijnzaad 1995).

When states become parties to CEDAW, they can either commit to the treaty as a whole, or they can submit reservations to parts of the treaty, as long as these are not "incompatible with the object and purpose" of the Convention (CEDAW art. 28 (2)). However, the Convention does not specify who is authorized to determine such incompatibility (see Chap. 4). In the absence of an unambiguous authority in this regard, Committee experts, States Parties representatives, and academic experts have tackled the question of what constitutes incompatibility. Two important dimensions are, first, the breadth of a reservation—the narrower it is, the more likely it is compatible with the treaty, and the broader it is, the less likely.[13] Secondly, it has been suggested that reservations should be declared impermissible if they are entered against the core of the Convention (Cook 1990; Lijnzaad 1995). By most accounts, article 2 (on state obligations to eliminate discrimination against women), 9 (on equal rights regarding nationality), 15 (on equality before the law), and 16 (equality in marriage and family matters) form the core articles of the Convention[14]; all of these articles, and most substantially article 16, have attracted reservations.[15]

The practice of entering reservations, and in particular those that have to be deemed inadmissible has been harshly criticized as rendering the Convention meaningless (e.g., Byrnes 2002; Clark 1991; Cook 1990). A lot of attention has also focused on the many reservations that have been entered based on religious and cultural grounds, often in specific reference to Islam (Connors 1996b; Mayer 1999). When the Committee itself focused on the link between incompatible reservations and Islam in its early years, it provoked a heated response from Muslim states rather than a constructive discussion (Byrnes 1989; Zwingel 2005b). Connors (2012a) suggests not shying away from this matter. However, in order to avoid hostility against what could be perceived as a biased attitude toward Islam, this discussion should be informed by the diversity of interpretations in regard to women's rights that exist *within* Islam (see also Krivenko 2009).

One the positive side, it should be noted that the number of reservations entered to CEDAW is comparable to (and not higher than) those entered in regard to other human rights treaties (Bayefski 2001). Also, a significant number of States Parties have narrowed or removed reservations entered upon ratification. This has happened more often for CEDAW than for other human rights treaties; however, it has rarely affected incompatible reservations, in particular not those entered in regard to article 16 (Connors 2012a). Finally, it is remarkable that 24 States Parties to CEDAW have taken the time to object to reservations,[16] yet it remains unclear if objections, some of them extremely carefully crafted, have much effect. Lijnzaad (1995) identifies a modest influence of objections on withdrawal of reservations.

To categorize this second dimension of principled connectivity with the Convention, the 134 or 71% of States Parties with no reservations[17] received a score of 2, the six with narrow or compatible reservations[18] received a score of 1, and the 27 with incompatible reservations[19] received a score of 0. "Incompatible reservations" include: reservations directed at the Convention in general; reservations concerning articles 2, 9, 15, and 16 in full or in regard to more than one subparagraph; and reservations directed at three or more articles of the Convention. All other reservations were considered compatible. Further, to recognize the process of narrowing or removing reservations, States Parties that converted an incompatible reservation into a compatible one[20] received a score of 0.5; and states that withdrew their reservations altogether[21] received a 1.5.

This last group of 17 states together with those states that never entered a reservation represent 80% of all CEDAW States Parties. The remaining 20% are comprised of 6% with compatible and 14% with incompatible reservations.

If we break down reservations by world region, Latin America and the Caribbean stands out with only one state, Bahamas, having a compatible reservation in force. States from more Developed Regions have four compatible and three incompatible reservations in place (see endnote 18 and 19, respectively), and Switzerland narrowed its reservations from incompatible to compatible. Eight African states maintain reservations, two of which—Lesotho and Tunisia—narrowed them and made them compatible with the Convention. Six reservations remain incompatible (see endnote 19). Finally, States Parties from Asia and the Pacific have 20 reservations in place 18 of which are incompatible (see endnote 19). Of the remaining two, one is compatible (entered by the Democratic People's Republic of Korea), the other is narrowed from incompatible to compatible (entered by Kuwait). Looking at reservations through the lens of regime type, 15 of the 37 reservations in place as of 2014 fall upon democracies and 22 upon non-democracies. The gap becomes more pronounced with respect to incompatible reservations (9 democracies vs. 18 non-democracies). Regime type has also influenced the withdrawal of reservations—16 out of 17 withdrawals have been undertaken by democracies (see endnote 21). Thus, reservations that are incompatible with the Convention are mostly entered by States Parties from Asia and the Pacific (18 vis-à-vis 6 from Africa and 3 from Developed Regions) and by undemocratic regimes (18 vis-à-vis 9 democratic ones).

Membership in the OP

Of the 188 States Parties to CEDAW in 2014, 105 ratified the Convention's OP. This is not a low number if compared to other treaties that have an OP attached (Smith-Cannoy 2012, p. 45), but it still shows that 44% of the States Parties (83 out of 188) do not want to take on the additional commitment of dealing with communications and inquiries related to their duties under the Convention. In order to operationalize this third dimension of principled connectivity, States Parties that became members of the OP between 2000 and 2007, that is, rather swiftly after its entry into force, received a score of 2, those states that ratified between 2008 and 2014 received a 1, and the ones that have not ratified the OP received a 0.

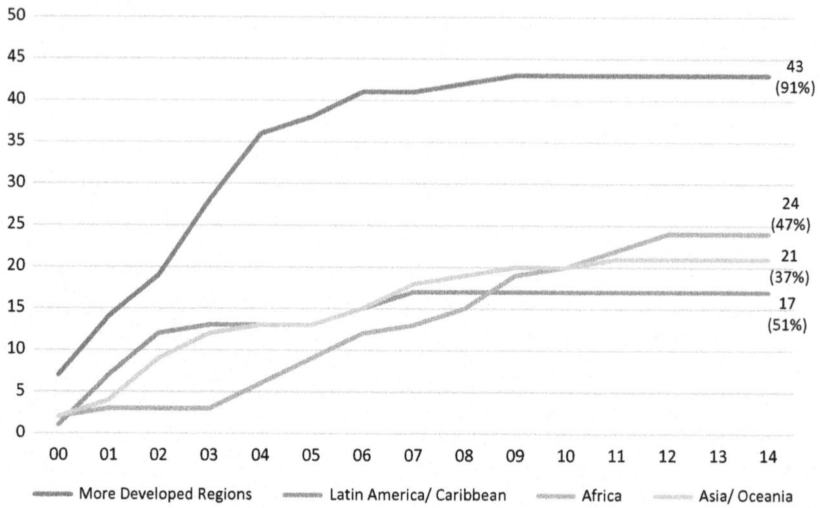

Fig. 7.3 States Parties to the OP to CEDAW per world region, 2000–2014

The group of states that ratified the OP early is the largest. Until 2007, 89 States Parties ratified the OP; only 16 more did so between 2008 and 2014. However, the group of 83 non-States Parties remains large. If it is true, as Smith-Cannoy (2012) suggests, that OP ratification processes are significantly slower than treaty ratification processes, then a further increase in membership can be expected. The regional break-up of OP adherence shows unevenness (see Fig. 7.3); 43 of the 47 CEDAW States Parties from More Developed Regions, or 91% of this group, ratified the OP, and almost all of them did between 2000 and 2007.[22] The other three regions have a much lower percentage of OP States Parties: 17 out of 33 CEDAW States Parties in Latin America and the Caribbean (51%), 24 out of 51 (47%) in Africa, and 21 out of 57 (37%) in Asia and the Pacific. The Latin American and Caribbean OP member states all ratified before 2007.[23] The Caribbean is significantly underrepresented in regard to OP membership—only three out of 13 Caribbean states have ratified thus far. In Africa, states are almost evenly divided between the early and late segment of OP ratification—13 states ratified until 2007, and 11 from 2008 on. This is a parallel trend to Convention ratification—African states have taken comparatively long in crafting decisions regarding treaty adherence. The fact that as of 2015, 10 African CEDAW States Parties were signatories to the OP suggest that more African OP ratifications can be expected. Finally, of the 21 Asian and Pacific CEDAW States Parties that ratified the OP, 18 did so until 2007, and three between 2008 and 2014. Only one other Asian state, Indonesia, has thus far signed the OP.

Regime type explains the discrepancy between More Developed and all other regions. Democracies are most likely to ratify OPs to human rights treaties (Simmons 2009, p. 107), and that region assembles the highest number of democracies. Selective evidence from domestic debates about CEDAW OP ratification in Germany, Canada, the United Kingdom, and Australia show that established democracies are often open to ratification because they consider this as a step consistent with their international policies in regard to women's rights and because they assume their domestic policies to be in line with the Convention's requirements (Zwingel 2005b, p. 365f). However, established democracies are more likely than newly formed democracies to be targeted with complaints, because their citizens are highly educated about their rights (Smith-Cannoy 2012, p. 57f). While this constitutes a clear disincentive for ratification, it has not deterred established democracies from ratifying the OP to CEDAW. In conclusion, democracies of all regions form the largest group of CEDAW OP States Parties (81 out of 105). Conversely, States Parties that have not ratified the OP are more often than not non-democratic (47 out of 83). However, there are also 24 non-democratic States Parties to the OP, most of them from Africa (13) and Asia and the Pacific (7). Finally, there is a significant number of democracies (36) across all regions that have not ratified the OP.[24]

Trends of Principled Connectivity

If we look at all three dimensions—treaty ratification, reservations, and OP ratification—combined, states are represented across a spectrum from 0 to 7 points (see Fig. 7.4). There are more states in the higher groups, in particular in the groups receiving a score of 5, 6, and 7. If the spectrum is clustered into a low, medium, and high segment of principled connectivity, the group with a high level is the largest (88 states), followed by the medium score group (70 states). The gap toward the group with low principled connectivity (39 states) is significant, and maybe the 30 states in this group that are actual States Parties to the Convention should be a reason for concern; 22 have incompatible reservations with

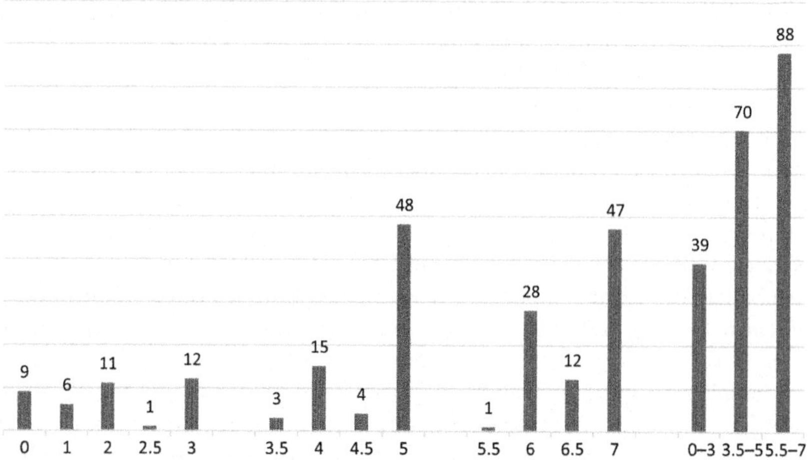

Fig. 7.4 Principled connectivity from lowest (0) to highest (7), based on CEDAW ratification, reservations, and OP ratification

the Convention in place, and none of them ratified the OP. A look at the list of states further reveals that states with a predominantly Muslim population form the majority in this cluster (see appendix 3).

The combined scores mirror the trends we have already seen for each individual dimension in regard to region and regime type. More Developed Regions has a high-medium-low connectivity score distribution of 73.5%–18.5%–8%, Latin America and the Caribbean 52%–45%–3%, Africa 32%–52%–15%, and Asia and the Pacific 28%–29%–43%. Thus, More Developed Regions forms the largest group in the high connectivity segment. Latin America and the Caribbean is almost equally represented in the high and medium segment and practically absent in the low segment. Africa is strongly represented in the medium segment, and Asia and the Pacific comprises the largest group in the low connectivity segment. In terms of regime type, democracies are strongly represented in the high connectivity segment where they make up 81% of all states; the medium connectivity segment is shared by 51% democracies and 49% non-democracies; and among the states with a low connectivity to the Convention, democracies are in the minority (28%).

Next to these patterns based on world region and regime type, how is principled connectivity with CEDAW related to the level of de facto gender equality in a given state? To find out about this relationship, I compared principled connectivity scores with GII scores of 2014. The GII is developed by UNDP and measures "the human development costs of gender inequality." This means that the *lower* the GII score, the more a country has *advanced* toward gender equality. The GII is based on five indicators—maternal mortality, adolescent fertility, ratio of female parliamentary participation, secondary education, and labor force participation. I use only 2014 data, which means that no development over time is implied. Also, the GII could not be calculated in 2014 for 45 of 197 states because data for at least one of the five indicators was not available. Thus, in the context of this analysis, GII scores should be understood as a temporary snapshot only (Fig. 7.5).

What can be seen in the juxtaposition of principled connectivity score and GII score is a *general* positive correlation, but the trend line shows that this is a modest tendency. The difference in GII average between states that have not ratified CEDAW and States Parties with the highest principled connectivity score is only 0.137 (the difference between 0.464 and 0.327, respectively).[25] Further, one would expect the treaty affinity groups with 4, 4.5, and 5 points to have a better average GII then the groups with 1, 2, and 3 points, but the opposite is the case. Likewise, the groups with scores 1 and 6.5 have a comparatively high average GII score.[26] Thus, in general, the assumption cannot be confirmed that only those states that already have reached a high level of de facto gender

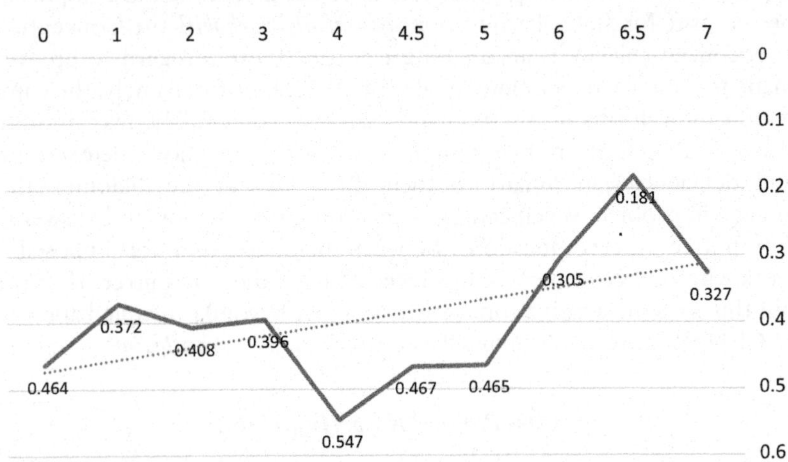

Fig. 7.5 Average GII score per principled connectivity score (0–7)

equality also show strong principled commitment to CEDAW. Rather, this connection to the Convention has been established out of a diversity of domestic gender regimes.

Substantive Connectivity

The second issue covered in this chapter is the *substantive* connectivity between States Parties and CEDAW. The two main dimensions of this substantive connection are States Parties' reporting habits and their frequency of having constructive dialogues with the CEDAW Committee. Both of these duties—submitting periodical reports and entering into dialogue with the Committee—are time-consuming dimensions of treaty implementation. According to CEDAW article 18, each State party has to submit a report on the status of implementation of the Convention the year after the treaty entered into force for that state, and every four years thereafter. The constructive dialogue with the Committee serves to discuss these reports and monitor treaty implementation on an ongoing basis; ideally, each submitted report should be discussed in a dialogue, even if the Convention does not explicitly say so.[27]

The constructive dialogue is the centerpiece of the CEDAW process. It constitutes the only face-to-face connection between international experts and domestic decision makers, and it provides guidance and expertise on a continuing basis. The dialogue is also the most important prerequisite for States Parties to *meaningfully work with* the Convention. It is conceptualized as an ongoing feedback loop in regard to progress made toward the overarching goal CEDAW stands for, namely, the elimination of all forms of discrimination against women. The task of States Parties is threefold. In their periodic reports, they diagnose their strength and deficiencies in regard to their goal. During the dialogue, they engage in problem specification by providing information and answering Committee experts' questions. Between dialogues, they are supposed to work with the recommendations received from the Committee. If carried out this way, substantive connectivity goes far beyond principled approval of CEDAW. It requires States Parties to *do impact translation.*

States Parties' Reporting Habits

It is well documented that States Parties' reporting discipline to human rights treaties in general and CEDAW in particular is not ideal (Bayefski 2001; Johnstone 2011; Leblanc et al. 2010; Zwingel 2005b). "Reporting habits" are documented here in two ways, namely in terms of *timeliness* of reporting and in regard to the *number of reports* submitted. The time period considered starts in 1982—the first year a State Party to CEDAW was due to submit a report, as the treaty entered into force in 1981—and ends in 2014, spanning a maximum of 32 years.[28] The first dimension captures the *number of years* a State Party has been *overdue per report*. If, for example, a state has been one year late with its initial report, three years late with the second, and not late for the third report, then it would be four years overdue, divided by three reports, resulting in a "lateness" of 1.3 years. This number gives an impression of reporting discipline of a country throughout the entire time of its treaty membership.[29] Lateness in reporting ranges from 0 to 14 years per report. There is actually only one State Party—the United Kingdom—that has never been late in reporting. However, there is a group of 21 states that have been only marginally late, that is a year or less per report. The number rises to 52 if we consider all States Parties that have been late two years or less per report. On the other end of the spectrum, Haiti holds the "lateness record" with 14 years per report.[30] In addition to Haiti, there are 6 other States Parties that are over 10 years late per report, and 48 more are overdue between 5 and 10 years (see appendix 4). Excessive delays in reporting undermine the duty of States Parties to account for their efforts to implement the treaty; as we will see, they also have a negative influence on the frequency of dialogues with the Committee.

The second dimension of States Parties' reporting habits captures how many reports have been submitted in relation to the number that should have been submitted according to CEDAW article 18. For example, Honduras should have submitted its initial report in 1984, followed by seven periodic reports until 2012. It did submit its first three reports in a timely fashion (1986, 1987, 1991) and combined its 4th, 5th, and 6th report (2006) as well as its 7th and 8th report (2015). This makes a submission of five reports out of eight or a reporting ratio of 0.63. While this particular performance is not ideal, it can still be considered substantial. If we divide reporting ratio into four levels from high to low (1–0.75; 0.74–0.5; 0.49–0.25; 0.24–0), there are 32 States Parties in the highest group, with five[31] making it to the ideal ratio of 1. 68 States Parties fall into the second category, which means that they have submitted between a half and three quarters of the reports they should have submitted. There are 59 States Parties in the third group (less than a half to one quarter of reports submitted), and 20 in the last group, which comes close to non-reporting.[32] In addition, there are 9 States Parties that have not submitted reports at all, but with the exception of one outlier,[33] none of them is more than 10 years overdue.

The reasons States Parties do not submit reports are typically not made transparent, but there is evidence that a lack of "state capacity," that is, lack of resources, expertise, and coordination between government entities is the most general explanatory factor (Heyns and Viljoen 2001; Leblanc et al. 2010). Many states have resorted to submitting combined reports. In a limited amount of cases, this is legitimate because it follows a request by the Committee[34]; in most cases, however, it is the practical consequence of long-delayed reporting. The degree to which combining reports undermines the constructive dialogue varies. For example, a one-time combination of two reports does not have a significant impact on reporting periodicity. However, there are 77 cases of 3 or more combined reports.[35] Broken down, there are 46 cases of three combined reports, 15 of 5, 10 of 5, 5 of 6, and one case of 7 combined reports. Almost all States Parties with that many combined reports submitted fall into the two lowest reporting ratio categories (0.49–0.0).

Taking these two dimensions of reporting habits together, it becomes clear that across the board, reporting discipline is a far cry from what it should be. Individual States Parties perform unevenly. Accordingly, there is a significant number of States Parties (52 or 28%) that are only moderately late in reporting—that is, two years or less per report; however, 79 States Parties (42%) are more than two but under five years overdue, 48 States Parties (26%) 5–10 years, and seven States Parties (4%) even more than 10 years—and again, that is lateness *per report*. Further, States Parties divide almost evenly between those that have submitted half or more of the ideal number of reports (100 or 53%) and those with a ratio below that or no reports submitted (79 and nine States respectively, which amounts to 88 or 47%).

Dialogue Frequency

Punctual or delayed reporting affects frequency of constructive dialogues, that is, the most important connection between CEDAW and domestic impact translation. To calculate "dialogue frequency," I have verified the time span between the State Party's first possible year for a dialogue and 2014 and divided it by the number of dialogues it has had.

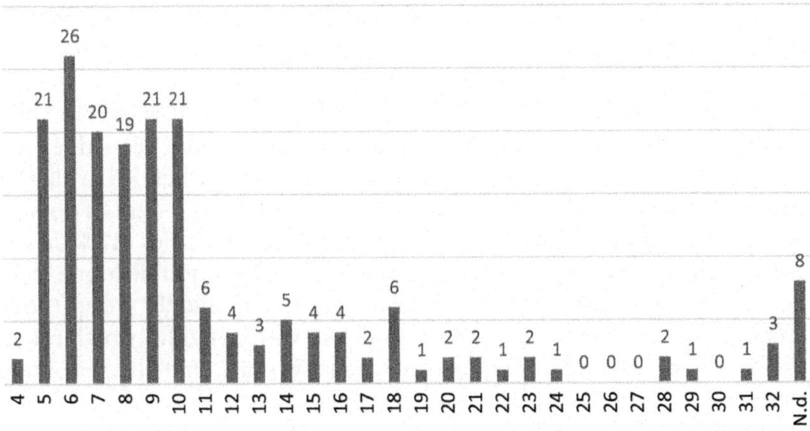

Fig. 7.6 Dialogue frequency of CEDAW States Parties in years, 1982–2014

For example, Argentina could have had its first dialogue in 1986, thus the time span considered is 28 years. In this time, it has had five dialogues with the Committee, which brings it to a dialogue frequency of 5.6 years. Figure 7.6 illustrates the distribution of States Parties' dialogue frequency.

A couple of things are noteworthy here. First, there are only two States Parties that indeed have had average dialogue intervals of four years. Thus, the ideal is a de facto exception. The main reason for this is delayed reporting, but there are other factors as well, in particular the inability of the Committee in its early years to consider all reports submitted due to limited meeting time (see Chap. 4). Second, most States Parties have a dialogue frequency between five and ten years (128 or 68%). Third, while the number of States Parties with larger average intervals is much smaller (50 or 27%), it is somewhat alarming that some of these intervals are decades long—the affected States Parties ratified the Convention early and have had only one constructive dialogue. Finally, the number of States Parties with no dialogue at all is not excessively high (8 or 4%), but a reduction would nevertheless be desirable.

I divide this distribution into three groups: States Parties with a dialogue frequency of up to eight years fulfill the spirit of the treaty in terms of monitoring frequency; this cut-off number is rather high, partly because the calculation is somewhat arbitrary—a state that has a dialogue frequency of eight years in 2014 had one of six years in 2012 if it had no dialogue in these two years. Group 1 is made up of 88 States Parties. The second group with a dialogue frequency of between 9 and 16 years fulfills the spirit of the treaty in part. It is made up of 68 States Parties. The third group of states with a dialogue frequency of 17 or more years does not fulfill the spirit of the treaty and consists of 24 States Parties. All in all, this means that less than half of all States Parties—88 or 47%—are in contact with the Committee often enough; for the 24 States Parties (13%) in the last group, the dialogue frequency comes close to a non-dialogue, rendering the monitoring procedure meaningless. The middle group (36%) seems to be torn between those two poles, with roughly two thirds of them having a dialogue frequency of 9 or 10 years, and the remaining third of 11–16 years (see Appendix 5 for a list of states per interval).

There is a clear connection between reporting discipline and dialogue frequency. The data shows that the closer a State Party comes to punctual and regular delivery of reports, the more likely it will benefit from adequate dialogue frequency. Conversely, weak reporting discipline prolongs these intervals. Concretely, of the 100 States Parties with adequate reporting discipline (defined here as up to two years reporting lateness and a reporting ratio of 0.5 or higher), 82 reached a dialogue frequency of eight years or less, and 18 had longer intervals between constructive dialogues. Among the best performers, that is States Parties with a reporting lateness of one year or less and/or a reporting ratio of 0.75 or higher, this trend is more pronounced. Of the 37 States Parties that fall in that group, only three had a dialogue frequency of over eight years. Similarly, if we look at the 88 States Parties with a dialogue frequency of eight years or less, 81 (92%) are in the top half of both reporting timeliness and reporting ratio. On the other end, of the 24 States Parties with inadequate dialogue frequency of 17 years and more, 23 (96%) had a reporting lateness of more than two years or a reporting ratio of 0.49 or less. In sum, good reporting discipline shortens the intervals between dialogues.

Substantive Connectivity in Relation to World Region, Regime Type, and Affinity to Gender Equality

The first part of this chapter examined if and how States Parties' location, regime type, and affinity to gender equality affect principled connectivity. These same dimensions will now be examined for substantive connectivity, represented by dialogue frequency. As for the regional dimension, 70% of

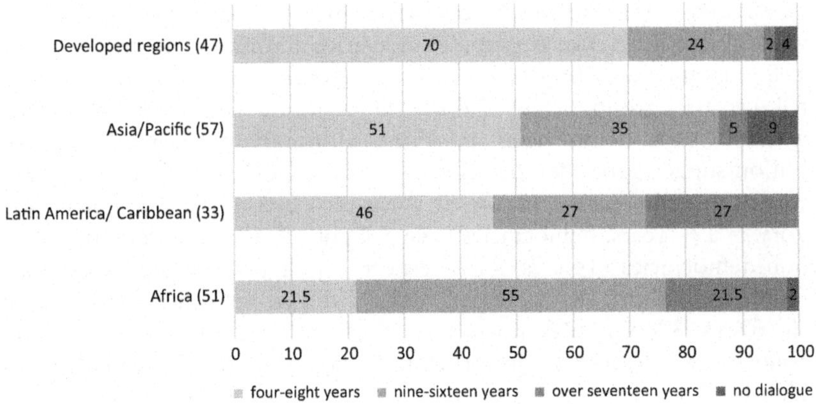

Fig. 7.7 Dialogue frequency per world region (in %)

States Parties from More Developed Regions have a dialogue frequency of eight years or lower, followed by 51% from Asia and the Pacific, 46% from Latin America and the Caribbean, and 21.5% from Africa. Only Africa has a majority of States Parties (55%) placed in the 8-to-16-year dialogue frequency interval; for the other regions, 24–35% of States Parties fall into that category. Finally, African and Latin American and Caribbean States Parties make up almost all states in the category of 17+ years of dialogue frequency (Fig. 7.7).

This regional performance of substantive connectivity differs somewhat from regional principled connectivity. States Parties from More Developed Regions have the best dialogue frequency, a result that one could expect after the results from principled connectivity. Second best are States Parties from Asia and the Pacific—this is surprising given that this region had the lowest level of principled connectivity. Apparently, a more distant relationship to the core principles of the Convention does not have to preclude States Parties from engaging in a sustained dialogue with the Committee. Next are States Parties from Latin America and the Caribbean—here, the opposite conclusion can be drawn, namely that high principled connectivity does not automatically result in high substantive connectivity and frequent contact with the monitoring body. Finally, States Parties from Africa have had the most difficulties reaching a good level of substantive connectivity.

Regime type correlates moderately with dialogue frequency. There is a noticeable difference between democracies and non-democracies in the 4–8 years interval: 50% of all democracies versus 41% of non-democracies fall into that group. There is also a difference in the 9–16 years interval with 31% of all democracies and 45% of all non-democracies. This distribution suggests that democracies tend to have shorter dialogue intervals than non-democracies. However, if we look at the last frequency category of 17+ years, democracies have a slightly *higher* representation than non-democracies (14% vs. 11%, respectively) and there are also slightly more democracies that have not had a dialogue with the Committee at all (5% vs. 3% of non-democracies). Thus, when it comes to substantive connectivity, democratic government is not a unanimous indicator for high-level performance.

Finally, shorter dialogue intervals correlate with better GII scores. The average 2014 GII score among the States Parties for which the GII could be calculated was 0.311 in the 4–8 years interval, 0.423 in the 9–16 years interval, and 0.509 for the 17+ years interval. Other than in the case of principled connectivity, where no straightforward connection to GII scores could be established, substantive connectivity to CEDAW parallels with de facto gender equality as measured by the GII. This seems logical. It is feasible for a state displaying considerable distance to gender equality norms to support CEDAW in principle—maybe, but not necessarily, as a "false positive." However, such a state will have difficulties in reporting, since report writing requires gender-related expertise and state investment in corresponding institutions. Conversely, a state that embodies a higher level of de facto gender equality typically has the infrastructure in place to design, develop, and document gender equality policies. Hence, it is prepared to present its work and have it monitored.

Concrete Examples of Principled and Substantive Connectivity

How do these general trends translate into concrete cases? Let's first look at the two states with the largest populations, India and China, both surpassing 1.2 billion, because these states' connectivity with CEDAW is potentially relevant for a large number of women. Both belong to the region of Asia and the Pacific. India is a democracy and China is not. India has a 2014 GII value of .563, China one of .202. This means that, as a tendency, Chinese women live under more gender equal conditions than Indian women, even if the fact that they do not live in a democracy influences their enjoyment of human rights.

In terms of principled connectivity, the two states are far apart from each other. Both are States Parties to CEDAW, yet China ratified earlier (1981) than India (1993). China has entered no reservations. India, in contrast, has incompatible reservations against art. 5 (a) and 16 (1) in place, declaring that the government does not interfere "in the personal affairs of any Community without its initiative and consent."[36] Neither state has ratified the OP. Their principled connectivity score results in a medium 5 for China and a low 2 for India. Thus, China accepts the full scope of the Convention and has done so for a long time, while India took longer to ratify and never fully committed to CEDAW. Neither in India nor in China do women have access to complaint mechanisms under CEDAW.

In terms of substantive connectivity, the two states are relatively even. China is 3.4 years late per report and has submitted 55% of the ideal number of reports, that is, five out of nine. India is 3.8 years late per report, and has submitted 50% of reports (three out of six; an exceptional report submitted upon request of the Committee regarding the Gujarat riots is not counted here). Thus, both countries lag behind in their reporting duties, but the ratio of 50% or more of reports submitted shows that they are continuously reporting rather than having long lapses between reports. Indeed, China submitted reports in 1983, 1989, 1997, 2005, and 2012, and India in 1999, 2005, and 2012. This steadiness has led to a reasonable dialogue frequency with the Committee of 6.4 years (China) and 6.67 years (India), respectively (see Table 7.1).

Table 7.1 Selected large States Parties, principled and substantive connectivity

	Democratic	*GII value*	*Principled connectivity*	*Substantive connectivity*		
				Reporting lateness	*Ratio of reports*	*Dialogue frequency*
China	N	0.202	5	3.4	0.55	6.4
India	Y	0.563	2	3.8	0.5	6.67
Brazil	Y	0.441	6.5	6.6	0.38	9.7
Russian Federation	N	0.314	7	1.8	0.78	6.4

To get an impression from other world regions as well, let's analyze two more states with large populations, Brazil (Latin America and the Caribbean) and the Russian Federation (More Developed Regions). Brazil is a democracy and has a 2014 GII value of .441; the Russian Federation is not a democracy and reaches a 2014 GII value of 3.14. In terms of principled connectivity, the two states are rather even. Russia reaches 7 points with early treaty ratification without reservations and early OP ratification; Brazil reaches 6.5, the only difference to Russia being that it ratified the Convention with reservations on subsections of articles 15 and 16, which it later withdrew.

In spite of these similarities, these two states' level of substantive connectivity differs significantly. Brazil is not only extremely late in terms of reporting—6.6 years per report—it has also submitted only 38% of its reports (three out of eight). This low percentage is a result of Brazil submitting its 1st through 5th report combined. Between 1985, when it should have submitted its first report, and 2002, when it submitted the combined report, it had no interaction with the Committee; it has subsequently picked up its responsibilities and submitted two more reports in 2005 and 2010. However, the dialogue frequency over the entire time of its treaty membership is 9.7 years. The Russian Federation, in contrast, is 1.8 years late per report and has submitted 78% of its reports (seven out of nine). It has reported steadily over time—1983, 1987, 1991, 1994, 1999, 2009, and 2014—and as a result, its dialogue frequency is 6.4 years (see Table 7.1).

This compilation of cases shows that the state with the highest principled connectivity (Russian Federation) also shows the best reporting discipline. While China and India with medium- and low-principled connectivity levels lag in terms of timely reporting, they still maintain sufficient periodicity so that all three states reach adequate dialogue frequency. Brazil, on the other hand, shows high principled connectivity in combination with inadequate reporting. This results in a much longer dialogue interval than for the other three states. Finally, it is interesting that in this compilation of states, the non-democracies fare better than the democracies in terms of substantive connectivity; they also have better GII values.

Patterns of Decreasing Commitment

I have argued that within the overarching concept of norm translation, impact translation depends fundamentally on the connections that are made between international norms and domestic contexts. This chapter has zoomed in on the connections that states—the official contract partners, according to international law—have established to the Convention. A few general observations can be made. First, official connectivity is channeled through statehood—in territories with ambiguous or contested statehood women cannot claim their rights through CEDAW. This is also true for states that refuse to make a connection to the Convention.

Second, making a connection to an international treaty implies a lot of work for a government, ranging from scrutinizing the treaty and deciding on the domestic position to it to delivering periodic reports and engaging in regular encounters with the Committee. While states' records in this regard are mixed, it is important to keep in mind the sheer volume of governmental work that is required to make a treaty resonate. Thus, governmental norm translation, if done well, is labor intensive. Many states shy away from this duty or set different priorities, but many also lack the resources necessary. Notably, least developed states are overrepresented among those States Parties with low substantive connectivity levels (see appendices 4 and 5).

Third, patterns of principled and substantive connectivity differ significantly. Most importantly, they show that it is easier to *declare* strong commitment to CEDAW than to *substantively engage* with its monitoring procedure. In more detail, states display a variety of positions in regard to principled connectivity, ranging from rejection of treaty membership to comprehensive adherence to its provisions. More states show high adherence than low adherence or rejection. Principled affinity depends in part on regional location—states from More Developed Regions and Latin America and the Caribbean are on a higher level than states from Africa and Asia and the Pacific. Also, democratic government makes higher levels of principled connectivity more likely. De facto gender equality, in contrast, is not unambiguously related to principled connectivity to CEDAW. While states in the highest connectivity segment have a marginally better average GII score that those in the lowest, the states in the middle segment have the worst average GII score. In general, one can observe that on the aspirational level, the majority of states construct themselves as adherents to the idea of cooperative sovereignty, willing to comply with international standards.

In terms of substantive connectivity, States Parties are more spread out. Their reporting discipline ranges from ideal to non-existent. As a consequence, we see a variation of dialogue intervals ranging from 4 to 32 years. This means that, while about half of the States Parties benefit from regular dialogues with the Committee, a significant portion of them is nowhere near adequately engaging in the monitoring procedure. I would argue that this lack of engagement is more problematic than entering reservations to the treaty, as a State Party that interacts with the Committee on a regular basis *and* has a reservation in place can take advantage of the Committee's guidance, whereas a State Party that does not submit reports and is not scheduled for a dialogue cannot. Substantive connectivity has a regional pattern somewhat different from principled connectivity. More Developed Regions have, again, a good record; States Parties from Asia and the Pacific have the second best average dialogue frequency, despite low principled connectivity; and both Latin America and the Caribbean and Africa have a lower level of substantive than of principled connectivity. Further, substantive connectivity is *less* directly influenced by regime type than principled connectivity and *more* directly influenced by de facto gender equality.

Fourth, in addition to the different levels of principled and substantive connectivity, there also seems to be only a weak connection between the two; not all states follow a scaffolding logic where they *first* talk the talk and *then* walk the walk. Sixty percent of States Parties in the highest principled connectivity category fall into the group with adequate reporting discipline and good dialogue frequency; 40% do not—Brazil (see earlier in this chapter) is an example of this group. Of States Parties with low principled connectivity, 50% have good dialogue frequency. Apparently, *low level* principled connectivity translates almost as much in substantive reporting and dialogue commitment as a *high level* of it. The concrete cases of India, China, and the Russian Federation confirm this trend—they differ in terms of principled connectivity from low to high, but all three are almost even in terms of substantive connectivity (even if the higher level of reporting discipline of the Russian Federation should be noted).

Finally, this chapter has shown that States Parties' commitments to CEDAW decrease the more substantive the duties become. So far, we have looked at international compliance—report writing and entering the constructive dialogue—and not yet at domestic-level impact translation. However, impact translation is even more demanding and labor intensive than establishing a meaningful connection to CEDAW, and in addition, it is confronted with potential domestic resistance. As Chap. 8 shows, States Parties become, even in the best of cases, rather eclectic in their strategies of CEDAW impact translation.

Notes

1. Withdrawal of membership is not specified in the Convention, but the Vienna Convention on the Law of Treaties allows for this option in principle. However, the process is cumbersome and formal withdrawals from international treaties are extremely rare (Kroworsch 2012).
2. An international organization could nevertheless declare itself bound by the treaty. Rudolf (2011) argues that such a step could have significant practical consequences.
3. Other forms of fluid statehood can be found in regard to overseas and dependent territories. For example, New Zealand has long included the Cook Islands and Niue in its reports, but these two territories have moved toward sovereignty (Kroworsch 2012). The Cook Islands became a State party to CEDAW in 2006.
4. Some states—for example, Finland and Japan—have scrutinized and amended laws in the process of ratification. In these cases, ratification actually constitutes domestic implementation of the Convention, but this kind of ratification process is not required and certainly not the norm.
5. This description applies to most of the non-States Parties to CEDAW. The Holy See has declared the obligations under the Convention inacceptable (Kroworsch 2012, p. 551). For a presentation of the Iranian domestic debate on women's rights as a problematic Western concept, in general, and CEDAW ratification, in particular, see Stachursky (2013). Somalia/Somaliland present a cultural context shaped by a mix of Islamic and tribal traditions both of which are hard to reconcile with CEDAW (UNICEF/The Academy for Peace and Development 2002).For Sudan, Tønnessen (2011) shows that Islamist feminist organizations promote ways of female empowerment that follow an interpretation of Islam that is not compatible with CEDAW; the government of Tonga has recently signaled its intent to ratify the Convention with reservations, but this announcement has drawn significant religious opposition (Moala 2015). Palau signed the Convention in 2011, yet it is not clear if and how it has further proceeded toward ratification.
6. One incompatibility is the balancing of the protection of privacy and free speech from government interference with governmental responsibility to prevent discrimination. The USA prioritizes the first norm, CEDAW the second.
7. The entry into force date is when a treaty becomes legally binding for a given state, usually three months after ratification.
8. An updated list of ratifications, accessions, and successions to CEDAW can be found in the United Nations Treaty Collection at https://treaties.un.org/ , Chapter IV, Human Rights.

9. This assumption does not apply to all states, in particular not if they came into being after the Convention was adopted. Cases in point are the Czech Republic, Slovakia (both 1993), or Timor-Leste (2002).
10. This cut-off date excludes South Sudan, which ratified CEDAW in April 2015.
11. See Chap. 4, p. 78 and United Nations 2010.
12. This classification is based on Polity IV data (available at: http://www.systemicpeace.org/polity/polity4.htm) and own research where Polity IV did not provide data.
13. An example for a narrow reservation is Austria's reservation regarding article 11 concerning "night work of women and special protection of working women ... within the limits established by national legislation." It affects only two subsets of one CEDAW article and was withdrawn in the context of legal reform. An example for a broad reservation is the Government of Malaysia's declaration "that Malaysia's accession is subject to the understanding that the provisions of the Convention do not conflict with the provisions of the Islamic Shariah law and the Federal Constitution of Malaysia." This reservation subordinates the Convention *as a whole* to the national legal framework.
14. See, among other sources, a proposal of Canada for the States Parties meeting in 1986 (UN Doc. A/41/608, p. 6), the 1998 statement of the CEDAW Committee declaring articles 2 and 16 the core provisions of the Convention (UN Doc. A/53/38, p. 47), Cook (1990) and Lijnzaad (1995, p. 304), who suggests to also include article 11 in the core.
15. An updated list of all reservations to CEDAW can be found together with ratifications in the United Nations Treaty Collection at https://treaties.un.org/, Chapter IV, Human Rights.
16. As of 2014, these were Austria, Belgium, Canada, Czech Republic, Denmark, Estonia, Finland, France, Germany, Greece, Hungary, Ireland, Italy, Latvia, Mexico, Netherlands, Norway, Poland, Portugal, Romania, Slovakia, Spain, Sweden, United Kingdom of Great Britain and Northern Ireland. The almost exclusive provenience from More Developed Regions—Mexico is the only exception—is striking. Clark (1991) suggests that most states refrain from this practice because there is a possibility of negative repercussions, especially if an objection is directed toward an influential state.
17. This group includes States Parties that have entered a reservation to CEDAW art. 29 (1), which concerns a mechanism of dispute settlement between states as the Convention explicitly allows to opt out of this provision (art. 29 [2]).
18. Australia, Austria, Bahamas, Democratic People's Republic of Korea, Liechtenstein, and United Kingdom of Great Britain and Northern Ireland.

19. Algeria, Bahrain, Bangladesh, Brunei Darussalam, Egypt, India, Iraq, Ireland, Israel, Jordan, Lebanon, Libya, Malaysia, Maldives, Malta, Mauritania, Micronesia, Monaco, Morocco, Niger, Oman, Pakistan, Qatar, Saudi Arabia, Singapore, Syria, and United Arab Emirates.
20. Kuwait, Lesotho, Switzerland, and Tunisia.
21. Belgium, Brazil, Canada, Cook Islands, Cyprus, Fiji, France, Germany, Jamaica, Luxembourg, Malawi, Mauritius, New Zealand, Republic of Korea, Spain, Thailand, and Turkey.
22. Only Switzerland and Australia ratified in 2008 and 2009, respectively. Australia first refused to join the OP because it saw it as another sign of UN ineffectiveness (Zwingel 2005b).
23. For a summary of selected Latin American ratification discussions, see Zwingel (2005b).
24. A large number of these is located in the Caribbean (Bahamas, Barbados, Dominica, Grenada, Jamaica, Saint Lucia, Saint Vincent and the Grenadines, and Trinidad and Tobago), and Asia. Among them are the three large democracies India, Indonesia, and Pakistan.
25. As lack of data for the GII is more frequent among states in the lowest segment of principled treaty connectivity, this difference may be larger under conditions of ideal data availability.
26. Scores 2.5 and 3.5 are not visualized in Fig. 7.5 because GII data was only available for one state. This led to a distortion of the overall picture.
27. Article 20 only stipulates that the Committee meets "to consider the reports submitted in accordance with article 18," without any specification of dialogue frequency.
28. All data for this calculation was taken from OHCHR's website (www.ohchr.org), Human Rights Bodies, country-specific information. It includes initial and periodic reports but not the additional follow-up reports the Committee has requested since 2008 (see Chap. 4).
29. States Parties have often submitted combined reports; in such cases, "lateness" was counted for each report individually, except when the combination of reports was explicitly requested by the Committee.
30. Haiti's initial report was due in 1982, but the government submitted its first through seventh report in 2008. This amounts to 98 late years divided by seven reports.
31. Denmark, Finland, Lithuania, the Netherlands, and the United Kingdom.
32. Haiti belongs to this group (ratio of 0.22), but so does Guinea-Bissau (ratio of 0.13) as it should have submitted eight reports since 1986 but instead presented one combined 1st to 6th report in 2008; Malaysia reaches a ratio of 0.2 with one report (combined 1st and 2nd) out of five submitted.

33. This outlier is Dominica. It has not submitted a report in 32 years and is the only State party that entered into a dialogue with the Committee that was not based on a report (see Chap. 4).
34. This happens, for example, when a State meets with the Committee for the constructive dialogue in 2009, and its next report is due in 2010. The Committee, rather than obliging the State to submit its next report just a year later would typically ask the State party to submit *the next two reports* together in 2014.
35. Some states also combine reports more than once, for example, Guinea and Trinidad and Tobago (two times three combined reports) and Colombia, Cuba, Iceland, Kenya, Tunisia, Vietnam, and Zambia (three times two combined reports).
36. See United Nations Treaty Collection at https://treaties.un.org/, Chapter IV, Human Rights.

CHAPTER 8

Some Patches in the Quilt: Cases of Impact Translation

The previous two chapters focused on *connections* between CEDAW and domestic contexts—Chap. 6 elucidated the work of norm translators aiming to anchor the Convention within *societies*, and Chap. 7 showed patterns of connectivity that *states* have established with the instrument. Both of these dimensions are prerequisites for impact translation of the Convention; changes *because of* CEDAW are unlikely if these connections are weak or not established. This chapter takes the last step in the stretched transnational perspective developed in this book to analyze CEDAW. It looks at dynamics of impact translation, that is, concrete use and repercussions of the Convention in domestic discourses, institutions, and policies.

Drawing on a growing body of literature that documents and assesses impact of CEDAW in many of its States Parties, the first part of this chapter gives an overview of these processes and shows that the Convention has been used often, for a variety of purposes, by different actors, and always within constraints. To provide a more comprehensive picture of how impact translation develops, the second part of the chapter looks at two States Parties, Chile and Finland, in detail and over an extended time span. Both states have taken their responsibilities under the Convention seriously, and in both cases, domestic civil society actors have connected to and worked with the Convention. Beyond this similarity of "best case" connectivity, the two countries are different in several aspects, in

S. Zwingel, *Translating International Women's Rights*,
Gender and Politics, DOI 10.1057/978-1-137-31501-4_8

particular in regard to geographical location and level of gender-related development. Studying the ways in which actors in Chile and Finland have made use of the Convention will therefore yield further insights into the varieties of impact translation.

The Difference CEDAW Makes: Assessments of Impact

Parallel to the general rising interest regarding diffusion of international norms, the number of studies that have traced the domestic impact of CEDAW has grown significantly. While these studies share a general theme, they often follow different rationales and are difficult to categorize. I chose to present them here along three characteristics: the understanding of impact or compliance they develop; the ways in which they consider the content of the Convention; and their depiction of actor constellations.

In the framework of norm translation developed here, impact translation describes an agency that uses international norms to influence domestic affairs. What scholars see as fitting into this category, however, varies widely. For example, Heyns and Viljoen define "impact" in their study on repercussions of Human Rights treaty bodies broadly as "*any influence* that these treaties may have had in ensuring the realization of the norms they espouse in the individual countries" (Heyns and Viljoen 2001, p. 485, emphasis added). At the same time, the authors address the difficulty in drawing a direct causal link between legislative change and the treaty body system. This difficulty seems to be the reason for the breadth of their definition, which probably yields over-optimistic findings, even if the tone of the study remains cautious and also identifies absence of impact. A number of documentations follow the "any influence" rationale, among them UNIFEM's *Brining Equality Home* (1998) and the International Center for Research on Women's *Recognizing Rights, Promoting Progress* (2010). Both present CEDAW "success stories" in different fields, including reference to the Convention in legislation, public policies and institution building, court rulings, and education and mobilization. These activities address different issues covered by the Convention, among them family law, land rights, sexual harassment, inheritance rights, violence against women, and reproductive rights.[1] On the other end of the spectrum, Dairiam (2004) develops an ambitious understanding regarding the obligations States Parties have in regard to CEDAW. She understands compliance as a *systematic process* toward de jure and de facto equality, disaggregated into a list of concrete steps to be taken. She finds states making inadequate implementation efforts—they are not as comprehensive as they should be but rather selective and ad hoc (see also den Boer 2012). Covering middle ground between these two approaches, I developed in my earlier work on CEDAW a spectrum of five categories of compliance from high, moderate/high, moderate, moderate/low, to low (Zwingel 2005b). This model is based on Cortell and Davis' (2000) categorization of domestic repercussions of international norms as inducing change in national discourses, state institutions and public policies. The majority of the 43 States Parties analyzed fell into the middle categories (moderate/high: 5, moderate: 19, moderate/low: 14), only one case in the highest, and four in the lowest. This categorization weighs impact translation, but since it relies on only those States Parties where documentation existed at the time, it probably over-represents higher levels of compliance, assuming that cases of no or negligible impact translation are less likely to be documented.

The second characteristic of CEDAW impact studies is their focus on treaty content. Some look for repercussions of the Convention in general while others focus on one or a few selected dimension(s). The line between these two approaches is not easy to draw as the more comprehensive studies rarely cover impact of *all* articles of the Convention, also because some treaty provisions are worked with much more than others.[2] Instead, they ask how the Convention has been used in a given context and then document this use. Depending on country specific priorities and actor constellations, CEDAW has been used to amend directly discriminatory laws, often in the fields of nationality, the family, and inheritance (Byrnes and Freeman 2012; Goonesekere 2007; Jivan and Forster 2009; Pradhan Malla 2000); to secure women's right to land ownership in predominantly rural societies (Byrnes and Freeman 2012; Freeman 1994); to include gender equality provisions in Constitutional reforms (Foster 2000; Miošić-Lisjak et al. 2009; Simmons 2009); to draft anti-discrimination policies and gender equality laws, often with a focus on employment (Nousiainen and Pentikäinen 2013; Yoneda 2000); and to overcome indirect forms of discrimination and come closer to *de facto* equality where the *de jure* situation is generally satisfactory (Byrnes 2013; Lamarche 2013; Roerink and van Dijk 2000). Studies focusing on one of the Convention's provisions analyze how domestic actors have responded to them; prominent issues are: VAW (Avdeyeva 2007; den Boer 2012; McQuigg 2007), health (Aniekwu 2006), reproductive health (Cook 2013; Shalev 2001), employment

(Rawstron 2014), education (Rawstron 2014; Sudduth 2009), land rights (Banks 2009; Harrison 2002; Nagarajan and Parashar 2013), and gender stereotyping (Biholar 2013; Cusack and Timmer 2011).

The third dimension in the CEDAW impact literature lays its focus on specific actors and their implementation strategies, including enabling and constraining context factors. Increasingly, there are considerations of domestic actors opposing international women's rights norms (Baldez 2013; Farhoumand-Sims 2009; Roald 2009), but most scholarship, in particular if the focus is on a traceable connection between international impulses and domestic action, studies affirmative forms of impact translation.[3] The actor focus may be predominantly on NGOs and their implementation strategies (Afsharipour 1999; McPhedran et al. 2000; UN/ESCAP 2000), or the application of the Convention by the judiciary (Bond 2014; Freeman et al. 2012; Ross 2008; Shivdas and Coleman 2010; United Nations/DAW 2000b), or governmental actors (den Boer 2012; McQuigg 2007), or a mix of all actors involved in impact translation (Hellum and Aasen 2013; Tanaka-Naji 2009). There are also a growing number of assessments on the ways in which the Committee's views issued under the Optional Protocol (OP) have influenced States Parties' compliance with CEDAW (see Chap. 5).

Most of these impact studies integrate a discussion of domestic context factors influencing implementation, both in enhancing and impeding ways (Heintz et al. 2006). Some studies also critically discuss the discrepancies between CEDAW and domestic normative contexts, including the weaknesses of the Convention, or the need to acknowledge normative differences rather than assume that treaty implementation is superior to non-implementation (Jivan and Forster 2009; Merry 2006; Sudduth 2009). Finally, there are some "miscellaneous" studies that focus on actors a bit more removed from direct impact of the Convention. The recollections of Committee experts falls in this category—they often reflect on their own diverse personal implementation efforts and those that they remember as particularly noteworthy (Schöpp-Schilling and Flinterman 2007); another type of analysis does not evaluate the impact of the Convention itself, but of programs designed to enhance CEDAW implementation, often by development agencies such as the Canadian International Development Agency (CIDA) or by UNIFEM. These reports focus on the effectiveness of the support program but are also revealing about the processes of CEDAW norm translation that are supposed to be enhanced (Miošić-Lisjak et al. 2009; UNIFEM/Universalia Management Group 2008; Chap. 6).

To summarize, CEDAW impact studies ask three sets of questions: What exactly is impact translation and how far does it go—is it nonexistent, sporadic, significant or even comprehensive? Which of the provisions of the Convention are actually being translated? Who does (or inhibits) this work? There are some "famous" incidents of impact translation that are covered extensively, for example the Unity Dow "citizenship case" in Botswana in which the High Court used CEDAW to declare the citizenship act unconstitutional[4]; the adoption and later strengthening of the Equal Employment Opportunity Law in Japan, a process in which advocates and femocrats used CEDAW successfully against strong domestic opposition (Kobayashi 2004; Tanaka-Naji 2009; Yoneda 2000); the amendment of Nepal's discriminatory inheritance laws triggered by civil society mobilization that drew on CEDAW (IWRAW AP 2005; Chap. 6); the Indian judiciary using CEDAW and the BPFA to demand national legislation to protect women from sexual harassment in the workplace (Mehra 2013; UNIFEM 1998); and the integration of CEDAW priciples in the new Constitutions of Brazil, Colombia, and South Africa (Foster 2000; Simmons 2009; UNIFEM 1998).

These are just a few examples out of the abundant literature. While the pluri-contextual phenomenon of impact translation is being covered more and more comprehensively, it also becomes more difficult to represent all this work in a single book. Hence, I have compiled a collection of CEDAW impact assessments sorted by state, which can be read as an extension to this book. It is available online at http://libguides.fiu.edu/cedaw_impact.[5] I hope this collection will be useful for other scholars, activists, and interested readers and that it satisfies their curiosity regarding country-specific dynamics around CEDAW. I further hope that this collection will remain dynamic and expand through input from other experts in this field.

CEDAW Impact Translation in Chile and Finland: Two Cases of High Connectivity with the Convention

The notion of impact translation I use is that an action, policy, or program that furthers women's rights has to be empirically connected to the Convention. This means that all the meaningful initiatives undertaken in the name of gender equality that are not connected to CEDAW are not considered part of this process. The most unequivocal link between domestic gender equality initiatives and the Convention is if these are a response to the respective State Party's ratification process and constructive dialogue with the Committee. Therefore, the case studies that follow trace these dynamics and identify policy and other implications resulting from it.

Chile and Finland were selected as cases because they are well connected to CEDAW based on the criteria established in Chaps. 6 and 7. In both states, there has been governmental and civil society engagement with the Convention, which allows for more avenues of norm translation work. Further, both states have a high level of principled and substantive connectivity with the Convention principled.[6] They ratified the Convention during the 1980s so that it entered into force in 1986 for Finland and in 1990 for Chile. Their reporting discipline has been excellent—Finland has been late one year, and Chile 0.17 years per report (see Table 8.1). Also, the reporting ratio is ideal for Finland (seven out of seven) and almost ideal for Chile (five out of six). Accordingly, both states have a high dialogue frequency with the Committee of 5.4 and 5.75 years, respectively. Finland has had five constructive dialogues with the Committee, and Chile four. For each country, domestic NGOs have contributed to three dialogues.

Context Factors: Political, Socio-Economic, and Gender-Related Development

The two states were also selected because they are located in different world regions and represent different regime types and levels of gender-related development. The intention behind this is to analyze diverse contexts that have established a high connectivity to the Convention and showcase implementation dynamics unfold under varying conditions. One dimension, however, that was kept relatively similar is a high level of general

Table 8.1 Dimensions of substantive connectivity to CEDAW per country

	Reporting discipline		*CEDAW dialogues*	*Dialogue frequency*	*NGO input to dialogue*
	Late (years per report)	*Reporting ratio*			
Chile	0.17	5:6	1995, 1999, 2006, 2012	5.75	1999, 2006, 2012
Finland	1	7:7	1989, 1995, 2001, 2008, 2014	5.4	2001, 2008, 2014

human development. This allows for the observation of impact translation in states where sufficient resources are available, and hence, where lack of resources cannot be an argument for implementation inactivity.

Politically, Chile and Finland are both democratic, but they represent different types of democracies. Finland has been a stable and inclusive democracy since its independence from Russia in 1917. Women have had political agency from early on; they were granted active *and* passive voting rights in 1906 (Marakowitz 1996; Sulkunen 2007). Chile returned to democratic rule in 1990 after 17 years of dictatorship and thus classifies as a newly established democracy, despite a long if exclusionary democratic tradition since its independence in 1810. Literate women acquired the right to vote in 1949, and unconditional suffrage for *all* adults was introduced only in 1970; previously, illiterate men and women, the majority of the population at the time, had been excluded from this right (Covarrubias 1978; Valenzuela 1999).

To illustrate the levels of development, including gender-related development, I use UNDP's most recent Human Development Index (HDI)[7] and Gender Inequality Index (GII), which measures the "human development costs of gender inequality" (UNDP 2015; see Chap. 7). While composite indices as the HDI and GII problematically simplify complex realities (Liebowitz and Zwingel 2014), they still allow to give a general picture of vastly differing realities informed by comparative data. As Table 8.2 shows, Chile and Finland have a very high HDI of .822 and .879, respectively. This places them on ranks 41 and 24 out of 187 countries calculated. Once the HDI is adjusted for different levels of inequality within each indicator, the picture changes. Finland remains almost on the same level (.83), which indicates that it has low levels of inequality. Chile,

Table 8.2 HDI indicators per country, 2014

	HDI	*Inequality-adjusted HDI*	*Life expectancy*	*Expected years of schooling*	*Mean years of schooling*	*GNI per capita (PPP US$)*
Chile	0.822 (rank 41)	0.661 (loss: 19.6%)	80	15.1	9.8	20,804
Finland	0.879 (rank 24)	0.83 (loss: 5.5%)	80.5	17	10.3	37,366

in contrast, sees a loss of 19.6% of human development due to inequalities and has a significantly lower inequality-adjusted HDI than HDI (.661 vs. .822). In terms of the three indicators on which the HDI is based, both countries have a high life expectancy of around 80 years and a mean duration of schooling of about 10 years. Only in regard to mean income is Finland significantly ahead of Chile.

The GII paints a more disparate picture of both countries. Finland shows an excellent level of reproductive health—a maternal mortality ratio of 5 per 100,000 live births and an adolescent birth rate of 9.2 per 1000 live births—a female political participation rate almost reaching parity (42.5% female parliamentarians), and full and gender equal education up until the secondary level. In labor force participation, there is an 8% gap between women and men. Chile's record is more mixed. It shows good results in a relatively low maternal mortality rate of 25 per 100,000 live births and a level of secondary school enrollment around 75% with only a minimal gender gap (3.1%). However, both the low political representation of women on the national level (13.9%) and the 15% gap between women and men participating in the labor force[8] are clear markers of gender inequality. Concerning is also the teenage pregnancy rate of 55.3 per 1000 live births. This number suggests a lack of information about and access to contraception that not only affects the reproductive health of teenage girls, but also their educational and employment opportunities. Accordingly, the overall "loss of development due to gender inequality" is much smaller in Finland (0.075) than in Chile (0.355) (Table 8.3).

These numbers are a good baseline to assess the level of gender (in)equality in both contexts, even if they leave much out, in particular phenomena that cannot be (or are not) counted, such as quality of employment, pay level, gender-based violence, power relations within the family, informal political participation, and intersectional discrimination of women or men due to other axes, such as race, class, sexual orienta-

Table 8.3 GII indicators per country, 2014

	GII	*Maternal mortality ratio*	*Adolescent birth rate*	*Female seats in parliament (%)*	*Secondary education (%), female/male*	*Labor force participation rate (%), female/male*
Chile	0.355	25	55.3	13.9	73.3/76.4	49.0/ 74.6
Finland	0.075	5	9.2	42.5	100/100	56/64.3

tion, or disability (Liebowitz and Zwingel 2014). In general terms, however, we can see that Finland constitutes a context with a long tradition of working toward gender equality as well as a high development level—thus, both normative and material conditions are favorable in regard to CEDAW impact translation (Nousiainen and Niemi-Kiesiläinen 2001). Chile is a context where a high development level has been achieved, but it is accompanied by manifold exclusions and inequalities (Schild 2013). Its GII value can be interpreted in two ways: either as an expression of structural opposition to gender equality norms, with the Catholic Church as an authoritative voice and conservative, male-dominated political institutions (Guzmán et al. 2010; Valdés 2010); or as the result of contesting these structures, with more and more women and gender equality advocates gaining ground in the political decision making. After all, Chile's GII expresses higher levels of gender inequality than Finland's, but lower levels than that of many other states, among them India and Brazil (see Chap. 7).

CEDAW and Gender Difference. Impact Translation in Chile

Chile ratified CEDAW in 1989 in the last days of the dictatorship. All democratic governments have shown high commitment in reporting to CEDAW and submitted the first through fourth reports in a timely manner in 1991, 1995, 1999, and 2004; the sixth and seventh report were, upon the request of the CEDAW Committee, combined and submitted in 2011. Chile has had four opportunities to enter into a constructive dialogue with the Committee in 1995, 1999, 2006, and 2012. Each time, it sent high ranking and well-informed delegations, typically headed by the Chilean women's policy agency (WPA). While Chilean NGOs were absent at the first encounter between the government and the CEDAW Committee, the 1999 dialogue saw two concise shadow reports from domestic NGOs. The dialogue in 2006 was enhanced by one comprehensive report co-authored by 10 NGOs, and in 2012, there were six NGO reports, three of them with a comprehensive focus, and three of them issue-specific, including on the situation of lesbian, bisexual, and transgender (LBT) and Mapuche (indigenous) women, as well as a contribution from the National Human Rights Institute.[9] This impressive level of participation notwithstanding, the substance of the dialogues shows, in the words of a Chilean feminist Teresa Valdés, "many old and new debts of Chile with CEDAW, and reveal[s] a country marked by social inequalities and gender discrimination with a democratic deficit in participation and representation, with conservative and authoritarian enclaves that do not recognize the objectives of the Convention" (Valdés 2013, p. 171).

Actors Dealing with CEDAW

Chile's WPA the *Servicio Nacional de la Mujer* (SERNAM - National Women's Service) is the institution that coordinates the interaction between the government and the CEDAW Committee. According to its founding law (No. 19.023) of 1991, it is part of SERNAM's mandate to evaluate public policies with the end to guarantee the implementation of the Convention. Its staff members take this task seriously and understand that "the preparation of the report is not the most important thing, but the period between one report and another" (Interview 21). However, the position of the WPA within the executive is rather weak—it is not an independent ministry but integrated into the Ministry of Planning, has a limited budget, and was created to design and coordinate public gender policies, not to carry them out; this authority lies in the respective resorts that often lack gender consciousness (Baldez 2001; Waylen 1996).[10] Precisely because of this precarious position, CEDAW as well as other international treaties have served as strong argumentative support for the work of SERNAM. As one staff member explains, "the international instruments on human rights of women are nothing but fundamental.... The international component, everything that has to do with the accumulated experience of the world's women's movement,...all these achievements are weapons that we can rest on" (Interview 21).

Women's NGOs who aim to raise awareness regarding women's rights have also increasingly turned to the Convention. As influential sectors of society and the political system do not endorse women's rights because they see them in conflict with family values, CEDAW provides an important tool for women's organizations (La Morada et al. 1999). For example, one of the organizations that have contributed to CEDAW shadow report writing, the *Foro abierto de salud y derechos sexuales y reproductivos*, works for the improvement of women's sexual and reproductive rights. In a context where motherhood is constructed as quasi-sacred, where many women do not have access to birth control, and where abortion is illegal under all circumstances but nonetheless clandestinely (and unsafely) performed in about one third of all pregnancies (CEM et al. 2006), much of the *Foro abierto's* work is dedicated to influencing public opinion and introducing rights-based language on women's reproductive health and autonomy. CEDAW has served the *Foro abierto* as an international framework that adds legitimacy to their work, which is often marginalized and sometimes even ridiculed (Interview 26 and 27).

On the other side of the spectrum, conservative voices regularly articulate opposition to the Convention. One concrete incident is the debate over ratifying the OP to CEDAW. The Chilean government showed a clear commitment to take this step[11]; however, representatives and sympathizers of the Catholic Church framed ratification as alien to Chilean traditions. Some arguments brought forward against ratification were that the OP would lead to the denaturalization of the concept of marriage and force Chile to legalize abortion. When the Senate's Commission on Foreign Relations debated the issue in early 2002, Cardinal Errazuriz of Santiago personally presented the church's position to the Commission, while a representative of SERNAM was denied the right to make a statement (Human Rights Watch 2003; Red de Salud de las Mujeres Latinoamericanas y del Caribe 2002). Ever since, the government has postponed consideration of the matter, assuming that approval would be unlikely.

Taken together, we see that several actors try to make sense of CEDAW domestically, and thus, engage in some kind of impact translation. Among state institutions, CEDAW is a strong reference for SERNAM, but its influence does not go far beyond the WPA.[12] Within civil society, some sectors support gender equality norms, but there are also "hard core" segments that resist these norms (UNDP 2010, p. 24). The latter are overrepresented in positions of authority and political decision making.

Crucial Issue Areas

Of the many issues that have been discussed during the constructive dialogues between Chile and the CEDAW Committee, I select four, namely the abolishment of discriminatory laws, political participation, reproductive health, and VAW. They have been of persistent relevance in the dialogue, and the influence of the Committee's position is clearer than in other fields. I did not include issues of female employment and labor market integration even if they have been discussed in each dialogue, with both NGO shadow reports and the Committee consistently criticizing that women's disadvantage in the labor market is directly linked to the burden of reproductive work that they have to shoulder largely by themselves[13] (Instituto Nacional de Derechos Humanos 2012; Liebowitz and Zwingel 2014). Governmental measures in this field focus on improving women's working conditions particularly in precarious sectors such as seasonal and domestic work, but they rarely make reference the international women's rights framework. The selection also excludes fields that have not figured prominently in the dialogue, for example, health care and pension policies. While these have had a tremendous impact on the lives of women

(Staab 2012), the connection to CEDAW is difficult to make. Finally, I leave out issues that have only come up in recent dialogues and where governmental reaction is difficult to observe, such as trafficking, exploitation of prostitution, and intersectional discrimination. In regard to such "new issues," however, the CEDAW dialogue has often been useful for NGOs to initiate difficult domestic debates—publicizing and overcoming discrimination against LBT women is on field in which this "boomerang strategy" has been used (OTD and IGLHRC 2012).

In regard to all four issues addressed here, the government has shown problem awareness since its first encounter with the Committee, but the development of policy responses has varied. In order to show its commitment to overcome legal discrimination, the government has presented a number of reforms throughout the dialogues, among them, the inclusion of a gender equality clause in the Constitution and the abolishment of some directly discriminatory laws such as the prohibition for women to work underground (UN Doc. CEDAW/C/CHI/3). These legal changes were part of the democratic transition and undertaken with the international human rights framework in mind, but gender equality advocates nevertheless saw shortcomings, such as the absence of a general legal definition of discrimination and a comprehensive anti-discrimination law (CEM et al. 2006; Corporación Humanas et al. 2012; La Morada et al. 1999). The most important concern in this field has been the discriminatory legal base in regard to marriage. At the time of the first dialogue, the only marriage regime that existed in Chile assumed a male head of household who administered the joint property of the spouses (*sociedad conyugal*), and there was no possibility of divorce. At the time of the second dialogue in 1999, two other, more egalitarian marriage regimes were available,[14] but the discriminatory *sociedad conyugal* remained the most common version of marriage, as either of the other two options has to be explicitly chosen by the couple (UN Doc. CEDAW/C/CHI/3). Both the Committee and NGOs have criticized this continuing de facto discrimination and asked for correction, but by the time of the 2012 dialogue, it was still not clear if the law was going to be amended (UN Doc. CEDAW/C/CHL/CO/5-6). Also, it took until 2004 that divorce became legal—before, marriages could only be annulled, which had particularly negative economic consequences for women. According to NGO complaints in the 2006 dialogue, practical impediments made it difficult to have access to divorce (e.g. dysfunctional family courts), but by 2012, these problems had largely been addressed so that divorce was legally *and* practically accessible. In the context of the debate about a civil union law, the Committee urged the government to make it inclusive and non-discriminatory, in particular with regard to same sex couples (Concluding Observations, UN Doc. CEDAW/C/CHL/CO/5-6). In the 2012 dialogue, NGOs criticized the hesitant approach of the government (Corporación Humanas et al. 2012), but as of 2015, a civil union law including same-sex couples was passed (Díaz-Romero 2015). Taken together, there has been some improvement in regard to the regulation of intimate relationships following the Committee's comments, in particular in regard to divorce and the wide coverage of civil unions. However, most heterosexual marriages are still not based on legal equality. This is a matter that has been problematized by several international human rights mechanisms, not only CEDAW (Gatica 2011), but thus far, to no avail.

Participation of women in formal political arenas has traditionally been low in Chile—after reinstatement of democratic elections, the percentage of female Parliamentarians has risen from 5.8% in 1990 to 15.8% in 2013. This is well below the current world average of 22.3% (Interparliamentary Union 2015). Over the course of the dialogues, we see the government respond to this fact by creating SERNAM and introducing various gender equality policies. However, non-governmental voices have pointed to the ineffectiveness of such steps undertaken by a conservative political establishment parts of which are insensitive or at times even outright hostile towards the idea of gender equality (CEM et al. 2006). In 2006 and 2012, the Committee therefore suggested introducing temporary special measures (TSMs) to counterbalance traditions that constitute a structural barrier for women to access political institutions. There had been attempts in that direction, for example, a quota bill introduced to Parliament in 1997, but it was not considered a priority issue and archived in 2005 (CEM et al. 2006). This unsatisfactory situation made the Committee request follow-up information on the matter, indicating that the persistent underrepresentation of women in political decision making needed to be urgently addressed (Concluding Observations, UN Doc. CEDAW/C/CHL/CO/5-6). In response, Chile reported that an electoral reform law adopted in January 2015 stipulates a 60–40 gender quota for party lists in the next four national elections (UN Doc. CEDAW/C/CHL/CO/5-6/Add.1). It is reasonable to assume that the consistent pressure of the Committee in regard to TSMs helped the second Bachelet government[15] break resistance in this matter.

The field of reproductive rights and health has been the one where Committee experts (and NGOs) have most consistently clashed with the State Party. From the first dialogue on, the government has recognized an unmet need for contraceptives, expressed most problematically in a high prevalence of teenage pregnancies and illegally performed abortions (UN Doc. CEDAW/C/CHI/1). Abortion is criminalized in Chile under all circumstances and the government has stated in each dialogue that this situation is unlikely to change. Therefore, it has concentrated its efforts on reducing teenage pregnancies. This is a problem that affects lower class girls more negatively than girls of affluent background, in particular because it often means the end to their education. To address this situation, the government made it illegal for schools to dismiss pregnant students[16]; further, it introduced sexuality education in public schools, but due to resistance from conservative sectors, this education excluded information about and access to contraceptives (UN Doc. CEDAW/C/CHI/3). Later reports describe how access to contraceptives has widened, but limitations in regard to range of methods and target groups have remained (CEM et al. 2006). In 2010, Law No. 20.418 on the right to receive information on and access to contraceptives entered into force. The methods covered include emergency contraception, which had caused a lot of controversy[17]; the law also reiterates that abortion is not a contraceptive and remains illegal. NGOs keep pointing out that Chilean women's reproductive rights are not recognized (Instituto de la Mujer 1999). They have insisted on the need of women to have access to a range of contraceptives and the possibility of abortion. At the same time, they criticized public policies for not addressing male responsibility for birth control. NGOs had authored a reproductive rights bill based on international standards, including CEDAW, but it was not considered by the legislature (CEM et al. 2006). The law that did pass (No 20.418) does not envision women's reproductive self-determination. The position of the Committee has been close to that of NGOs. From the first dialogue on, it has tried to explain to the government that reproductive rights for women entail full information about and access to contraceptives, and that the criminalization of abortion makes it more likely that the procedure is performed under unsafe conditions. This, in turn, jeopardizes the lives and health of women, as unsafe abortions constitute a major cause of maternal mortality in Chile (Concluding observations, UN Docs. CEDAW/C/CHL/CO/4 and CEDAW/C/CHL/CO/5-6). The Committee has also pointed out that restricted access to contraception reinforces the need for abortion, even if it carries the risk of imprisonment and death. It may seem that the constructive dialogue has had little influence on public policies in this field as the domestic discourse is dominated by ideas that are hard to reconcile with the international women's rights framework. However, engaging with these standards has supported the marginalized position of women's NGOs, which is important in an atmosphere where publicly talking about sexuality and the prevention of pregnancies is difficult. The engagement with CEDAW has further allowed SERNAM, in clear demarcation to more radical claims brought forward by NGOs, to work on incremental changes, in particular in regard to the importance of birth control and responsible sexual relationships. As of 2015, there are signs that partial decriminalization of abortion may become a reality. A bill is being debated in the legislature that specifies three indications—danger for the life of the mother, non-viability of the fetus, and pregnancy as result of rape—based on which an abortion can be legally performed (Díaz-Romero 2015).

In the field of VAW, the dialogue shows a promising development in the sense that problem recognition within the government has deepened and that this recognition has been translated into increasingly meaningful protective measures. In its second report, the government presented the 1994 Law on Intra-Family Violence (No. 19.325). This law was a remarkable achievement given that it was confronted with considerable resistance, but it was also watered down from a bill addressing gender hierarchies expressed in domestic violence into a law dealing with violence within the family, as if it was committed and experienced by all family members alike (Interview 29). Materially speaking, it was not helpful to the (almost exclusively) female victims, as it was passed without providing funds for shelters and psychological services, and as its primary focus was on reconciliation between the spouses. NGOs therefore called it ineffective (La Morada et al. 1999). In the dialogue in 2006, the government reported that the law had been amended to correct some of its deficiencies, including the built-in lack of financial resources. The figures of women experiencing violence remained high, which brought the government to increase the number of advice centers across the country, but it still had not created any publicly run shelters for women (UN Doc. CEDAW/C/CHI/4). The NGO response to this situation was a criticism of what they see as an incoherent and underfunded policy (CEM et al. 2006). Only in its last report could the government report that, since 2007, shelters had been set up. It had also increased the number of violence prevention centers and has a more comprehensive definition of VAW in place (UN Doc. CEDAW/C/CHL/CO/5-6). NGOs remain critical—one important blank in the government's violence policy is that lesbian, bisexual, and transgender women are not recognized as potential victims (OTD and IGLHRC 2012). The Committee recognized the governmental effort but criticized that the legal framework conceptualized VAW as too narrow and confined to the private sphere. It therefore asked the government to provide follow-up information on its efforts to a more comprehensive VAW policy. The government responded to this request by presenting a National Action Plan on violence and the set-up of a commission to revise the current law on domestic violence (No. 20.066) (UN Doc. CEDAW/C/CHL/CO/5-6/Add.1). It seems that the ongoing guidance of the Committee in regard to VAW has helped the Chilean government better determine and carry out its responsibilities vis-à-vis female victims of violence.

Assessing the Process

Impact translation processes in all four fields—abolishment of discriminatory laws, in particular in regard to marriage, political representation of women, reproductive rights, and VAW—are slow, sometimes extremely slow, and up against normative resistance. Chile is a context where gender difference is a much more acceptable model than gender equality, and one of the major defining features of femininity is motherhood. Those norms enshrined in CEDAW that come closer to this idea can be translated better into the domestic context. Political representation and elimination of VAW both resonate with a motherly notion gender difference. Female politicians can be positively constructed (and often construct themselves) as "care takers" of the country (Franceschet 2001); and in regard to VAW, once the prevalence is admitted, a gender difference perspective would assume the need of protection of women as the weaker sex, in particular at home, where they should be able to carry out their role as nurturing mothers unharmed. However, equal rights provisions of the Convention, in particular within marriage and the family, and female autonomy in regard to their reproductive functions resonate less with domestic gender norms. This is particularly true for the latter field, as reproductive rights are often constructed as diametrically opposed to motherhood.

CEDAW may appear rather powerless vis-à-vis this domestic constellation, but it has provided an important frame of reference for governmental and non-governmental women's rights advocates. Governmental gender equality advocates have a useful tool in CEDAW as it is seen as less radical than newer instruments such as the 1995 BPFA, which was extremely controversial in Chile (Interview 21). Thus, SERNAM has, from a weak position within the government, used CEDAW to support incremental measures that are reconcilable with the conservative political climate. Examples for this are manifold legal changes, some of which materialized into meaningful public policies, in particular in the field of domestic violence, and to a lesser degree, in sexuality education for teenagers. This strategy of creating change from within the parameters of a deeply patriarchal system has its limits—for example, Chilean policies aimed at helping women better reconcile work and family responsibilities do not sufficiently address, and thus largely perpetuate, the role of women as primary family care takers (Instituto Nacional de Derechos Humanos 2012; Liebowitz and Zwingel 2014). In matters where domestic discourses collide with CEDAW, SERNAM is even more cautious and very carefully weighs which parts of the international framework are worthwhile to work with. In the field of reproductive rights, this has meant sidelining the notion of female sexual and reproductive autonomy and emphasizing the right to information on and access to contraceptive methods. This norm resonates with domestically acceptable ideas of responsible motherhood, and SERNAM's strategy was successful in slowly widening the availability of contraceptives.

Women's NGOs, on the other hand, use international norms not within the parameters of the political system, which they do not consider representative of a much more open-minded society (CEM et al. 2006); they promote "unfitting" gender equality norms in order to expand discursive spaces and influence public discourses and beliefs in the long term. For them, the principle of non-discrimination is opposed to the stereotypical elevation of motherhood; instead, they claim female autonomy in all fields of life—including when it comes to decisions on continuing or ending a pregnancy. CEDAW's international framework has also helped them push issues of intersectional discrimination on the domestic agenda, such as in regard to the living situations of indigenous women, immigrant women, and LBT women. These openings notwithstanding, it is also clear that many segments of Chilean society remain unimpressed by the idea of gender equality and non-discrimination—the difficulty to regulate marriages and civil unions on a basis of equality is indicative of this continuing support of patriarchal values (Interview 19, UNDP 2010).

Impact Translation in Finland

Finland signed CEDAW in 1980 and ratified it in 1986 after a thorough process of legal review and adjustment of legal provisions deemed inconsistent with the Convention. It has submitted seven almost timely reports in 1988, 1993, 1997, 1999, 2004, 2007, and 2012 and entered into five constructive dialogues with the CEDAW Committee in 1989, 1995, 2001, 2008, and 2014. In all encounters, it sent high-ranking delegations, coordinated by the Ministry for Foreign Affairs, which is responsible for reporting to all human rights treaty bodies. While it is a Finnish tradition to consult with NGOs during the preparation of governmental reports, NGOs have also directly contributed to the last three constructive dialogues by submitting independent reports. For the 2001, 2008, and 2014 dialogues, a collective of NGOs coordinated by the Coalition of Finnish Women's Associations (NYTKIS) submitted a joint report. In 2014, four additional issue specific NGO reports addressing the situation of disabled women, sexual minorities, sex workers, and victims of human trafficking were submitted, and both the Finnish NHRI and the Ombudsman for Equality provided a separate statement.[18]

Finnish governments frequently declare gender equality to be part of Finnish national identity, and they want to showcase their commitment in this field not only domestically but also internationally. For example, Finland has sent two experts to the Committee, one of them being the fourth male expert in this position. Nominating a male expert indicates that women's rights expertise is constructed as a general rather than a women-only issue and is extremely rare among CEDAW States Parties (see Chap. 4). Despite such favorable factors, gender equality experts detect a "Finnish dilemma of equality" (Parvikko 1992, p. 89; Nousiainen and Niemi-Kiesiläinen 2001). Gender equality is widely appreciated and at the same time, assumed to be (almost) achieved. This attitude makes it difficult to admit the structural character of gender-based discrimination as well as recognize gender differences. NGO reports speak in this context about a dominant notion of "gender neutrality" that stands in the way of transformational anti-sexist public policies, which is particularly problematic in regard to VAW (NYTKIS 2014). Further, the concept of gender equality is somewhat resistant to the idea of other, intersecting dimensions of discrimination such as race, ethnicity, and gender expression (Holli and Kantola 2007).

Actors Dealing with CEDAW

Both governmental and non-governmental actors engaging with CEDAW are supportive of the international women's rights framework—other than in Chile, there is no explicit opposition to the Convention, however,

NGOs also point out that it is not well known domestically (NYTKIS 2014). Finland established its first WPA, the Council for Equality in 1972, which is "ahead of the curve" in global comparison (True and Mintrom 2001). It is primarily a parliamentary advisory body (Council for Equality 1997). In 1987, the Ombudsman for Equality and the Board for Equality were created as enforcement mechanisms for the 1986 Equality Act. Since 2001, the Gender Equality Unit within the Ministry of Social Affairs and Health is responsible for the design of governmental gender equality policies and gender mainstreaming. This institutional expansion is indicative of governmental support; also, the nomination of a Minister for Gender Equality (as a second portfolio for the Minister of Social Affairs) has strengthened the attention to gender issues on the cabinet level (Holli and Kantola 2007). While the executive and legislative branches have established ties to CEDAW, the judiciary is less involved, also because according to Finnish legal tradition, it is not an actor that invokes provisions of international treaties (Nousiainen and Pentikäinen 2013). However, Finnish courts have made reference to CEDAW in at least three occasions (UN Doc. CEDAW/C/FIN/Q/7/Add.1).

Women who organize their interests outside of state institutions have done so, traditionally, with a strong orientation toward the state (Jallinoja 1986). This has led to a high representation of women in political parties as well as a number of consolidated women's organizations and networks that interact regularly with the state—the contribution of NGOs to the government's reports to CEDAW is one expression of this close relationship. More recently, networks on new issues have emerged (Holli and Kantola 2007). Maybe most remarkable are the organizations with a focus on LBTI rights and representing the rights of sex workers; the latter find themselves outside of the mainstream of Finnish gender equality advocacy.

Ratification Process and Crucial Issue Areas

In the context of ratifying CEDAW, Finland undertook a legislative review to assess compatibility of domestic law with the treaty. This procedure resulted in unusually comprehensive changes (Nousiainen and Pentikäinen 2013; Zwingel 2005b). A number of laws were amended, among them, the Child Custody and Right to Access Act (No. 361/83), the Guardianship Act (No. 368/83), the Nationality Act (No. 584/84), and the Family Name Act (No. 694/85); the most transformative change, however, was the adoption of the Act on Equality between Women and Men (No. 609/86). It became the first legal prohibition of gender-based discrimination,[19] and its reliance on the Convention made the scope of the law rather broad (UN Doc. CEDAW/C/Add. 56; Interview 31). Adopting this act was by no means uncontroversial—influential public voices opposed it because they did not think Finland needed it (Interviews 31 and 32). At the time, Finland was not part of the European Community due to its policy of international neutrality, thus, it could not connect to the supranational gender equality framework developed there. CEDAW was, therefore, a welcome instrument to add legitimacy to and help implement proposals that the Council for Equality had been lobbying for previously, and it decided to use the Convention proactively. Thus, it was argued that the Convention demanded legal reform as well as effective redress against gender-based discrimination, and that Finland needed to come up to the level of the other Nordic states—at the time, all of them had gender equality legislation in place. Another strategy that helped pass the act was that the Council worked hard to ensure that the legal review process was coordinated at a high political level, and it influenced the composition of the multi-ministerial working group undertaking this task (Interview 32).

The most important and recurring themes that have been dealt with in the dialogue between the Committee and Finland are: the coverage of gender equality legislation; equal employment and family responsibilities; VAW; and trafficking and prostitution.[20] In all of these fields, the CEDAW dialogue is a useful assessment tool, but just as in Chile, concrete impact on domestic policies is not always visible. This is particularly true after 1995, when Finland became a member state of the European Union (EU); CEDAW lost some of its significance because the European legal framework is more directly applicable to its member states.

Legal protection from gender-based discrimination has been provided since 1986 when the Act on Equality between Women and Men was adopted. Other forms of discrimination were addressed much later, namely with the Non-Discrimination Act (No. 21/2004) in 2004. This is a reflection of the high priority paid to gender equality in Finland, but in the dialogue with the CEDAW Committee, it has also become clear that there is rigidity in this focus that makes it difficult to address other forms of discrimination that may aggravate the situation of certain groups of women. As detailed in Chap. 4, the Committee has increasingly emphasized the responsibility of States Parties in regard to intersectional forms of discrimination. Since the Finnish gender equality act conceptualizes men and women principally as two homogeneous collectives, the Committee asked the delegation as early as in the first dialogue to provide information on minority women. Finland provided information on Romani, Sami, immigrant, and disabled women in its 2nd through 7th reports. However, it is striking that this information has remained almost identical over this extended period of time (1993–2012)—for example, it is repeatedly stated that minority women are discriminated against on the labor market and experience more violence than majority women. At the same time, there are hardly any governmental initiatives presented to address these problems—for example, several reports state that existing shelters are not prepared to meet the special needs of minority women, yet this problem is not corrected (UN Docs. CEDAW/C/FIN/6; CEDAW/C/FIN/CO/6/Add.1). Further, there was some debate about consolidating the Equality and Non-Discrimination Acts, but they were eventually kept separate because women's organizations feared consolidation would water down and marginalize gender equality work (NYTKIS 2008). In the view of the Committee, however, this two-track solution bears the risk that intersectional discrimination is not adequately addressed (UN Doc. CEDAW/C/FIN/CO/6). NGOs also criticized that the Finnish equality framework is decidedly heteronormative and that sexual minorities are not included (NYTKIS 2008). The government reported in its 7th report that it was considering including protection from discrimination based on sexual orientation and gender identity into the Gender Equality Act (UN Doc. CEDAW/C/FIN/7). The fact that NGOs representing LBTI women made their own voices heard in the 2014 dialogue suggests that they do not find their rights sufficiently addressed domestically[21] and that they consider the CEDAW dialogue a forum that potentially adds weight to their claims.

The second field, equal employment policies, is at the heart of Finnish public gender policies and figures prominently in all CEDAW reports. What the dialogues reveal is that while public policies have been committed to creating a more gender equal employment situation, the major obstacles and problems to achieve this goal have remained largely unchanged. The core obstacles are, first, a vertically and horizontally segregated labor market that leaves women in low paying employment sectors and extremely underrepresented at the top management level (2% as of 2000, UN Doc. CEDAW/C/FIN/4). Second, there is a high concentration of women employed under fixed-term contracts—these contracts lack benefits and protection, and pregnant fixed-term contract employees are often illegally dismissed. Third, the task to reconcile work with family responsibilities rests primarily on women—despite the fact that women have almost the same employment ratio as men, parental leave is taken in over 90% of all cases by the mothers[22] (UN Docs. CEDAW/C/FIN/5 and CEDAW/C/FIN/7). A result of these imbalances is a gender pay gap of about 20%, which has only recently started to diminish at a glacial pace.

The government has not been passive in this regard—in each CEDAW report, it has presented new measures to complement the ones already in place. The Equality Act, which starts out with a rather broad mandate addressing working life, education, training, and decision making, and which has, in the Ombudsman for Equality, a mechanism for implementation, has been regularly evaluated and amended. In its 1993 report, Finland informed the Committee that indirect discrimination, unequal treatment related to pregnancy and parenthood, and sexual harassment in the workplace had been added to the scope of the act (UN Doc. CEDAW/C/FIN/2). Further, employers have been required to prepare an equality plan, and the level of compensations in cases of discrimination was increased (UN Docs. CEDAW/C/FIN/3, CEDAW/C/FIN/4). It has also happened, however, that an amendment has added new supervisory duties to the office for the Ombudsman, but no additional resources were provided (UN Doc. CEDAW/C/FIN/5). In a letter to CEDAW, the Ombudsman criticized this omission as serious impediment to implement the legal framework (Ombudsman for Equality 2014). NGOs and the Committee recognize governmental efforts, but they criticize that general societal structures of discrimination against women that play out on the labor market are not addressed (Finnish NGOs 2000). Accordingly, the Committee has consistently urged the government to increase its efforts to eliminate stereotypes and bridge the gender-segregation of the labor market (UN Docs. A/56/38 and CEDAW/C/FIN/CO/6). NGOs have proposed more proactive measures to overcome the skewed parental leave ratio and expand the leave that parents can take together to 18 months, six of which would be reserved for the father (NYTKIS 2008, 2014).

The field of VAW shows an interesting development. In the first dialogue in 1989, the Committee requested information on VAW, especially in the domestic sphere (UN Doc. A/44/38), but the delegation could not present such information because it was not collected. As a member of that delegation recalls,

> the Minister responded that she was very sorry but she couldn't provide any information and she promised to do it in the next report. And then the Council for Equality...invited different authorities, from the Ministry of

> the Interior, the police, the Ministry of Justice, social workers, doctors, and started to...investigate what should be done. (Interview 31)

The second report did contain information on VAW as well as on governmental measures taken, including defining domestic violence as a major crime and training of law enforcement officers (UN Doc. CEDAW/C/FIN/2). In the third dialogue, it became clear that the Finnish government intensified its efforts in regard to VAW; for example, it undertook several studies to better understand the full scope of VAW, and it had adopted the Act on the Restraining Order (No. 898/1998) that had been frequently used (UN Doc. CEDAW/C/FIN/4); however, NGOs criticized that VAW was not fully understood as a serious human rights violation. This was evident, among other things, in the insecure and insufficient funding for shelters and prevention projects (Finnish NGOs 2000). However, government and NGOs agree on a rather broad understanding of VAW that includes the commercialization of sex, trafficking in women, and prostitution; NGOs describe these phenomena as violations of human dignity (UN Doc. CEDAW/FIN/4; Finnish NGOs 2000).

Since the 2008 dialogue, governmental efforts seem to have reached a plateau. While the reports contain some further improvements, in particular the extension of restraining orders to persons living in the same household (UN Doc. CEDAW/C/FIN/6), it also becomes clear that VAW remains on a high level and that support services for victims are insufficient. The NGO report makes it more explicit than the governmental report[23] that most shelters are run by non-governmental organizations based on precarious funding. They criticize government policies as ignorant regarding the vulnerabilities of women experiencing violence—in their view, the 2006 reconciliation law in cases of intimate partnership violence is indicative of this ignorance (NYTKIS 2008; Amnesty International 2014). The Committee has been concerned about VAW all along, but it is noteworthy that it selects this area both in its 2008 *and* 2014 Concluding Observations as the one where it requests follow-up information from the government (UN Docs. CEDAW/C/FIN/CO/6 and CEDAW/C/FIN/CO/7). This means that it considers the inadequate response to VAW the most alarming obstacle to the implementation of the Convention in Finland. The government response to the first follow up request in 2010 and its 2012 report do not show much new initiative; in particular, it could not report *any* change in the provision of shelter space. In 2012, the number remained at the level of 2008, namely at 125 family spaces, a number far below the 500 spaces recommended by the Council of Europe (UN Docs. CEDAW/C/FIN/CO/6/Add.1 and CEDAW/C/FIN/7). NGOs add that there are hardly any secret shelter spaces and that the needs of immigrant and other minority women are not sufficiently addressed (Human Rights Center 2014; NYTKIS 2014). In their interpretation, it all comes down to the inability of the government to see women as victims (NYTKIS 2008).

In regard to trafficking in women and prostitution, the CEDAW dialogue with Finland is interesting because it exemplifies a field where women's rights norms are contested even among women's rights advocates. From the second dialogue on, the dominant domestic position shared by the government and NGOs has been that trafficking in women and prostitution hang together and that as a consequence, the selling and buying of sexual services is in itself coercive. In the words of NGOs, "the prevention of prostitution is an issue of human rights protection" (Finnish NGOs 2000, p. 16). Both the government and the majority of women's NGOs further agree that the commercialization of sex in the media, including the objectification of women, contribute to this problem (UN Doc. CEDAW/C/FIN/4; Finnish NGOs 2000). The government presented efforts to curb trafficking in women and "moving prostitution" from the Baltic States and Russia and reported about the criminalization of several forms of purchasing sexual services, including from minors and in public places (UN Docs. CEDAW/C/FIN/4 and CEDAW/C/FIN/5). In its sixth report, it presents a 2006 amendment of the law on human trafficking that criminalizes the purchase of sex from a victim of human trafficking or procurement (UN Doc. CEDAW/C/FIN/6). The majority of women's NGOs are dissatisfied with this law. They would have preferred full criminalization of the purchase of sexual services and claim that the law is biased toward the perspective of voluntary sex workers, which represent a small minority of prostitutes (NYTKIS 2008). It is only in the 2014 dialogue with the Committee that the prohibitionist NGO position is complemented by voices that represent the perspective of sex workers. In particular the report of *Pro tukipiste* explains the negative consequences that criminalization has on providers of sexual services, and that the needs of sex workers, many of whom are immigrant women, are not addressed (Pro tukipiste 2014).

Thus far, the Committee has followed the prohibitionist Finnish majority position, even if the Convention accommodates a regulatory position toward prostitution. Art. 6 asks states to suppress "all forms of traffic in women and exploitation of prostitution of women." This implies an understanding that prostitution can be exploited *or not*. The Committee has, in its concluding observations regarding Finland, shared concerns voiced by the government and NGOs, and supported the interpretation that connects trafficking in women and prostitution of any kind (UN Doc. A/56/38). In 2014, it endorsed the idea of absolute criminalization and asked for measures that are victim oriented. It did not follow the reasoning of the pro-sex worker organizations (UN Doc. CEDAW/C/FIN/CO/7). It is not clear why the Committee takes this prohibitionist position, considering that this is only one possible interpretation of the Convention. It could be that the majority of its current members are indeed convinced that this is the best interpretation of the spirit of the Convention. Or maybe experts take the position that the Committee should follow domestic interpretations of the Convention as much as possible in an attempt to accommodate cultural differences under the umbrella of CEDAW. However, the Committee has no tradition of being so adaptive because this strategy runs the risk to produce inconsistent concluding observations. Often, the Committee has clarified its interpretation of a treaty provision in form of a General Recommendation; this could be useful in regard to prostitution as well, since it has become such a contested field among women's rights advocates.

Assessing the Process

Finland is, comparatively speaking, an enabling context for CEDAW implementation. There is no openly voiced and fundamental resistance to the Convention, even if there is disagreement on certain details. However, the strong support of gender equality has been identified by analysts and advocates as potential bias against grasping societal structures that discriminate against and victimize women—this seems to function like a "glass wall" preventing substantive gender equality.

In the four fields presented, CEDAW has played a trigger role in regard to equality legislation and VAW. In both of these fields, however, the Committee has formulated more far-reaching claims than the Finnish government was ready to address. In the first field, this is the challenge of intersectional discrimination; in the second, it is the lack of confronting the problem with the amount of resources that are necessary. This reluctance is most likely based on a misinterpretation of the phenomenon of violence and how it affects women and society as a whole. In the field of equal employment, the Committee has stressed the point of underlying discriminatory structures, due to gender stereotypes and intersectional discrimination, but this has had little domestic effect. In the field of trafficking and prostitution, CEDAW has been more of an accompanying voice, but may have the potential to enable a more inclusive debate in the future; the increase of non-governmental participation in the dialogue points in that direction.

All in all, while CEDAW seems to have become somewhat eclipsed by the EU in regard to domestic influence, it does have "future potential" in Finland because of its broad scope that the Committee has constantly further developed (Nousiainen and Pentikäinen 2013). There are many areas in which CEDAW could help Finnish society to move closer toward substantive equality—VAW, reconciliation policies, and addressing women in their diversity stand out the most.

Decreasing Commitment and "Normative Incompleteness"

Impact translation describes how a globally codified set of norms is used domestically and ultimately, how it affects the real lives of people. The evidence of CEDAW impact translation presented in this chapter allows for better characterization of this process. The most general observation is that the engagement with a treaty decreases the more demanding compliance duties become. Chapter 7 described that many states' high level of principled affinity with the Convention does not always translate into adequate reporting discipline. This chapter has shown that governmental and non-governmental actors in several States Parties have made use of the Convention to influence domestic gender relations, but this happens in an unsystematic manner. This is also true for the two in-depth case studies. Their high levels of substantive connectivity with the Convention translated into selective and partial impact translation. Perhaps it is a fitting metaphor for CEDAW norm translation to think of the Convention as a well where people fetch water. The first person scoops water out of the well and passes it to the next person, and that one to the next, and so on. In the process of passing the container, some water is spilled. As this happens each time the water pot changes hands, there is not much water left at the end. However, spillage can be minimized if care is used in this process. Following the argument I made in the introduction, meaningful connections between unconnected discourses and practices will help spread the notion of women's rights.

I do not intend to introduce this metaphor to spread pessimism; rather, it helps to analytically deal with the dynamic of decreasing engagement. One the one hand, treaty standards and human rights in practice are two different phenomena—the standards can be perfect, but the practice, which is the most important dimension of human rights, cannot. In Goodale's words, human rights practice is "characterized by contradictions, uncertainties, and a kind of normative incompleteness" (2007, p. 26). Thus, it should not be seen as a defeat that state policies and human relations do not entirely conform with human rights standards, as long as the standards are taken seriously. In the "CEDAW as a well" metaphor, people do benefit from the water, if in imperfect, possibly improvable, ways. On the other hand, we can analyze these imperfect processes of impact translation and identify factors that enhance or inhibit treaty resonance (or, in the metaphor, factors that reduce or increase water spillage). I would like to highlight two such factors based on the findings of the chapter, namely domestic context characteristics and actor constellations on the one hand, and opportunity structures on the other.

Given the fact that 189 states have ratified the Convention, it is almost redundant to say that CEDAW implementation happens in a wide variety of cultural contexts and that some of these contexts are more open and some more reluctant to engage in this process. The two case studies confirm this finding, but they are also two examples with more meaningful impact translation processes than can be expected from the entirety of States Parties. Both states take CEDAW seriously, have established a regular dialogue with the Committee and have, comparatively speaking, a high level of resources that would allow them to produce de facto change in accordance with CEDAW. However, they are different in two crucial dimensions. First, Finland has a more stable and inclusive democratic tradition than Chile, thus, it is more difficult in Chile to represent all and in particular, non-elite interests in political decision making. Second, Finland is a strong proponent of gender equality, whereas in Chile, the notion of gender difference is more dominant. Accordingly, Finland is a context that resonates very well with the Convention, which is also visible in the fact that there is no direct opposition to CEDAW. State policies have truly engaged in promoting gender equality, and resources have been provided on a high level, visible in the expansion of funding of the WPAs. It is also noteworthy that the Committee has constantly asked Finland to provide information on the effect of legal changes and public policies, and the Finnish reports made great efforts to deliver this information. Nonetheless, the strong support of gender equality has made it harder for Finnish actors to deal with issues where discrimination against women is based on gender difference, such as in regard to VAW, and where it is reinforced by other dimensions of discrimination. Hence, even a state as well-equipped and normatively close to CEDAW as Finland remains beneath the expectations of the Committee when it comes to establishing a sufficient infrastructure for female victims of violence, making anti-discrimination legislation comprehensive, and in its response to the needs of minority women.

In Chile, the dominant notion of gender difference is more difficult to reconcile with CEDAW. In regard to VAW and political representation, it has been possible to detect and take measures against discrimination against women, in the spirit of CEDAW and at the same time, in maintaining the notion of women being different from men (i.e., in need of protection, better decision makers). However, the normative clash between the Convention and the ways reproductive rights and family relations are perceived has led to very little impact translation in those fields. Here it is interesting to take note of the actor constellations in Chile, with a relatively weak WPA and women's rights NGOs, on the one hand, and a strong presence of conservative politicians as well as the Catholic Church, on the other. In all fields, de facto changes fall far short of legal changes—this is particularly noteworthy in the field of VAW, where problem recognition in the spirit of the Convention has unfolded, but this has only extremely slowly translated into real life support for women experiencing violence.

The other factor that influences impact translation is opportunity, depending on the perception of domestic actors. Such an opportunity can arise in the process of ratification itself, as in the case of Finland, where this "window" was used to thoroughly scrutinize legal compatibility. Other opportunities arise from comprehensive legal reforms, in particular, constitutional reforms as in South Africa or Colombia. But fundamental changes are not the only triggers for impact. Often, NGOs have used the Committee's concluding observations to pressure governments, and governments themselves react to Committee assessments. States Parties have also engaged in considerable impact translation activities in response to complaints under the OP where the Committee found a breach of the Convention—the measures taken by Brazil to deal better with maternal mortality or those taken by Austria to provide better protection for victims of domestic violence are encouraging examples (see Chap. 5). Hence, while many dynamics can create favorable opportunity structures, the *change making* has to be done by someone. At the end of the day, impact translation of CEDAW always depends on governmental and non-governmental norm translators.

Notes

1. There are numerous websites that replicate this strategy. Some of them are documentations compiled in the context of the Convention's 30th anniversary celebration (for example, Waldorf 2009).
2. For example, States Parties often use CEDAW in their efforts to combat violence against women, partly because the Committee is so insistent on it (see Chap. 4), partly because the expertise developed by the Committee is a useful source of guidance in a relatively new policy field (see both case studies in this chapter). A CEDAW provision that is rarely invoked is equality in sports and cultural activities (art. 13).
3. As discussed in Chap. 6, actors who reject CEDAW are more likely to voice protest internationally than domestically because this would run the risk of adding visibility to the instrument at home (Interview 24).
4. This act discriminated women married to foreign men as they could not pass on their citizenship to their children, whereas Batswana men married to foreign women could do so. It was changed after the High Court's decision (Unity Dow v Attorney-General of Botswana, 1992, Botswana High Court).
5. I thank Mark Pacho for his help in creating this collection and making it publicly available.
6. Finland reached the highest level of principled connectivity (7 points) due to its early ratification of the Convention without reservations and early ratification of the OP, while Chile made it to the middle level (5 points): It ratified the Convention early and without reservations but did not ratify the OP due to vehement domestic opposition.
7. The HDI defines three dimensions of human development: a long and healthy life, access to knowledge, and a decent standard of living. These three dimensions are measured in life expectancy at birth, mean years of education among the adult population, expected years of schooling for children of school-entry age, and Gross National Income (GNI) per capita.
8. The data on labor force participation collected by UNDP is problematic because it is based on national statistics, and they do not always count the same types of employment. For example, national statistics may or may not include informal, seasonal, or irregular labor force participation.
9. All documents for the 2012 dialogue are available online at www.ohchr.org.
10. In 2014, President Bachelet signed a bill to create an upgraded and independent WPA, the *Ministerio de la Mujer y Equidad de Género* (Díaz-Romero 2015).
11. Chile was both engaged in the drafting process of the OP and the first government to sign the document in 1999 (Molina 2000; Zwingel 2005b).
12. For example, CEDAW could be used in judicial proceedings, but the judiciary has not shown inclination to implement women's rights norms or

even the principle of non-discrimination generally speaking (Zwingel 2005b; Interviews 28, 29, and 30). There is one exception to this norm: the Constitutional Court once made reference to CEDAW art. 12, building on the Constitutional provision that men and women should have equal access to health care, to declare unconstitutional the practice of private health care providers that charged disproportionally higher fees for women's care than for men's (Cook and Undurraga 2012, p. 325).

13. The significant increase of child care facilities under the first Bachelet government (2006–2010) has started to alleviate some of this burden (UN Doc. CEDAW/C/CHI/5-6).
14. According to the first model, joint ownership only applies to jointly acquired assets; the second provides for a complete separation of assets.
15. Michelle Bachelet, president from 2006 to 2010 and reelected in 2014, is known for her proactive stance regarding public gender policies (Stevenson 2012).
16. This prohibition was first introduced for public schools only (UN Doc. CEDAW/C/CHI/3) and later applied also to private schools (UN Doc. CEDAW/C/CHI/4).
17. This controversy was about whether emergency contraception is a contraceptive or an abortive measure and if, in the wake of different assessments of this question, health care providers that are opposed to this method can be forced by the government to offer it (Bordalí Salamanca and Zúñiga Añazco 2009).
18. All documents for the 2008 and 2014 dialogues are available online at www.ohchr.org.
19. It was only in 1995 that discrimination based on several grounds, including sex, has become prohibited in the Constitution (UN Doc. CEDAW/C/FIN/3).
20. Uncharacteristically for CEDAW dialogues, reproductive health and rights have never played a prominent role in the encounters with Finland because the country's policies are considered to be in compliance with the Convention (UN Doc. CEDAW/C/5/Add. 56; Parvikko 1992).
21. Examples are the difficult process of legal gender recognition for trans women, which demands sterilization and single civil status (Amnesty International 2014), heteronormative school curricula, and a high prevalence of LGBT youth being bullied (SETA—LGBTI Rights in Finland 2014).
22. There has been a rise, however, in fathers taking paternity leave, which has been extended from four to six weeks maximum (UN Doc. CEDAW/C/FIN/7).
23. As the governmental report is written in cooperation with NGOs, it often presents NGO work without clarifying that this is *not* a governmental effort. Arguably, this is a weakness of collaborative report writing (Nousiainen and Pentikäinen 2013).

CHAPTER 9

Conclusion: How Far Can CEDAW Reach? Lessons for a Better Understanding of Norm Translation

In this book, I have asked how far the Convention on the Elimination of All Forms of Discrimination against Women (CEDAW) can reach. The detailed answer to this question is exposed in the preceding eight chapters; in this final reflection, I want to bundle the most important findings and reflect on the contribution of my work to the broader debate on the power and influence of norms. Finally, I propose a few areas for further research.

How far *can* CEDAW reach? In the introduction, I embedded this question in the realization that a UN-adopted Convention on women's rights is rather far removed from the real-life problems many women are facing, and that its relevance depends on the strength of the connections that can be established between the international *discourse* on women's rights and the manifold contextualized *practices* regarding women's rights around the globe. Accordingly, two dimensions are relevant when examining the reach of CEDAW: the dimension of *content* (does the Convention contain all necessary norms to eliminate discrimination against women and work for gender equality?); and the dimension of *connectivity* (have norm translators created strong enough connections with the Convention that it can invoke social change?).

Following the text of the Convention, the original scope of content of CEDAW entails three major principles—elimination of discrimination against women, equality between men and women, and state responsibility to achieve both goals—and these principles are specified in 16

S. Zwingel, *Translating International Women's Rights*,
Gender and Politics, DOI 10.1057/978-1-137-31501-4_9

substantial articles (see Chap. 3). This scope is a historical snapshot that was further developed and substantiated through Committee interpretation, mostly with a focus on expanding and deepening the meaning of all three principles (see Chaps. 4 and 5). Prominent examples in this development are the inclusion of violence against women (VAW) into the scope of the Convention, addressing intersectional discrimination, and the extended responsibility of States Parties to deal with indirect and structural forms of discrimination. Thus, despite the absence of VAW in the text of the treaty, the Committee has integrated it into the scope of the Convention as a particularly severe form of discrimination against women covered by CEDAW art. 1. Ever since the Committee issued General Recommendation 19 providing this interpretation, VAW has been a cornerstone in its scrutiny of States Parties. In the context of this development, the Committee has also strengthened the principle of due diligence of States Parties in respect to violations of women's rights committed by non-state actors (as most violent acts against women are committed within their private relations). Secondly, the idea that reaching substantive gender equality means to think of men and women as two collectives that need to be balanced against each other was expanded. Working for gender equality now also implies recognizing differences among women—some experience discrimination "only" because of their gender, but others need to navigate additional layers of discrimination based on their race, class, disability, sexuality, nationality, religion, and other dimensions. From this recognition, it follows that States Parties have to address these intersectional forms of discrimination so that multiple disadvantaged women can enjoy their rights. Finally, the Committee has expanded its expectation towards States Parties to *proactively* work against underlying structures of sexism. This means that they have to go far beyond eliminating discriminatory laws, even if that remains an important duty; in addition, they have to combat gender stereotypes and apply temporary special measures in areas where the playing field is so tilted that equality of opportunity does not result in equality of outcome—as we have seen, this applies to many fields, including political decision making (see Chaps. 4 and 8).

Both the Convention's original content and the Committee's interpretation of it have attracted criticism, mostly from positions that are critical of gender equality. Such positions, voiced in the drafting process and later on, think that the Convention goes too far in uprooting a natural gender order that is based on male–female complementarity, and that it fails to recognize the important role women play for society and the family *in distinction from men*. From this perspective, CEDAW is sometimes called "radically feminist" or otherwise criticized as not really representing the manifold needs of the world's women (Chaps. 3 and 6). In addition to this interpretation, there are also voices supporting gender equality that criticize CEDAW. They claim that the Convention's focus on women's rights is insufficient for a profound transformation toward gender equality. Rosenblum (2011), for example, argues that CEDAW reinforces the gender binary and constructs women as exclusive victims of gender-based discrimination. He insists, however, that *all* possible gender identities need to be included in a gender equality project—for example, male and transgender persons—and that the forms of discrimination to be eliminated should be experience-based rather than identity-based. In short, a Convention that focuses *only* on discrimination against women is not comprehensive enough to work toward gender equality.

Where is CEDAW situated on this spectrum? Rosenblum makes a valid point about the silence of CEDAW regarding gender-based discrimination that is not experienced by women. Indeed, reflections on masculinities and male experiences are hardly recognized as a relevant matter in international law; based on androcentric underpinnings, the male experience is considered the human standard, also in human rights law (see Chap. 3). CEDAW is, without a doubt, part of this discourse, even if it starts out to correct it and shine a spotlight on female experiences. However, Rosenblum's criticism does not take into consideration that the Committee has widened its focus to recognize the diversity of women (see Chaps. 4 and 8). His is a radical position—"radical" in the sense of "addressing root causes". It is, however, one among many in the universe of positions regarding gender equality, and the focus of CEDAW has been to specify the meaning of women's rights in a way that accommodates as many interpretations of gender equality as possible, including, to a certain degree, those that favor gender difference. There is significant tension in this endeavor—some of the Committee's interpretations have been unequivocal and draw a clear line of what constitutes a violation of the Convention, for example, polygyny or female genital mutilation (FGM) or girl marriages. In regard to these practices, it does not recognize any context-specific traditions as justification. Other interpretations show the Committee's inclination to be inclusive rather than setting a precise standard; examples are its cautious position regarding abortion as a dimension of reproductive health, discriminatory experiences of LBT women, and the exploitation of prostitution (Chaps. 4 and 8). Thus, what the Committee tries to do is widen the scope of women's rights and, at the same time, accommodate context-sensitive interpretations of the Convention to a certain degree. It is important to understand this "meaning making" the Committee is undertaking as an embedded process. Committee experts, involved non-governmental organizations (NGOs), States Parties and UN agencies are having this conversation in a broader global discourse on gender norms. This context, as we have seen in Chap. 3, has its own shifting priorities; it has been supportive for a widening of the women's rights framework as the importance of gender awareness has been pushed in more areas of international policy making, for example, security policy. This global discourse has, however, also lost some of its transformational passion of collective empowerment of women and increasingly conforms to neoliberal models of development.

The second dimension of the reach of CEDAW is the web of connections norm translators have created around it. Initially, the Convention was called the "poor cousin" among the treaty bodies because it appeared isolated (Chap. 4). This starting point for CEDAW suggests that the idea of women's rights was not yet well embedded in international governance institutions—indeed, a lot of awareness raising had to be done to make gender equality internationally relevant (Chap. 3). Once the Convention was adopted, several actors worked to increase its international authority and legitimacy, including Committee experts, UN femocrats, and women's rights advocates within and outside of state institutions (Chaps. 4, 5, and 6). It is due to this sustained global discourse translation work that CEDAW has grown into an international standard and monitoring instrument that has retained a high level of relevance over several decades—without this work, the Convention might as well have turned into a paper tiger, as many international agreements do. Even more important than these efforts to create international authority for CEDAW is the translation work that connects the Convention to domestic contexts. This impact translation work has been undertaken by many different types of advocates. It starts with the Committee experts continuously and competently advising States Parties. It is sustained by transnational connections established between the Committee and non-governmental domestic advocates—this work, most comprehensively undertaken by IWRAW Asia Pacific, connects the Convention not only to States Parties, but also to societal actors (Chap. 6). Finally, domestic women's rights advocacy and governmental implementation work are the most context-specific and change-oriented elements in this chain of translating CEDAW. Chapters 6, 7, and 8 have shown, however, that translation work has its limits and is not only favoring CEDAW.

Both internationally and domestically, resistance to CEDAW is being articulated. Supporters of CEDAW may have a weak stance domestically, as we have seen in the case of Chile (Chap. 8). Also, governmental translation work is typically partial rather than comprehensive, and this is true even under the best of domestic circumstances (Chap. 8).

I suggest seeing this incompleteness of impact translation not as a deficiency but rather as a requirement for a meaningful process of appropriation of global norms, even if it is clear, based on the patterns of connectivity presented in Chap. 7, that not all cases of incomplete impact translation are an expression of engagement with the Convention. CEDAW stands for one set of norms among many that each State Party and its society is juggling with—the "receiving end" of global norms deserves some leeway to make domestic sense of this "external package," even more so if we consider the dynamic character of global norms, and that they may be in dissonance with other "norm packages" emanating from global discourses. Principles of democratic decision making demand that norms agreed upon elsewhere cannot take on abstract legitimacy in a given context. Rather, a locale's dealing with outside influences is a matter of self-determination (Massey 2005; Chap. 1). I think it is consistent with this position, however, to also influence States Parties that do not engage meaningfully with the Convention (and as a consequence, do not show noteworthy impact translation dynamics) to take their commitments towards international women's rights standards seriously. In the rationale presented in this book, this means to establish and reinforce transnational connections that allow such meaningful engagement both on the state and society level.

This book contributes in at least three ways to the vibrant debate on norm diffusion, localization, or translation. First, it supports the argument that norms should be framed as processes rather than things and that we should think of them as fluid (Krook and True 2012). Norms change and maintain meaning, they expand and narrow, lose and regain authority. They are in constant motion and under ongoing inter-personal negotiation, sometimes explicitly, sometimes implicitly. Accordingly, a methodological approach that searches exclusively for clearly identifiable effects caused by clearly demarcated norms can reach only so far. Also, the notion of norms as inter-personally constituted through negotiations connects intergovernmental arenas with national, local, and transnational debates. Thus, in the broad scholarly debate on the power of norms, my contribution joins in with approaches that look at global norms in a de-centered, de-essentializing fashion.

Secondly, the picture I painted of norm translation as intricate, cumbersome, and labor-intensive processes adds to our understanding of norms and their potential influence. This picture is guided by a framework—I divided the processes described into two broad movements, global discourse translation and impact translation—but it also is the result of empirically tracing different layers of norm creation and application of norms and of stitching together normative trajectories. This work shows that it is worthwhile to take a close look at the evolution and cross-fertilization of different strands of agency as it reveals crucial dynamics that are not easily visible from a macro-level perspective that is predominantly interested in general patterns. For example, I have shown that the adoption of the Convention was not a concluding point of global norm creation but rather the opening of a debate that is ongoing. It took more than one-and-a-half decades and a lot of work geared towards strengthening the global discourse to make CEDAW a widely recognized international standard of women's rights. I have further described the many efforts that have gone into creating transnational ownership of the Convention, a process sustained by a small number of individuals with a vision that ended up creating a surprisingly robust and functional structure for treaty impact (that the treaty itself does not provide for). I have shed light on the difficulties to create substantial commitment to the Convention—again, there are some surprising findings, for example, that States Parties, even those that take gender equality seriously and are highly committed to the Convention, do not follow through with their commitments. Finland and its deficient public policies in regard to VAW exemplify this dynamic. The reasons for that lay in deeply engrained gender norms, in the case of Finland the difficulty to construct women as vulnerable. In other domestic contexts, resistance to CEDAW implementation is based on other gendered traditions. In the case of Chile, the strongest ones are seeing women as *predominantly* vulnerable, not suited for public leadership, but almost exclusively responsible for parenting and reproductive work.

The third contribution of this book is to unambiguously stress the advantages of non-coercive mechanisms of norm translation over coercive ones. This applies in particular to human rights norms because they aim at changing societal structures, a process that is always long term (in other areas, there may be norms that can be realized through more superficial processes). While these non-coercive mechanisms are infused with power, in particular with the power of defining what is right and wrong, they do not simply impose these definitions; they offer them, work on them, adjust them, teach States Parties (who have legally committed to them) how to use them, and support these actors' efforts. I want to stress this quality because instruments like human rights treaties are often framed as ineffective or weak vis-à-vis other, more coercive instruments such as humanitarian interventions. The latter regularly create what Kapur (2006) calls the "dark side" of human rights—the construction and alienation of "others" that do not readily accept their liberal logic. While humanitarian interventions have the goal to end suffering and mistreatment, they routinely violate the rights of the alleged violators as well as many of those they set out to "rescue." For those who experienced the violence committed in the name of human rights, this framework will never be legitimate. I do not deny that instruments like CEDAW may also create exclusions, but this study has shown the networks created around the Convention have worked to *include* disenfranchised perspectives. I think these attempts have, in the sense of Butler's vision introduced in Chapter 1, worked against forces that deny some humans access to humanity and construct them as threats. Connecting this translation work to Spivak's thoughts, maybe one can go so far as to say that the Convention has enabled learning for both the subaltern and the rightening subject, learning that allows to stand up against structures of oppression, and learning that helps recognize privilege. Learning that connects.

Finally, the findings in this book suggest two areas of future research. One is the relationship between different sets of international norms; here, I have focused on the connectivity of norms between different contexts, and most norm diffusion literature takes that stance. But we know little about how, for example, the human rights framework and the discourse of international financial stability influence each other, or if they do at all. If such a connection existed, how would money lending institutions and stock brokers deal with the idea that collective wellbeing should supersede commercial profit? And would this conversation add a more material basis to the ideational human rights framework? In many policy areas, advocates have tried to make connections between global justice agendas and the geopolitical interests of sovereign states; these attempts, for example, in the field of global climate politics or immigration, could be usefully analyzed within a framework of norm translation.

Secondly, I suggest producing more studies that carefully trace the evolution of justice-oriented sets of norms. This is cumbersome work—"ant work" instead of "hawk work," as one of my former IR professors would say. It is not work that yields grand narratives or represents the world in quantifiable categories. As a matter of fact, this type of research is methodologically premature, and it could use interdisciplinary stimulation. As Chap. 2 shows, anthropological human rights research has provided fascinating ways to understand and follow norm translation processes. I think a continuing exploration of how to combine different approaches coming from anthropology, sociology, international relations, and the work of practitioners will yield even more far-reaching results. Hopefully, they will also contribute to the imperfect making of human rights practice.

Appendix 1: List of Interviews

Interview 1, Former Under-Secretary General of the UN, Helsinki, Finland, 2001
Interview 2, Chief of DAW Women's Rights Section, New York, USA, 2000
Interview 3, CEDAW expert from Mexico, New York, USA, 2000
Interview 4, Chief of Special Procedures branch of OHCHR, Geneva, 2010
Interview 5, CEDAW expert from the Republic of Mauritius, Geneva, Switzerland, 2010
Interview 6, CEDAW expert from the Netherlands, Geneva, Switzerland, 2010
Interview 7, CEDAW expert from Israel, Geneva, Switzerland, 2010
Interview 8, CEDAW expert from Italy, New York, USA, 2010
Interview 9, UNIFEM staff member, New York, USA, 2000
Interview 10, HRC expert from Finland, New York, USA, 2002
Interview 11, CEDAW expert from New Zealand, New York, USA, 2000
Interview 12, CEDAW expert from Bangladesh, 2010, Geneva, Switzerland
Interview 13, Representative of IWRAW AP (NGO), Geneva, Switzerland, 2010
Interview 14, CEDAW expert from South Africa, New York, USA, 2000
Interview 15, HRC and former CEDAW expert from Australia, New York, USA, 2000

S. Zwingel, *Translating International Women's Rights*,
Gender and Politics, DOI 10.1057/978-1-137-31501-4

Interview 16, CEDAW expert from Germany, New York, USA, 2000
Interview 17, CEDAW expert from Croatia, Geneva, Switzerland, 2010
Interview 18, CEDAW expert from Ghana, Geneva, Switzerland, 2010
Interview 19, CEDAW expert from Ghana, New York, USA, 2000
Interview 20, SERNAM staff member, Santiago, Chile, 2001
Interview 21, SERNAM staff member, Santiago, Chile, 2001
Interview 22, Head of IWRAW (NGO), Minneapolis, USA, 2000
Interview 23, Representative of IWRAW AP (NGO), via email, 2002
Interview 24, Representative of REAL Women of Canada (NGO), 2012
Interview 25, CEDAW expert from Jamaica, Geneva, Switzerland, 2010
Interview 26, Representative of La Morada (NGO), Santiago, Chile, 2001
Interview 27, Representative of Foro de Salud y Derechos Reproductivos (NGO), Santiago, Chile, 2001
Interview 28, Lawyer and Expert on the HRC, Santiago, Chile, 2001
Interview 29, Lawyer, expert on women's rights, Santiago, Chile, 2001
Interview 30, Judge, expert on women's rights, Santiago, Chile, 2001
Interview 31, Ombudsman for Equality, Helsinki, Finland, 2001
Interview 32, Former Secretary for the Council of Equality, Helsinki, Finland, 2001

Interviews that were not conducted in English (i.e., conducted in German or Spanish) were translated into English by the author.

Appendix 2: List of Decided Communications Until June 2014

S. Zwingel, *Translating International Women's Rights*,
Gender and Politics, DOI 10.1057/978-1-137-31501-4

Case/complaint	*Position state*	*View committee*	*Dissent*	*Recommendations*	*Follow up*
1/2003 B.J. v. Germany **(8/2002)** Discrimination in/after marriage; Arts. 1, 2, 3, 5, 15, 16	Inadmissible[a, b, c] (lack of grievance)	Inadmissible[a, b] (7/2004, 23 months)	Regarding[b]	–	–
2/2003 A.T. v. Hungary (10/2003) Domestic violence/state neglect of due diligence Arts. 2, 5, 16	Recognition that domestic remedies are not effective	Interim measure Admissible Merits: goes along with complaint Arts. 2, 5 and 16 (1/2005, 15 months)	–	C: Provide safe place to live G: More effective measures to combat VAW	Closed, further monitoring in Constructive dialogue (36th session, 2006)
3/2004 Nguyen v. The Netherlands (12/2003) Discriminatory maternity leave benefits Art. 11	Inadmissible[a, c] (lack of grievance —no sex-based discrimination)	Admissible No merits (8/2006; 32 months)	Points to indirect discrimination	Dissenting: Study dimensions of indirect discrimination	–
4/2004 A.S. v. Hungary (2/2004) Sterilization without consent (Roma woman) in public hospital Arts. 10, 12, 16	Inadmissible[b, c] (measure was lifesaving)	Admissible Merits: goes along with complaint Arts. 10, 12, 16 (8/2006, 28 months)	–	C: Compensation G: Training and legal enforcement of reproductive rights	Compensation paid; after long negotiations, case closed in 47th session (2010)
5/2005 Goekce (deceased) v. Austria (12/2004) Domestic violence resulting in death/ state neglect of due diligence Arts. 1, 2, 3 and 5	Inadmissible[b, c] (due diligence complaint not substantiated)	Admissible Merits: goes along with complaint Arts. 2 a, c, f and 3, 1 and GR 19 (despite VAW law) (8/2007, 32 months)	–	G: Review implementation of law (safety of victim over rights of perpetrator); train law enforcement officers	Compliance with Committee's recommendations, case closed 45th session (2010)
6/2005 Yildirim (deceased) v. Austria **(12/2004)** Domestic violence resulting in death/ state neglect of due diligence Arts. 1, 2, 3 and 5	Inadmissible[b, c] (due diligence complaint not substantiated)	Admissible Merits: goes along with complaint Arts. 2 a, c f and 3, 1 and GR 19 (despite VAW law) (8/2007, 32 months)	–	See 5/2005; also: better collaboration of authorities with NGOs in the field	See 5/2005; case closed 45th session (2010)

7/2005 Munoz-Vargas y Sainz de Vicuna v. Spain (2/2005) Acquisition of aristocratic family title Arts. 1 and 2	Inadmissible[a, b, c] (lack of grievance)	Inadmissible[a] (8/2007, 30 months)	1: Inadmissible[c] (Not a human rights matter) 2: Admissible	–	–
8/2005 Kayhan v. Turkey (8/2004) Discrimination in public employment (head scarf) Art. 11	Inadmissible[a, b, d] (similar case dismissed before European Court of Human Rights)	Inadmissible[b] (domestic proceedings without claim of gender-based discrimination) (1/2006, 17 months)	–	–	–
10/2005 N.S.F v. UK (9/2005) Asylum request on gender-based grounds denied (Pakistani national)	Inadmissible[b] (no claim of gender-based discrimination)	Inadmissible[b] (follows state position) (5/2007, 20 months)	–	–	–
11/2006 Ragan Salgado v. UK (4/2005) Discriminatory citizenship act: mother cannot transmit British nationality to her son born in 1954. Arts. 1, 2, and 9	Inadmissible[a, b] (Amendment of law in 1981)	Inadmissible[a, b] (follows state position); also: when son becomes major, discrimination of mother ends. (1/2007, 21 months)	–	–	–
12/2007 Groupe d'Intérêt pour le Matronyme v. France (5/2006) Discriminatory name law (complaint of daughters of divorced parents) Art. 16, in particular 16 1(g)	Inadmissible because of France's reservation to art. 16 1(g); and[c] (children are not discriminated based on gender)	Inadmissible[c] (follows state position) (8/2009, 39 months)	Admissible: See discrimination considering articles 2, 5 and 16(1).	Dissenting: Eliminate discriminatory family laws; allow two complainants to change their names	–
13/2007 SOS Sexisme v. France (7/2006) Discriminatory name law (see 12/2007, complaint of divorced mothers and unmarried women) Art. 16, in particular 16 1(g)	Inadmissible because of France's reservation to art. 16 1(g); and[c] (only one child is still minor)	Inadmissible for childless women and for those with adult children (victim status ends with their majority); and for mother of minor child, inadmissible[b] (8/2009, 37 months)	Only inadmissible[b]	–	–

(continued)

(continued)

Case/complaint	*Position state*	*View committee*	*Dissent*	*Recommendations*	*Follow up*
15/2007 Zheng v. the Netherlands (1/2007) Chinese victim of trafficking; application for asylum rejected Art. 6	Inadmissible[b] (case still pending) and[c]	Inadmissible[b] (case before Committee not identical with that before domestic authorities) (10/2008, 21 months)	Admissible: State asks too much of victim; more diligence can be expected	Dissenting: Acknowledge victim status of complainant; train corresponding authorities	–
17/2008 Pimentel v. Brazil (11/2007) Maternal death due to lack of adequate health care services (woman of African descent) Arts. 2 and 12	Inadmissible[b] (trial pending) and[c] (OP 4(2)b—substandard health care, not an issue under the Convention)	Admissible Merits: goes along with complaint Arts. 2 c, e; 12; 1 and GRs 24 and 28 (7/2011, 44 months)	–	C: Compensation for family G: Combat preventable maternal mortality for all women	Compensation paid; structural improvement in process (NGO source), ongoing (2014)
18/2008 Tayag Vertido v. Philippines (11/2007) Court decision in rape case based on stereotypes; re-victimization Arts. 1, 2, 5 and GR 19	Inadmissible[b]	Admissible Merits: goes along with complaint Arts. 2 c, f; 5 a; 1 and GR 19 (7/2010, 32 months)	–	C: Compensation G: Faster procedures; revision of law (focus on "lack of consent"); training of judiciary	Lukewarm government response; rejection of compensation; ongoing (2014)
19/2008 Kell v. Canada (6/2008) Discriminatory housing/property rights (Native woman) Arts. 1, 2, 14, 15, 16	Inadmissible[a, b, c] (no gender-based discrimination)	Admissible Merits: State failure to prevent gender-based and intersectional discrimination Arts. 2, 16; 1 (2/2012, 44 months)	Inadmissible[b]; discrimination is not proven	C: Compensation G: Training of law enforcement with view on rights of aboriginal women	Ongoing (2014)
20/2008 V.K. v. Bulgaria (10/2008) Domestic violence/state neglect of due diligence Arts. 1, 2, 5, 16 and GR 19	Admissible; due diligence complaint not substantiated	Admissible Merits: State applies restrictive notion of domestic violence and fails to effectively protect victims Arts. 2 c, d, e, f, 5, 16 (1); 1 and GR 19 (7/2011, 33 months)	–	C: Compensation G: Appeal law (one month provision, move burden of proof away from victim); train judiciary; provide more shelters	Ongoing (2014)

22/2009 T.P.F. v. Peru (6/2009) Abortion denied to minor which prevents surgery; results in paralysis Arts. 1, 2 (c) and (f), 3, 5, 12 and 16 (e)	Inadmissible[b]	Admissible Merits: Right to health denied (follows complaint; abortion also necessary in regard to girl's mental health) Arts. 2, 3, 5, and 12 (10/2011, 28 months)	–	C: Compensation G: Review laws so that therapeutic abortion is accessible; train personnel; allow abortion in case of rape	Ongoing (2014)
23/2009 Abramova v. Belarus (4/2009) Sexual harassment in detention Arts. 1, 2 (a), (b), (d), (e), (f), 3, 5(a).	Inadmissible[b]	Admissible Merits: Goes along with complaint Arts. 1, 2 (a), (b), (d), (e), (f), 3, 5(a) (7/2011, 27 months)	–	C: Compensation G: Improve situation of female prisoners	Ongoing (2014)
25/2010 M.P.M. v. Canada (3/2010) Deportation of Mexican national (gender-based violence expected) Arts. 2 c, d, 3, 15 and 16	Inadmissible[c] (author already left for Mexico)	Inadmissible[c] (follows state) (2/2012, 23 months)	–	–	–
26/2010 Herrera Rivera v. Canada **(9/2010)** Deportation of Mexican national (gender-based violence expected) Arts. 1, 2 a–d, 5 a and 24	Inadmissible[b, c] (no duty under CEDAW to not deport)	Inadmissible[b] (10/2011, 13 months; also, Committee had asked for interim measures of protection)	–	–	–
27/2010 Mukhina v. Italy **(3/2010)** Child custody case	No statement	Inadmissible[c] (unsubstantiated) (10/2011, 19 months)	–	–	–
28/2010 R.K.B. v. Turkey **(7/2009)** Discriminatory employment termination; stereotypical approach of courts to the case Arts 1, 2 a, c, 5 a, 11, 1 a, d	Inadmissible[c] (not related to Convention and not substantiated)	Admissible; goes along with complaint Arts 1, 2 a, c, 5 a, 11, 1 a, d (2/2012, 31 months)	Supportive (focus on equality of outcome)	C: Compensation G: Implement labor code in practice and train lawyers/judges on CEDAW and gender stereotypes	Ongoing (2014)

(*continued*)

(continued)

Case/complaint	*Position state*	*View committee*	*Dissent*	*Recommendations*	*Follow up*
29/2011 Sankhe v. Spain **(12/2010)** Discrimination in getting a work permit as Senegalese citizen 1, 2 a–g, 3, 6, 9(1), 10(a), 11(1) (a) and (d), 11 2c, 15 1 and 2, 16 1 c, d, and f	Inadmissible[b, c] (unequal treatment allegation ill-founded)	Inadmissible[b] (10/2013, 34 months)	–	–	–
31/2011 V.P.P. v. Bulgaria (12/2010) Sexual assault against child with long term mental health consequences; inadequate state reaction Arts. 1, 2 a–c, e–g, 3, 5, 12, 15	Rejects accusation that due diligence duties are neglected but says little to the case per se	Admissible, goes along with complaint Arts. 1, 2 a–c, e–g, 3, 5, 12, 15 (10/2012, 22 months)	–	C: Compensation G: Repeal discriminatory laws; prevent re-victimization and ensure de facto application of law	Ongoing (2014)
32/2011 Jallow v. Bulgaria (11–2010) Domestic violence and child abuse, migrant woman; lack of state support Arts. 1, 2, 3, 5 and 16, 1 (c), (d), (f) and (g)	Inadmissible[b, c]	Admissible; goes along with complaint Arts. 1, 2, 3, 5 and 16, 1 (c), (d), (f) and (g) (7/2012, 20 months)	–	C: Compensation G: Ensure access for victims of domestic violence to services, esp. migrant women; train law enforcement/judges on these issues	Ongoing (2014)
33/2011 M.N.N. v. Denmark **(5/2010)** Rejection of Ugandan asylum seeker who faces risk of circumcision if deported Arts. 1, 2c–d, 3.	Inadmissible[c, d] (not within scope of Convention—extraterritoriality)	Interim measures. Inadmissible[c] (risk is not substantiated) but in case of substance of claim, state has extraterritorial responsibilities (7/2013, 38 months)	–	–	–

34/2011 R.P.B. v. Philippines **(5/2011)** Acquittal of rape case of deaf girl despite clear evidence Arts. 1, 2 c, d, f and GR 18/19	Inadmissible[b, c]	Admissible (2/2014, 33 months) Merits: Goes along with complaint (access to justice obstructed, judgment based on stereotypes) Arts. 1, 2 c, d, f and GR 18/19	–	C: Compensation and free counseling G: Review rape legislation; provide adequate assistance in court proceedings; train judiciary and legal professionals	Ongoing (2014)
35/2011 M.E.N. v Denmark **(10/2011)** Rejection of Burundi asylum seeker who faces risks for life if deported Arts. 1, 2c, d, and 3	Inadmissible[b, c] (extraterritoriality)	Inadmissible[b] (no reference to gender based HR violations); reiterates its position on extraterritorial duties (7/2013, 21 months)	Admissible (author has made her risk as a woman sufficiently clear)	–	–
36/2012 De Blok et al. V Netherlands **(11/2011)** Lack of public maternity leave for self-employed females (limited time frame) Art. 11 2b	Inadmissible[c] (state responsibility not substantiated under CEDAW)	Admissible (self-employed women are not excluded from access to public maternity leave) Art. 11 2 b (2/2014, 27 months)	–	Provide compensation for authors and others in their situation (all in all, situation is fixed since 2008 new legislation)	Ongoing (2014)
38/2012 J.S. v. the U.K. **(2/2011)** Right of mother to pass on British nationality art. 9 (and 1, 2, 3)	No victim standing (male author); inadmissible[b, c] (reservation against art. 9)	Inadmissible[b] (10/2012, 20 months)	–	–	–
39/2012 N. v. Netherlands **(2/2012)** Rejection of Mongolian asylum seeker who faces gender-based violence if deported Arts. 1, 2 e, 3 and 6	Inadmissible[b, c]	Inadmissible[c] (not made sufficiently clear that Mongolian state cannot protect; otherwise, Netherlands would have had duties under Convention) (2/2014, 24 months)	–	–	–

(continued)

(continued)

Case/complaint	*Position state*	*View committee*	*Dissent*	*Recommendations*	*Follow up*
40/2012 M.S. v. Denmark **(3/2012)** Pakistani national and her family's asylum rejection (based on sexual harassment as member of religious minority)	Inadmissible[c] (too extraterritoriality; not substantiated; not applicable for male family members—no victim status)	Inadmissible[c] (severity of problem not substantiated) (7/2013, 16 months)	–	–	–
44/2012 M.K. D. A.-A. v. Denmark **(9/2012)** Filipino woman's custody rights violated vis-à-vis Danish father Arts. 1, 2 d, 5 and 16 d	Inadmissible[d, c] (state decided in her favour; other reasons)	Inadmissible because of lack of victim status—mother and son returned to Philippines; but recognizes that until then, her rights were violated (10/2013, 13 months)	–	–	–

[a]Inadmissibility based on art. 4, 2 (e) (facts that are subject of communication occurred prior to entry into force of OP for State party)

[b]Inadmissibility based on art. 4, 1 (lack of exhausting domestic remedies)

[c]Inadmissibility based on art. 4, 2 (b) and (c) (matter is incompatible with Convention, or ill-founded or not sufficiently substantiated)

[d]Inadmissibility based on art. 4, 2 (a) (matter is or was already under international investigation)

C Case-specific

G General

Appendix 3: Principled Connectivity With CEDAW

0	Holy See, Iran, Niue, Palau, Somalia, South Sudan, Sudan, Tonga, USA
1	Brunei Darussalam, Micronesia, Monaco, Oman, Qatar, United Arab Emirates
2	Algeria, Bahrain, India, Lebanon, Malaysia, Mauretania, Morocco, Pakistan, Saudi Arabia, Singapore, Syrian Arab Republic
2.5	Kuwait
3	Bahamas, Democratic People's Republic of Korea, Egypt, Iraq, Israel, Jordan, Kiribati, Malta, Marshall Islands, Nauru, State of Palestine, Swaziland
3.5	Cook Islands, Fiji, Switzerland
4	Afghanistan, Chad, Comoros, Djibouti, Eritrea, Gambia, Maldives, Myanmar, Niger, Papua New Guinea, São Tomé and Príncipe, Suriname, Tajikistan, Tuvalu, Uzbekistan
4.5	Jamaica, Lesotho, Malawi, Tunisia
5	Australia, Bangladesh, Barbados, Benin, Bhutan, Burundi, Central African Republic, Chile, China, Congo, Cote d'Ivoire, Cuba, Democratic Republic of the Congo, Dominica, El Salvador, Estonia, Ethiopia, Grenada, Guinea, Guyana, Haiti, Honduras, Indonesia, Ireland, Japan, Kenya, Lao People's Democratic Republic, Latvia, Liberia, Libya, Liechtenstein, Madagascar, Mozambique, Nicaragua, Republic of Montenegro, Saint Lucia, Saint Vincent and the Grenadines, Samoa, San Marino, Sierra Leone, Togo, Trinidad and Tobago, Turkmenistan, Uganda, Vietnam, Yemen, Zambia, Zimbabwe
5.5	Mauritius
6	Albania, Andorra, Angola, Armenia, Austria, Azerbaijan, Bosnia and Herzegovina, Botswana, Cambodia, Cameroon, Cape Verde, Czech Republic, Equatorial Guinea, Georgia, Ghana, Guinea-Bissau, Kazakhstan, Kyrgyzstan, Lithuania, Republic of Moldova, Seychelles, Slovakia, Solomon Islands, South Africa, The Former Yugoslavia Republic of Macedonia, Timor-Leste, United Kingdom of Great Britain and Northern Ireland, Vanuatu

(*continued*)

S. Zwingel, *Translating International Women's Rights*, Gender and Politics, DOI 10.1057/978-1-137-31501-4

(continued)

6.5	Belgium, Brazil, Canada, Cyprus, France, Germany, Luxembourg, New Zealand, Republic of Korea, Spain, Thailand, Turkey
7	Antigua and Barbuda, Argentina, Belarus, Belize, Bolivia, Bulgaria, Burkina Faso, Colombia, Costa Rica, Croatia, Denmark, Dominican Republic, Ecuador, Finland, Gabon, Greece, Guatemala, Hungary, Iceland, Italy, Mali, Mexico, Mongolia, Namibia, Nepal, Netherlands, Nigeria, Norway, Panama, Paraguay, Peru, Philippines, Poland, Portugal, Republic of Serbia, Romania, Russian Federation, Rwanda, Saint Kitts and Nevis, Senegal, Slovenia, Sri Lanka, Sweden, Ukraine, United Republic of Tanzania, Uruguay, Venezuela

Appendix 4: Substantive Connectivity Values

States	*Overdue per report (years)*	*Ratio submitted to due reports*	*Dialogue frequency (years)*
Afghanistan	5	0.33	10
Albania	3.75	0.8	9.5
Algeria	0.75	0.6	5.67
Andorra	5.33	0.4	7
Angola	7.17	0.43	13.5
Antigua and Barbuda	4	0.14	24
Argentina	0.86	0.88	5.6
Armenia	1.83	0.67	6.67
Australia	2.7	0.63	6
Austria	1.38	0.75	6.2
Azerbaijan	1.2	0.8	6
Bahamas	7.4	0.33	20
Bahrain	1.3	0.67	5.5
Bangladesh	1.1	0.75	5.8
Barbados	6.9	0.33	10.7
Belarus	2.7	0.55	6.4
Belgium	2	0.63	5.6
Belize	3.3	0.33	11.5
Benin	3.8	0.33	10.5
Bhutan	8.4	0.33	16
Bolivia	4.2	0.5	11.5
Bosnia and Herzegovina	4	0.33	10
Botswana	7	0.2	17
Brazil	6.6	0.38	9.7

(*continued*)

S. Zwingel, *Translating International Women's Rights*,
Gender and Politics, DOI 10.1057/978-1-137-31501-4

(continued)

States	*Overdue per report (years)*	*Ratio submitted to due reports*	*Dialogue frequency (years)*
Brunei Darussalam	4	0.5	7
Bulgaria	6.7	0.38	10.3
Burkina Faso	2	0.57	6.5
Burundi	4.5	0.33	10.5
Cambodia	5	0.33	10.5
Cameroon	3.2	0.6	6.3
Canada	1	0.88	6.2
Cape Verde	11.1	0.22	16
Central African Republic	12	0.17	22
Chad	8	0.2	18
Chile	0.17	0.83	5.75
China	3.4	0.55	6.4
Colombia	2.6	0.63	6.2
Comoros	10	0.2	19
Congo	9.7	0.25	15.5
Cook Islands	1.5	0.5	7
Costa Rica	6.5	0.43	13.5
Côte d'Ivoire	9	0.2	17
Croatia	3.6	0.5	10.5
Cuba	3.1	0.55	6.4
Cyprus	4.6	0.38	9.3
Czech Republic	0.83	0.83	5
Democratic People's Republic of Korea	4	0.25	12
Democratic Republic of the Congo	3.1	0.71	9
Denmark	0.25	1	5
Djibouti	6	0.25	14
Dominica	n.a.	n.a.	32
Dominican Republic	3.6	0.63	7.8
Ecuador	2.6	0.67	8
Egypt	3.3	0.55	8
El Salvador	3.4	0.67	8
Equatorial Guinea	3.7	0.5	9.6
Eritrea	3.6	0.6	18
Estonia	3.7	0.5	11
Ethiopia	5.6	0.33	10.7
Fiji	4.8	0.4	9
Finland	1	1	5.4
France	1.8	0.75	7.25
Gabon	6.7	0.38	15
Gambia	4.6	0.33	20
Georgia	2.2	0.6	6.3

(*continued*)

(continued)

States	*Overdue per report (years)*	*Ratio submitted to due reports*	*Dialogue frequency (years)*
Germany	2	0.625	7
Ghana	3.4	0.43	9
Greece	3.1	0.625	6
Grenada	11.2	0.16	23
Guatemala	4.6	0.625	7.75
Guinea	7.4	0.375	10.3
Guinea-Bissau	12	0.13	28
Guyana	6.7	0.44	8
Haiti	14	0.22	32
Honduras	3.3	0.63	15
Hungary	2	0.67	5.3
Iceland	2	0.63	9.3
India	3.8	0.5	6.67
Indonesia	3.3	0.5	7.25
Iraq	5.8	0.43	9
Ireland	3.1	0.43	9
Israel	1.8	0.67	7.3
Italy	3.2	0.63	7
Jamaica	3	0.5	7.25
Japan	0.63	0.88	7
Jordan	2.6	0.67	7
Kazakhstan	0.75	0.75	5
Kenya	3.1	0.5	7.25
Kiribati	5	n.a.	No dialogue
Kuwait	4	0.4	9.5
Kyrgyzstan	0.5	0.8	5.3
Lao People's Democratic Republic	10.4	0.22	16
Latvia	5.5	0.17	21
Lebanon	1.6	0.8	8
Lesotho	8	0.2	18
Liberia	10	0.25	29
Libya	4.6	0.43	12
Liechenstein	0.25	0.8	5.7
Lithuania	1.4	1	6.3
Luxembourg	2.2	0.71	6
Madagascar	4.43	0.43	12
Malawi	3.4	0.57	8.7
Malaysia	5.2	0.2	18
Maldives	3.8	0.5	10
Mali	5.7	0.375	14
Malta	5.75	0.33	11
Marshall Islands	5	n.a.	No dialgoue

(*continued*)

(continued)

States	*Overdue per report (years)*	*Ratio submitted to due reports*	*Dialogue frequency (years)*
Mauritania	2.3	0.5	6
Mauritius	4.7	0.375	9.7
Mexico	2.4	0.67	5.3
Micronesia (Federated States of)	5	n.a.	No dialogue
Monaco	4	n.a.	No dialogue
Mongolia	3.2	0.55	8
Morocco	0.5	0.5	6.7
Mozambique	3	0.4	16
Myanmar	1.4	0.6	8
Namibia	4	0.5	10.5
Nauru	2	n.a.	No dialogue
Nepal	3.2	0.5	7.3
Netherlands	0.17	1	5.5
New Zealand	0.86	0.75	4.6
Nicaragua	3.25	0.67	8
Niger	5	0.25	14
Nigeria	2.83	0.5	7
Norway	1.1	0.89	5.3
Oman	2	0.5	7
Pakistan	3.5	0.4	8.5
Panama	7.4	0.33	10.7
Papua New Guinea	9	0.2	18
Paraguay	2.6	0.57	8.7
Peru	1.9	0.75	5.1
Philippines	2.9	0.67	8
Poland	3.4	0.55	8
Portugal	2	0.89	8
Qatar	1	0.5	4
Republic of Korea	0.29	0.88	5.6
Republic of Moldova	1.8	0.6	6.3
Republic of Montenegro	3	0.5	7
Republic of Serbia	2.88	0.55	7.75
Romania	2.38	0.5	10.3
Russian Federation	1.75	0.78	6.4
Rwanda	4.6	0.44	8
Saint Kitts and Nevis	8	0.125	28
Saint Lucia	10.25	0.125	31
Saint Vincent and the Grenadines	6.1	0.22	32
Samoa	4	0.33	10.5
San Marino	5	n.a.	No dialogue
São Tomé and Príncipe	6	n.a.	No dialogue

(*continued*)

(continued)

States	*Overdue per report (years)*	*Ratio submitted to due reports*	*Dialogue frequency (years)*
Saudi Arabia	2.5	0.25	13
Senegal	8	0.43	14
Seychelles	10	0.17	21
Sierra Leone	7	0.29	12.5
Singapore	1.25	0.8	6
Slovakia	2.83	0.5	10
Slovenia	1	0.83	7
Solomon Islands	6	0.33	11
South Africa	3.25	0.4	8.5
Spain	1.3	0.88	5.8
Sri Lanka	5.7	0.44	8
State of Palestine			n.a.
Suriname	4.6	0.33	10
Swaziland	5	0.33	9
Sweden	1	0.77	6.4
Switzerland	1.6	0.6	8
Syrian Arab Republic	0.33	0.67	5
Tajikistan	4.6	0.33	10
Thailand	3	0.38	9.3
The Former Yugoslavia Republic of Macedonia	3	0.4	9.5
Timor-Leste	2	0.67	10
Togo	9.1	0.25	15
Trinidad and Tobago	7	0.33	23
Tunisia	4.7	0.38	9.3
Turkey	1.6	0.71	6.75
Turkmenistan	2.5	0.4	8
Tuvalu	3	0.5	14
Uganda	5	0.38	9.3
Ukraine	2.1	0.75	6.4
United Arab Emirates	1	0.67	9
United Kingdom of Great Britain and Northern Ireland	0	1	5.4
United Republic of Tanzania	3.5	0.5	9.3
Uruguay	5.6	0.44	10.7
Uzbekistan	1.6	0.8	6
Vanuatu	3.8	0.4	18
Venezuela (Boliviarian Republic of)	2	0.63	6
Vietnam	4.87	0.63	10.3
Yemen	1.25	0.75	9.7
Zambia	3	0.38	9.3
Zimbabwe	5.6	0.33	11

Appendix 5: Dialogue Frequency of CEDAW States Parties in Yearly Intervals (1982–2014)

4	New Zealand, Qatar
5	Algeria, Argentina, Bahrain, Bangladesh, Belgium, Chile, Czech Republic, Denmark, Finland, Hungary, Kazakhstan, Kyrgyzstan, Liechtenstein, Mexico, Netherlands, Norway, Peru, Republic of Korea, Spain, Syrian Arab Republic, United Kingdom of Great Britain and Northern Ireland
6	Armenia, Australia, Austria, Azerbaijan, Belarus, Burkina Faso, Cameroon, Canada, China, Colombia, Cuba, Georgia, Greece, India, Lithuania, Luxembourg, Mauritania, Morocco, Republic of Moldova, Russian Federation, Singapore, Sweden, Turkey, Ukraine, Uzbekistan, Venezuela
7	Andorra, Brunei Darussalam, Cook Islands, Dominican Republic, France, Germany, Guatemala, Indonesia, Israel, Italy, Jamaica, Japan, Jordan, Kenya, Nepal, Nigeria, Oman, Republic of Montenegro, Republic of Serbia, Slovenia
8	Ecuador, Egypt, El Salvador, Guyana, Lebanon, Malawi, Mongolia, Myanmar, Nicaragua, Pakistan, Paraguay, Philippines, Poland, Portugal, Rwanda, South Africa, Sri Lanka, Switzerland, Turkmenistan
9	Albania, Brazil, Cyprus, Democratic Republic of Congo, Equatorial Guinea, Fiji, Ghana, Iceland, Iraq, Ireland, Kuwait, Mauritius, Swaziland, Thailand, The Former Yugoslavia Republic of Macedonia, Tunisia, Uganda, United Arab Emirates, United Republic of Tanzania, Yemen, Zambia
10	Afghanistan, Barbados, Benin, Bosnia and Herzegovina, Bulgaria, Burundi, Cambodia, Croatia, Ethiopia, Guinea, Maldives, Namibia, Romania, Samoa, Slovakia, Suriname, Tajikistan, Timor-Leste, Vietnam, Panama, Uruguay
11	Belize, Bolivia, Estonia, Malta, Solomon Islands, Zimbabwe
12	People's Democratic Republic of Korea, Libya, Madagascar, Sierra Leone
13	Angola, Costa Rica, Saudi Arabia
14	Djibouti, Mali, Niger, Senegal, Tuvalu
15	Congo, Gabon, Honduras, Togo

(*continued*)

S. Zwingel, *Translating International Women's Rights*, Gender and Politics, DOI 10.1057/978-1-137-31501-4

(continued)

16	Bhutan, Cape Verde, Lao People's Democratic Republic, Mozambique
17	Botswana, Côte d'Ivoire
18	Chad, Eritrea, Lesotho, Malaysia, Papua New Guinea, Vanuatu
19	Comoros
20	Bahamas, Gambia
21	Latvia, Seychelles
22	Central African Republic
23	Grenada, Trinidad and Tobago
24	Antigua and Barbuda
25–27	
28	Guinea-Bissau, St. Kitts and Nevis
29	Liberia
30	
31	Saint Lucia
32	Dominica (without report), Haiti, Saint Vincent and the Grenadines
N. d.	Kiribati (9 years), Marshall Islands (7 years), Micronesia (9 years), Monaco (8 years), Nauru (2 years), San Marino (9 years), São Tomé and Príncipe (10 years), State of Palestine (0 years)

Bibliography

Abouharb, M. R., & Cingranelli, D. L. (2006). The human rights effects of World Bank structural adjustment 1981–2000. *International Studies Quarterly, 50*, 233–262.

Acar, F. (2007). Thoughts on the committee's past, hopes for its future. In H.-B. Schoepp-Schilling & C. Flinterman (Eds.), *The circle of empowerment. Twenty-five years of the UN Committee on the Elimination of Discrimination against Women* (pp. 340–345). New York: The Feminist Press.

Acharya, A. (2004). How ideas spread: Whose norms matter? Norm localization and institutional change in Asian regionalism. *International Organization, 58*(2), 239–275.

Afsharipour, A. (1999). Empowering ourselves: The role of women's NGOs in the enforcement of the women's convention. *Columbia Law Review, 99*(1), 129–166.

Alvarez, S. E. (2000). Translating the global. Effects of transnational organizing on local feminist discourses and practices in Latin America. *Meridians: Feminism, Race, Transnationalism, 1*(1), 29–67.

Amnesty International. (2014). *Finland. Submission to the UN committee on the elimination of discrimination against women, 57th session, February 2014*, London.

Amnesty International, Center for Women's Global Leadership, Human Rights First, Human Rights Watch, International Service for Human Rights. (2008). Letter to the chairperson of the committee on the elimination of discrimination against women, Re: Discrimination on the basis of sexual orientation and gender identity. https://www.humanrightsfirst.org/wp-content/uploads/pdf/080730-FD-cedaw-ngo-letter.pdf. Date accessed 30 July 2015.

Aniekwu, N. I. (2006). The Convention on the Elimination of All Forms of Discrimination against Women and the status of implementation on the right to health care in Nigeria. *Human Rights Brief, 13*(3), 34–39.

S. Zwingel, *Translating International Women's Rights*,
Gender and Politics, DOI 10.1057/978-1-137-31501-4

Antrobus, P. (2004). *The global women's movement. Origins, issues and strategies.* London: Zed Books.

Antrobus, P., & Sen, G. (2005). The personal is global: The project and politics of the transnational women's movement. In S. Batliwala & L. D. Brown (Eds.), *Transnational civil society. An introduction* (pp. 142–158). Bloomfield: Kumarian Press.

Aouij, E. (2007). In the Muslim world. In H.-B. Schoepp-Schilling & C. Flinterman (Eds.), *The circle of empowerment. Twenty-five years of the UN Committee on the elimination of discrimination against women* (pp. 86–87). New York: The Feminist Press.

Arbour, L. (2007). *Twenty-fifth anniversary of the work of the committee on the elimination of discrimination against women*, Statement by Ms. Louise Arbour, United Nations High Commissioner for Human Rights. http://www.un.org/womenwatch/daw/cedaw/cedaw25anniversary/Statement_HCHR.pdf. Date accessed 30 July 2015.

Avdeyeva, O. (2007). When do states comply with international treaties? Policies on violence against women in post-communist countries. *International Studies Quarterly, 51*, 877–900.

AWID. (2013). *Watering the leaves, starving the roots. The status of financing for women's rights organizing and gender equality*, by A. Arutyunova and C. Clark. Toronto: AWID.

Bagić, A. (2006). Women's organizing in post-Yugoslav countries: Talking about "donors". In M. Marx Ferree & A. M. Tripp (Eds.), *Global feminism. Transnational women's activism, organizing, and human rights* (pp. 141–165). New York/London: New York University Press.

Baldez, L. (2001). Coalition politics and the limits of state feminism in Chile. *Women and Politics, 22*(4), 1–28.

Baldez, L. (2013). *Blocking diffusion: Conservative backlash and the UN treaty on women's rights.* Paper presented at the 2013 annual meeting of the International Studies Association, San Francisco, April 3–6.

Baldez, L. (2014). *Defying convention. U.S. resistance to the U.N. treaty on women's rights.* New York: Cambridge University Press.

Banda, F. (2012). Article 10. In M. A. Freeman, C. Chinkin, & B. Rudolf (Eds.), *The UN Convention on the Elimination of All Forms of Discrimination against Women. A commentary* (pp. 253–278). Oxford: Oxford University Press.

Banks, A. M. (2009). CEDAW, compliance, and custom: Human rights enforcement in Sub-Saharan Africa. *Fordham International Law Journal, 32*, 781–845.

Basu, A. (1995). *The challenge of local feminisms. Women's movements in global perspective.* Boulder: Westview.

Bayefsky, A. (2001). *The UN human rights treaty system. Universality at the crossroads.* The Hague: Kluwer Law International.

Bellamy, A. (2009). *A responsibility to protect: The global effort to end mass atrocities.* Cambridge: Polity Press.

Berkovitch, N. (1999). *From motherhood to citizenship. Women's rights and international organizations.* Baltimore/London: John Hopkins University Press.

Bernard, D. P. (2007). The first twelve years. In H.-B. Schoepp-Schilling & C. Flinterman (Eds.), *The circle of empowerment. Twenty-five years of the UN committee on the elimination of discrimination against women* (pp. 266–267). New York: The Feminist Press.

Biholar, R. (2013). *Transforming discriminatory sex roles and gender stereotyping: The implementation of Article 5(a) CEDAW for the realisation of women's right to be free from gender-based violence in Jamaica.* Cambridge, Antwerp, Portland: Intersentia.

Binion, G. (1995). Human rights: A feminist perspective. *Human Rights Quarterly, 17*(3), 509–526.

Boerefijn, I. (2012a). Article 20. In M. A. Freeman, C. Chinkin, & B. Rudolf (Eds.), *The UN Convention on the Elimination of All Forms of Discrimination against Women. A commentary* (pp. 513–518). Oxford: Oxford University Press.

Boerefijn, I. (2012b). Article 21. In M. A. Freeman, C. Chinkin, & B. Rudolf (Eds.), *The UN Convention on the Elimination of All Forms of Discrimination against Women: A commentary* (pp. 519–526). Oxford: Oxford University Press.

Boerefijn, I. (2012c). Article 22. In M. A. Freeman, C. Chinkin, & B. Rudolf (Eds.), *The UN Convention on the Elimination of All Forms of Discrimination against Women: A commentary* (pp. 527–530). Oxford: Oxford University Press.

Boerefijn, I. (2012d). Article 18. In M. A. Freeman, C. Chinkin, & B. Rudolf (Eds.), *The UN Convention on the Elimination of All Forms of Discrimination against Women: A commentary* (pp. 489–507). Oxford: Oxford University Press.

Bond, J. (2014). *CEDAW in Sub-Saharan Africa: Lessons in Implementation,* Michigan State Law Review, 241–263.

Bordalí Salamanca, A., & Zúñiga Añazco, Y. (2009). Análisis del fallo del Tribunal Constitucional sobre la píldora del día después. *Anuario de Derechos Humanos,* 5, 173–182.

Boserup, E. (1970). *Women's role in economic development.* London: St. Martin's Press.

Brehms, E. (2009). Conflict among human rights norms. In D. P. Forsythe (Ed.), *Encyclopedia of human rights* (Vol. 1, pp. 387–393). Oxford: Oxford University Press.

Breitmeier, H., Underdal, A., & Young, O. R. (2011). The effectiveness of international environmental regimes: Comparing and contrasting findings from quantitative research. *International Studies Review, 13*(4), 579–605.

Bunch, C. (1990). Women's rights as human rights: Toward a re-vision of human rights. *Human Rights Quarterly, 12*(4), 486–498.

Burrows, N. (1985). The 1979 Convention on the Elimination of All Forms of Discrimination against Women. *Netherlands International Law Review, 32,* 419–460.

Buss, D. E. (2004). The Christian right, globalization, and the "natural family". In M. A. Tétreault & R. A. Denemark (Eds.), *Gods, guns, and globalization. Religious radicalism and the international political economy* (pp. 57–77). Lynne Rienner: Boulder/London.

Butler, J. (2004). Beside oneself: On the limits of sexual autonomy. In J. Butler (Ed.), *Undoing gender* (pp. 17–39). New York: Routledge.

Byrnes, A. C. (1989). The "other" human rights treaty body. The work of the committee on the elimination of discrimination against women. *Yale Journal of international Law, 14*, 1–67.

Byrnes, A. C. (2002). The Convention on the Elimination of All Forms of Discrimination against Women. In W. Bendeck, E. M. Kisaakye, & G. Oberleitner (Eds.), *Human rights of women. International instruments and African experiences* (pp. 119–172). London/New York: Zed Books.

Byrnes, A. C. (2012a). Article 1. In M. A. Freeman, C. Chinkin, & B. Rudolf (Eds.), *The UN Convention on the Elimination of All Forms of Discrimination against Women. A commentary* (pp. 51–70). Oxford: Oxford University Press.

Byrnes, A. C. (2012b). Article 2. In M. A. Freeman, C. Chinkin, & B. Rudolf (Eds.), *The UN Convention on the Elimination of All Forms of Discrimination against Women. A commentary* (pp. 71–99). Oxford: Oxford University Press.

Byrnes, A. C. (2013). The implementation of the CEDAW in Australia: Success, trials, tribulations and continuing struggle. In A. Hellum & H. S. Aasen (Eds.), *Women's human rights. CEDAW in international, regional, and national law* (pp. 323–357). Cambridge: Cambridge University Press.

Byrnes, A. C., & Bath, E. (2008). Violence against women, the obligation of due diligence and the optional protocol to the Convention on the Elimination of All Forms of Discrimination against Women—Recent developments. *Human Rights Law Review, 8*(3), 517–533.

Byrnes, A. C., & Connors, J. (1996). Enforcing the human rights of women: A complaints procedure for the women's convention? *Brooklyn Journal of International Law, 21*(3), 679–783.

Byrnes, A. C., & Freeman, M. A. (2012). *The impact of the CEDAW convention: Paths to equality* (UNSW law research paper no. 2012-7). http://ssrn.com/abstract=2011655

Çağlar, G., Prügl, E., & Zwingel, S. (Eds.). (2013). *Feminist strategies in international governance*. New York: Routledge.

Campbell, M. (2015). CEDAW inquiry into grave violence against aboriginal women in Canada. *Oxford Human Rights Hub*. http://ohrh.law.ox.ac.uk/cedaw-inquiry-into-grave-violence-against-aboriginal-women-in-canada/. Date accessed 30 July 2015.

Cardenas, S. (2007). *Conflict and compliance. State responses to international human rights pressure*. Philadelphia: University of Pennsylvania Press.

Caron, M. (2007). Challenging governments. In H.-B. Schoepp-Schilling & C. Flinterman (Eds.), *The circle of empowerment. Twenty-five years of the UN Committee on the Elimination of Discrimination against Women* (pp. 265–266). New York: The Feminist Press.

Carpenter, C. R. (2007). Setting the advocacy agenda: Theorizing issue emergence and nonemergence in transnational advocacy networks. *International Studies Quarterly, 51*(1), 99–120.

Cartwright, S. (1998). The Committee on the Elimination of Discrimination against Women. In K. D. Askin & D. M. Koenig (Eds.), *Women and international human rights law* (Vol. 2, pp. 165–181). Ardsley: Transnational.

Cartwright, S. (2007). Interpreting the convention. In H.-B. Schoepp-Schilling & C. Flinterman (Eds.), *The circle of empowerment. Twenty-five years of the UN Committee on the Elimination of Discrimination against Women* (pp. 30–35). New York: The Feminist Press.

Catholic Family and Human Rights Institute. (2007). CEDAW reality check, by A. Ruse. https://c-fam.org/cedaw-reality-check-3/. Date accessed 30 July 2015.

CEM, CEDEM, CLADEM, La Morada, Corporación DOMOS, Corporación Humanas, FLACSO, Foro-Red de Salud y Derechos Sexuales y Reproductivos-Chile, Instituto de la Mujer, MEMCH. (2006). Informe Sombra CEDAW, CHILE 2003–2006.

Chambers, C. (2006). Anthropology as cultural translation: Amitav Ghosh's *In an antique land. Postcolonial Text, 2*(3), 1–19.

Chappell, L. (2006). Contesting women's rights: Charting the emergence of a transnational conservative patriarchal network. *Global Society, 20*(4), 491–519.

Charlesworth, H. (1994). What are "Women's international human rights"? In R. Cook (Ed.), *Human rights of women. National and international perspectives* (pp. 58–84). Philadelphia: University of Pennsylvania Press.

Charlesworth, H. (1995). Human rights as men's rights. In J. Peters & A. Wolper (Eds.), *Women's rights, human rights: International feminist perspectives* (pp. 103–113). New York/London: Routledge.

Charlesworth, H. (2005). Not waving but drowning: Gender mainstreaming and human rights. *Harvard Human Rights Journal, 18*, 1–18.

Charlesworth, H. (2013). International human rights law: A portmanteau for feminist norms? In G. Çağlar, E. Prügl, & S. Zwingel (Eds.), *Feminist strategies in international governance* (pp. 21–36). New York: Routledge.

Charlesworth, H., & Chinkin, C. (2013). *The creation of UN women* (Regnet research paper no. 2013/7). Canberra: Centre for International Governance and Justice, Australian National University.

Chayes, A., & Chayes, A. H. (1995). *The new sovereignty. Compliance within international regulatory agreements.* Cambridge/London: Harvard University Press.

Chinkin, C. (1996). Women's rights as human rights under international law. In C. Gearty & A. Tomkins (Eds.), *Understanding human rights* (pp. 553–572). London/New York: Mansell.

Chinkin, C. (2012a). Article 3. In M. A. Freeman, C. Chinkin, & B. Rudolf (Eds.), *The UN Convention on the Elimination of All Forms of Discrimination against Women. A commentary* (pp. 101–122). Oxford: Oxford University Press.

Chinkin, C. (2012b). Violence against women. In M. A. Freeman, C. Chinkin, & B. Rudolf (Eds.), *The UN Convention on the Elimination of All Forms of Discrimination against Women: A commentary* (pp. 443–474). Oxford: Oxford University Press.

Chinkin, C., & Freeman, M. A. (2012). Introduction. In M. A. Freeman, C. Chinkin, & B. Rudolf (Eds.), *The UN Convention on the Elimination of All Forms of Discrimination against Women: A Commentary* (pp. 1–33). Oxford: Oxford University Press.

Chinkin, C., & Rudolf, B. (2012). Preamble. In M. A. Freeman, C. Chinkin, & B. Rudolf (Eds.), *The UN Convention on the Elimination of All Forms of Discrimination against Women: A commentary* (pp. 35–49). Oxford: Oxford University Press.

Clark, B. (1991). The Vienna Convention reservations regime and the Convention on Discrimination against Women. *The American Journal of International Law, 85*, 281–321.

Cohn, M. (2004). Resisting equality: Why the U.S. refuses to ratify the women's convention. *Thomas Jefferson Law Review, 27*, 15–26.

Cohn, C. (2008). Mainstreaming gender in UN security policy: A path to political transformation. In S. Rai & G. Waylen (Eds.), *Global governance: Feminist perspectives* (pp. 185–206). New York: Palgrave Macmillan.

Concerned Women for America. (2002). CEDAW Committee rulings, by W. Wright. http://www.cwfa.org/cedaw-committee-rulings/. Accessed 30 July 2015.

Connors, J. (1996a). NGOs and the human rights of women at the United Nations. In P. Willetts (Ed.), *The conscience of the world. The influence of non-governmental organizations in the UN system* (pp. 147–180). London: Hurst & Company.

Connors, J. (1996b). The women's convention in the Muslim world. In M. Yamani (Ed.), *Feminism and Islam. Legal and literary perspectives* (pp. 351–371). New York: New York University Press.

Connors, J. (2003). Introduction to the optional protocol and its mechanisms. In Deutsches Institut für Menschenrechte (Ed.), *The optional protocol to CEDAW. Mitigating violations of women's human rights* (pp. 17–21), 13–15 Mar 2003, Seminar Documentation, Berlin.

Connors, J. (2010). The system is in place—now a visionary approach is needed. Interview with Jane Connors, Chief of special procedures branch at the UN Office of the High Commissioner for Human Rights. *Zeitschrift für Menschenrechte/Journal for Human Rights, 4*(2), 152–162.

Connors, J. (2012a). Article 28. In M. A. Freeman, C. Chinkin, & B. Rudolf (Eds.), *The UN Convention on the Elimination of All Forms of Discrimination against Women: A commentary* (pp. 565–595). Oxford: Oxford University Press.

Connors, J. (2012b). Optional protocol. In M. A. Freeman, C. Chinkin, & B. Rudolf (Eds.), *The UN Convention on the Elimination of All Forms of Discrimination against Women: A commentary* (pp. 607–679). Oxford: Oxford University Press.

Cook, R. J. (1990). Reservations to the Convention on the Elimination of All Forms of Discrimination against Women. *Virginia Journal of International Law, 30*, 643–716.

Cook, R. J. (Ed.). (1994). *Human rights of women. National and international perspectives.* Philadelphia: University of Pennsylvania Press.

Cook, R. J. (1995). Women. In O. Schachter & C. C. Joyner (Eds.), *United Nations legal order* (Vol. 1, pp. 433–471). Cambridge: Cambridge University Press.

Cook, R. J., & Undurraga, V. (2012). Article 12. In M. A. Freeman, C. Chinkin, & B. Rudolf (Eds.), *The UN Convention on the Elimination of All Forms of Discrimination against Women: A commentary* (pp. 311–333). Oxford: Oxford University Press.

Cook, R. J. (2013). Human rights and maternal health: Exploring the effectiveness of the Alyne Decision. *Journal of Law, Medicine & Ethics, 41*(1), 103–123.

Corporación Humanas, CEDEM, CEM, Corporación Domos, Fundación Instituto de la Mujer, Observatorio Género y Equidad, Observatorio Ciudadano, Observatorio de Equidad de Género en Salud, Red Chilena contra la Violencia hacia las Mujeres. (2012). *Resumen Ejecutivo, Informe Alternativo para el Examen del Estado de Chile ante el Comité CEDAW en su 53° Sesión (Quinto y Sexto informe periódico combinado)*, Septiembre de 2012.

Cortell, A., & Davis, J. (2000). Understanding the domestic impact of international norms: A research agenda. *International Studies Review, 2*(1), 65–87.

Corti, I. (2007). Relationships with UN conferences, specialized agencies, programs, and funds. In H.-B. Schoepp-Schilling & C. Flinterman (Eds.), *The circle of empowerment. Twenty-five years of the UN Committee on the Elimination of Discrimination against Women* (pp. 36–50). New York: The Feminist Press.

Council for Equality. (1997). *A pioneer of equality. Goals, achievements, snapshots. 1972–1997.* Helsinki: Ministry of Social Affairs and Health.

Covarrubias, P. (1978). El Movimiento Feminista Chileno. In P. Covarrubias & R. Franco (Eds.), *Chile: Mujer y Sociedad* (pp. 615–648). Santiago: UNICEF.

Cusack, S., & Pusey, L. (2013). CEDAW and the rights to non-discrimination and equality. *Melbourne Journal of International Law, 14*, 54–92.

Cusack, S., & Timmer, A. (2011). Gender stereotyping in rape cases: The CEDAW Committee's decision in Vertido v The Philippines. *Human Rights Law Review, 11*(2), 329–342.

Dairiam, S. (2002). Equality and non-discrimination: The two essential principles for the promotion and protection of the human rights of women. In *Proceedings of a conference organized by the Centre for Comparative and Public Law and the Women's Studies Research Centre*, University of Hong Kong, Hong Kong, 20 Apr 2002.

Dairiam, S. (2004). *The status of CEDAW implementation in the ASEAN countries and selected Muslim countries*, IWRAW Asia Pacific Occasional Paper Series (Vol. 1). http://www.iwraw-ap.org/organisation/our-publications/training-materials/. Date accessed 15 Aug 2015.

Dairiam, S. (2007). From global to local: The involvement of NGOs, circle of empowerment. In H.-B. Schoepp-Schilling & C. Flinterman (Eds.), *The circle of empowerment. Twenty-five years of the UN Committee on the Elimination of Discrimination against Women* (pp. 313–325). New York: The Feminist Press.

Davis, K. (2002). Feminist body/politics as world traveller. Translating our bodies, ourselves. *European Journal of Women's Studies, 9*(3), 223–247.

de Haan, F. (2010a). Continuing Cold War paradigms in Western historiography of transnational women's organizations: The case of the Women's International Democratic Federation. *Women's History Review, 19*(4), 547–573.

de Haan, F. (2010b). A concise history of women's rights. *UN Chronicle, XLVII*(1). http://unchronicle.un.org/. Date accessed 30 July 2015.

Delbrück, J. (1981). Die Konvention der Vereinten Nationen zur Beseitigung jeder Form der Diskriminierung der Frau von 1979 im Kontext der Bemühungen um einen völkerrechtlichen Schutz der Menschenrechte. In I. Von Münch (Ed.), *Staatsrecht - Völkerrecht - Europarecht: Festschrift für Hans-Jürgen Schlochauer* (pp. 247–270). Berlin: Walter de Gruyter.

den Boer, A. (2012). *Counting what counts in the application of the women's rights convention: Violence against women in Asian states.* Paper prepared for the annual International Studies Association conference, San Diego.

Dhesca Brazil. (2014). Estado brasileiro cumpre reparacoes simbolicas do caso AlynePimentel.http://www.plataformadh.org.br/2014/04/29/estado-brasileiro-cumpre-reparacoes-simbolicas-do-caso-alyne-pimentel/. Date accessed 30 July 2015.

Díaz-Romero, P. (2015). Avances de género: bajo el agua y contra la corriente. Fundación Equitas, Barómetro de política y equidad, tema: género, June 2015. www.fundacionequitas.org/Barometro/VerPorTema?tema=género. Date accessed 15 Aug 2015.

Donnelly, J. (1986). International human rights: A regime analysis. *International Organization, 40*(3), 599–642.

Donnelly, J. (2013). *International human rights* (4th ed.). Boulder: Westview Press.

Donner, L. (1994). Gender bias in drafting international discrimination conventions: The 1979 women's convention compared with the 1965 racial convention. *California Western International Law Journal, 24*, 241–254.

Druelle, A. (2000). Right-wing anti-feminist groups at the United Nations. Institut de recherches et d'études feministes Université du Québec i Montréal. https://www.globalpolicy.org/component/content/article/177/31817.html. Date accessed 30 July 2015.

Edwards, A. (2011). Universal suffrage and the international human rights treaty bodies: Where are the women? In M. C. Bassiouni & W. A. Schabas (Eds.), *New challenges for the UN human rights machinery. What future for the UN treaty body system and the Human Rights Council procedures?* (pp. 151–170). Cambridge: Intersentia.

Englehart, N. A., & Miller, M. K. (2014). The CEDAW effect: International law's impact on women's rights. *Journal of Human Rights, 13*(1), 22–47.

Enloe, C. (1990). *Bananas, beaches and bases. Making feminist sense of international politics.* Berkeley/Los Angeles: University of California Press.

Epstein, C. (2012). Stop telling us how to behave: Socialization or infantilization? *International Studies Perspectives, 13*(2), 135–145.

Ernst, J. (1995). U.S. ratification of the Convention on the Elimination of All Forms of Discrimination against Women. *Michigan Journal of Gender & Law, 3*, 299–348.

Eschle, C., & Maiguashca, B. (2010). *Making feminist sense of the global justice movement.* Lanham: Rowman and Littlefield.

Evatt, E. (2002). Finding a voice for women's rights: The early days of CEDAW. *George Washington International Law Review, 34*(3), 515–553.

Evatt, E. (2007). Private global enterprises, international trade, and finance. In H.-B. Schoepp-Schilling & C. Flinterman (Eds.), *The circle of empowerment. Twenty-five years of the UN Committee on the Elimination of Discrimination against Women* (pp. 106–121). New York: The Feminist Press.

Ewelukwa, U. (2005). Centuries of globalization; centuries of exclusion. African women, human rights, and the 'new' international trade regime. *Berkeley Journal of Gender, Law and Justice, 20*, 75–149.

Fall, Y. (2001). Gender and social implications of globalization: An African perspective. In R. Kelly, J. Bayes, M. Hawkesworth, & B. Young (Eds.), *Gender, globalization, and democratization* (pp. 49–74). Lanham: Rowman & Littlefield.

FAO/IFAD/ILC. (2004). *Rural women's access to land and property in selected countries. Progress towards achieving the aims of Articles 14, 15 and 16 of the Convention on the Elimination of All Forms of Discrimination against Women (CEDAW)*, Rome.

Farha, L. (2008). Committee on the Elimination of Discrimination against Women. Women claiming economic, social and cultural rights—the CEDAW potential. In M. Langford (Ed.), *Social rights jurisprudence: Emerging trends in international and comparative law* (pp. 553–568). Cambridge: Cambridge University Press.

Farhoumand-Sims, C. (2009). CEDAW and Afghanistan. *Journal of International Women's Studies, 11*(1), 136–156.

Finnemore, M., & Sikkink, K. (1998). International norm dynamics and political change. *International Organization, 52*(4), 887–917.

Finnish NGOs. (2000). *The implementation of The Convention on the Elimination of All Forms of Discrimination against Women in Finland*, S. Mustakallio & M. Pentikäinen (Eds.). Helsinki.

Fitzpatrick, J. (1994). The use of international human rights norms to combat violence against women. In R. J. Cook (Ed.), *Human rights of women. National and international perspectives* (pp. 532–571). Philadelphia: University of Pennsylvania Press.

Flinterman, C. (2007). Strengthening women's human rights through individual complaints. In H.-B. Schoepp-Schilling & C. Flinterman (Eds.), *The circle of empowerment. Twenty-five years of the UN Committee on the Elimination of Discrimination against Women* (pp. 286–297). New York: The Feminist Press.

Foley, R. (2004). Muslim women's challenge to Islamic law. The case of Malaysia. *International Feminist Journal of Politics, 6*(1), 53–84.

Foster, L. A. (2000). South Africa. In M. McPhedran et al. (Eds.), *The first CEDAW impact study. Final report* (pp. 155–186). Toronto: York University, Centre for Feminist Research.

Foundation for Women's Rights Promotion and Development. (2015). CEDAW in action. http://www.cedaw.org.tw/en/en-global/home. Date accessed 18 Dec 2015.

Franceschet, S. (2001). Women in politics in post-transitional democracies. The Chilean case. *International Feminist Journal of Politics, 3*(2), 207–236.

Fraser, A. (1995). The Convention on the Elimination of All Forms of Discrimination against Women (the women's convention). In A. Winslow (Ed.), *Women, politics, and the United Nations* (pp. 77–94). Westport: Greenwood Press.

Fraser, A., & Tinker, I. (Eds.). (2004). *Developing power: How women transformed international development.* New York: The Feminist Press.

Freeman, M. A. (1994). Women, law, and land at the local level: Claiming women's human rights in domestic legal systems. *Human Rights Quarterly, 16*(3), 559–575.

Freeman, M. A. (2010). The Committee on the Elimination of Discrimination against Women and the role of civil society in implementing international women's human rights norms. *New England Journal of International & Comparative Law, 16*, 25–48.

Freeman, M. A. (2012). Article 16. In M. A. Freeman, C. Chinkin, & B. Rudolf (Eds.), *The UN Convention on the Elimination of All Forms of Discrimination against Women. A commentary* (pp. 409–442). Oxford: Oxford University Press.

Freeman, M. A., Chinkin, C., & Rudolf, B. (Eds.). (2012). *The UN Convention on the Elimination of All Forms of Discrimination against Women. A commentary.* Oxford: Oxford University Press.

Friedman, E. (1995). Women's human rights: The emergence of a movement. In J. Peters & A. Wolper (Eds.), *Women's rights, human rights: International feminist perspectives* (pp. 18–35). London/New York: Routledge.

Friedman, E. (1999). The effects of "transnationalism reversed" in Venezuela: Assessing the impact of UN global conferences on the women's movement. *International Feminist Journal of Politics, 1*(3), 357–381.

Friedman, E. (2003). Gendering the agenda: The impact of the transnational women's rights movement at the UN conferences of the 1990s. *Women's Studies International Forum, 26*(4), 313–331.

Galey, M. (1984). International enforcement of women's rights. *Human Rights Quarterly, 6*(4), 463–490.

Galey, M. (1995). Forerunners in women's quest for partnership. In A. Winslow (Ed.), *Women, politics and the United Nations* (pp. 11–27). Westport: Greenwood Press.

Garner, K. (2010). *Shaping a global women's agenda: Women's NGOs and global governance, 1925–85*. Manchester/New York: Manchester University Press.

Gatica, R. M. (2011). El destino de la sociedad conyugal. *Anuario de Derechos Humanos, 7*, 169–178.

Ghodsee, K. (2012). Rethinking state socialist mass women's organizations. The Committee of the Bulgarian Women's Movement and the United Nations decade for women, 1975–1985. *Journal of Women's History, 24*(4), 49–73.

Gilchrist, H. (2001). The optional protocol to the women's convention: An argument for ratification. *Columbia Journal of Transnational Law, 39*(3), 763–784.

González, A. (2000). Vigésimo Aniversario de la Convención sobre la Eliminación de todas las Formas de Discriminación contra la Mujer. In J. Hurtado & V. Matus (Eds.), *La Convención sobre la Eliminación de todas las Formas de Discriminación contra la Mujer* (pp. 5–8). Una Herramienta para la Acción, Santiago de Chile.

Goodale, M. (2007). Introduction. Locating rights, envisioning law between the global and the local. In M. Goodale & S. Merry (Eds.), *The practice of human rights. Tracking law between the global and the local* (pp. 1–38). Cambridge: Cambridge University Press.

Goodale, M. (2009). *Dilemmas of modernity. Bolivian encounters with law and liberalism*. Stanford: Stanford University Press.

Goodenough, P. (2010). Islamic nations fail to weaken women's rights resolution at U.N. Human Rights Council. *CNSNEWS.com*, 5 October. http://cnsnews.com/news/article/islamic-nations-fail-weaken-women-s-rights-resolution-un-human-rights-council. Date accessed 30 July 2015.

Goonesekere, S. (2007). Universalizing women's human rights through CEDAW. In H.-B. Schoepp-Schilling & C. Flinterman (Eds.), *The circle of empowerment. Twenty-five years of the UN Committee on the Elimination of Discrimination against Women* (pp. 52–67). New York: The Feminist Press.

Goonesekere, S. (2012). Article 9. In M. A. Freeman, C. Chinkin, & B. Rudolf (Eds.), *The UN Convention on the Elimination of All Forms of Discrimination against Women. A commentary.* (pp. 233–251). Oxford: Oxford University Press.

Gray, M., Kittilson, M., & Sandholtz, W. (2006). Women and globalization: A study of 180 countries, 1975–2000. *International Organization, 60*(2), 293–333.

Grewal, I. (2008). The transnational in feminist research: Concept and approaches. In H. Brabandt, B. Roß, & S. Zwingel (Eds.), *Mehrheit am Rand? Geschlechterverhältnisse, globale Ungleichheit und transnationale Handlun gsansätze* (pp. 189–199). Opladen: VS Verlag.

Grewal, I., & Kaplan, C. (1994). Introduction: Transnational feminist practices and questions of postmodernity. In I. Grewal & C. Kaplan (Eds.), *Scattered hegemonies. Postmodernity and transnational feminist practices* (pp. 1–33). Minneapolis/London: University of Minnesota Press.

Guzmán, V., Seibert, U., & Staab, S. (2010). Democracy in the country but not in the home? Religion, politics and women's rights in Chile. *Third World Quarterly, 31*(6), 971–988.

Hafner-Burton, E., Tsutsui, K., & Meyer, J. (2008). International human rights law and the politics of legitimation. Repressive states and human rights treaties. *International Sociology, 23*(1), 115–141.

Hainsfurther, J. (2009). A rights-based approach: Using CEDAW to protect the human rights of migrant workers. *American University International Law Review, 24*, 843–895.

Halley, J. E., Kotiswaran, P., Shamir, H., & Thomas, C. (2006). From the international to the local in feminist legal responses to rape, prostitution/sex work and sex trafficking: Four studies in contemporary governance feminism. *Harvard Journal of Law and Gender, 29*, 335–423.

Hannan, C. (2013). Feminist strategies in international organizations: The United Nations context. In G. Çağlar, E. Prügl, & S. Zwingel (Eds.), *Feminist strategies in international governance* (pp. 74–91). New York: Routledge.

Hannerz, U. (1996). *Transnational connections. Culture, peoples, places.* London/ New York: Routledge.

Harrison, C. M. (2002). Tough row to hoe: Can CEDAW's optional protocol help Muslim women in rural Bangladesh realize their right to development? *Praxis. The Fletcher Journal of Development Studies, 12*, 1–14.

Hathaway, O. (2002). Do human rights treaties make a difference? *Yale Law Journal, 111*(8), 1935–2042.

Hatuqa, D. (2014). "Paradigm shift": Palestinians join treaties. *Al Jazeera*, http://www.aljazeera.com/news/middleeast/2014/04/shift-palestinians-join-treaties-20144181119508l3313.html. Date accessed 30 July 2015.

Heintz, B., Mueller, D., & Schiener, H. (2006). Menschenrechte im Kontext der Weltgesellschaft. Die weltgesellschaftliche Institutionalisierung von Frauenrechten und ihre Umsetzung in Deutschland, der Schweiz und Marokko. *Zeitschrift für Soziologie, 35*(6), 424–448.

Hellum, A., & Aasen, H. S. (Eds.). (2013). *Women's human rights. CEDAW in international, regional, and national law.* Cambridge: Cambridge University Press.

Henkin, L. (1990). Law and politics in international relations: State and human values. *Journal of International Affairs, 44*, 183–208.

Heritage Foundation. (2009). CEDAW: How U.N. interference threatens the rights of American women, by G. Melton. http://www.heritage.org/Research/Reports/2009/01/CEDAW-How-UN-Interference-Threatens-the-Rights-of-American-Women?query=CEDAW:+How+U.N.+Interference+Threatens+the+Rights+of+American+Women. Date accessed 30 July 2015.

Hevener Kaufman, N. (1986). An analysis of gender based treaty law: Contemporary developments in historical perspective. *Human Rights Quarterly, 8*(1), 70–88.

Heyns, C., & Viljoen, F. (2001). The impact of the United Nations human rights treaties on the domestic level. *Human Rights Quarterly, 23*(4), 483–535.

Hill, D. (2010). Estimating the effects of human rights treaties on state behavior. *The Journal of Politics, 72*(4), 1161–1174.

Hintjens, H. (2008). UNIFEM, CEDAW, and the human rights-based approach. *Development and Change, 39*(6), 1181–1192.

Hiskes, R. (2010). Missing the green: Golf course ecology, environmental justice, and local "fulfillment" of the human right to water. *Human Rights Quarterly, 32*(2), 326–341.

Hofferberth, M., & Weber, C. (2012). *Lost in translation: A methodological critique of constructivist norm research.* Paper presented at the 53rd annual convention of the International Studies Association, San Diego.

Holli, A. M., & Kantola, J. (2007). State feminism Finnish style: Strong policies clash with implementation problems. In J. Outshoorn & Kantola, J. (Eds.), *Changing state feminism* (pp. 82–101). Houndmills: Palgrave Macmillan.

Holtmaat, R. (2012). Article 5. In M. A. Freeman, C. Chinkin, & B. Rudolf (Eds.), *The UN Convention on the Elimination of All Forms of Discrimination against Women. A commentary* (pp. 141–167). Oxford: Oxford University Press.

Human Rights Center. (2014). *Contribution by the Finnish NHRI: The examination of the 7th periodic report of Finland on the implementation of the CEDAW.*

Human Rights Watch. (2003). World report 2003, Chile. http://www.hrw.org/legacy/wr2k3/americas3.html. Date accessed 15 Aug 2015.

Humphrey, J. (1983). The memoirs of John P. Humphrey, the first director of the United Nations Division of Human Rights. *Human Rights Quarterly, 5*(3), 392–421.

Hussein, A. (2004). Crossroad for women at the UN. In A. S. Fraser & I. Tinker (Eds.), *Developing power: How women transformed international development* (pp. 3–13). New York: The Feminist Press.

IGLHRC. (2009). UN: CEDAW silent on LBT women in concluding observations. http://iglhrc.org/content/un-cedaw-silent-lbt-women-concluding-observations. Date accessed 30 July 2015.

IGLHRC. (2015). Shadow reports. http://iglhrc.org/our-publications/shadow-reports. Date accessed 30 July 2015.

Ignatieff, M. (2005). Introduction: American exceptionalism and human rights. In M. Ignatieff (Ed.), *American exceptionalism and human rights* (pp. 1–26). Princeton: Princeton University Press.

Instituto de la Mujer. (1999). *Presentación del Estado de Cumplimiento del CEDAW.* Santiago de Chile: Instituto de la Mujer.

Instituto Nacional de Derechos Humanos. (2012). Informe Complementario Comité de la CEDAW, 2012.

Inter Press Service. (2009). RIGHTS: Women's treaty a powerful force for equality, by L. Jansen. http://www.ipsnews.net/2009/12/rights-womens-treaty-a-powerful-force-for-equality/. Date accessed 30 July 2015.

International Center for Research on Women. (2010). *Recognizing rights, promoting progress. The global impact of the Convention on the Elimination of All Forms of Discrimination against Women.* Washington, DC: ICRW.

Interparliamentary Union. (2015). *Democracy through partnership between men and women.* http://www.ipu.org/iss-e/women.htm. Date accessed 15 Aug 2015.

Inter-Parliamentary Union/United Nations. (2003). The Convention on the Elimination of All Forms of Discrimination against Women and its optional protocol. Handbook for parliamentarians. http://www.ipu.org/PDF/publications/cedaw_en.pdf. Date accessed 30 July 2015.

IWRAW AP. (2002). *Annual report 2002.* Kuala Lumpur: IWRAW AP.

IWRAW AP. (2004). *Regional consultation on women's right to participate in political and public life, Jakarta, Indonesia, 9–12 December, Report.* http://www.iwraw-ap.org/organisation/activities/iwraw-asia-pacific-reports/, other reports. Date accessed 30 July 2015.

IWRAW AP. (2005). *Global consultation on the ratification and use of the optional protocol to the Convention on the Elimination of All Forms of Discrimination against Women, Kuala Lumpur, Malaysia, August 27–30, Report.* http://www.iwraw-ap.org/organisation/activities/iwraw-asia-pacific-reports/, other reports. Date accessed 30 July 2015.

IWRAW AP. (2006). *Addressing intersectional discrimination with temporary special measures,* Occasional Paper Series No. 8. http://www.iwraw-ap.org/organisation/our-publications/training-materials/. Date accessed 30 July 2015.

IWRAW AP. (2007a). *Exploring the potential of the UN human rights treaty body system in addressing sexuality rights,* Occasional Paper Series No. 11. http://www.iwraw-ap.org/organisation/our-publications/training-materials/. Date accessed 30 July 2015.

IWRAW AP. (2007b). Possible elements for inclusion in a general recommendation on Article 2 of CEDAW. Outcome document of the expert group meeting on CEDAW Article 2: National and international dimensions of state obligation. http://www.iwraw-ap.org/organisation/activities/iwraw-asia-pacific-reports/, other reports. Date accessed 30 July 2015.

IWRAW (2009). International women's rights action watch. http://www1.umn.edu/humanrts/iwraw/index.html. Date accessed 30 July 2015.

IWRAW AP. (2009). *Equity or equality for women? Understanding CEDAW's equality principles*, Occasional Paper Series No. 14. http://www.iwraw-ap.org/organisation/our-publications/training-materials/. Date accessed 30 July 2015.

IWRAW AP. (2015a). About us. http://www.iwraw-ap.org/organisation/about-us/. Date accessed 30 July 2015.

IWRAW AP. (2015b). Programmes. http://www.iwraw-ap.org/organisation/programmes/. Date accessed 30 July 2015.

IWRAW AP. (2015c). Governance. http://www.iwraw-ap.org/organisation/governance/. Date accessed 30 July 2015.

IWRAW AP. (2015d). IWRAW Asia Pacific reports. http://www.iwraw-ap.org/organisation/activities/iwraw-asia-pacific-reports/. Date accessed 30 July 2015.

Jackson, P., Crang, P., & Dwyer, C. (Eds.). (2004). *Transnational spaces. Routledge research in transnationalism*. London/New York: Routledge.

Jacobson, R. (1991). The Committee on the Elimination of Discrimination against Women. In P. Alston (Ed.), *The UN and human rights: A critical appraisal* (pp. 444–472). Oxford: Clarendon Press.

Jacobson, T. (2010). CEDAW Committee rulings pressuring 83 party nations to legalize abortion 1995–2010. Catholic Family and Human Rights Institute, Additional Research: CEDAW. http://t.c-fam.org/images/PDFs/20101022_CEDAWAbortionRulings95-2010.pdf. Date accessed 30 July 2015.

Jain, D. (2005). *Women, development, and the UN. A sixty-year quest for equality and justice* (United Nations Intellectual History Project Series). Bloomington: Indiana University Press.

Jallinoja, R. (1986). Independence or integration: The women's movement and political parties in Finland. In D. Dahlerup (Ed.), *The new women's movement. Feminism and political power in Europe and the USA* (pp. 158–178). London: Sage.

Jamal, A. (2005). Transnational feminism as critical practice. A reading of feminist discourses in Pakistan. *Meridians: Feminism, Race, Transnationalism, 5*(2), 57–82.

Jayawardena, K. (1986). *Feminism and nationalism in the Third World*. London: Zed Books.

Jenichen, A. (2013). How do women's rights norms travel? Peace-building operations as opportunity structures in Bosnia. In G. Çağlar, E. Prügl, & S. Zwingel (Eds.), *Feminist strategies in international governance* (pp. 198–213). New York: Routledge.

Jivan, V., & Forster, C. (2009). Challenging conventions: In pursuit of greater legislative compliance with CEDAW in the Pacific. *Melbourne Journal of International Law, 10*, 655–690.

Joachim, J. (2007). *Agenda setting, the UN, and NGOs. Gender violence and reproductive rights*. Washington, DC: Georgetown University Press.

Johnstone, R. (2006). Feminist influences on the United Nations human rights treaty bodies. *Human Rights Quarterly, 28*, 148–185.

Johnstone, R. (2010a). *Is the CEDAW still relevant? (Re)assessing CEDAW in 2010.* Paper presented at the 11th annual conference of the Association of Human Rights Institutes, Reykjavik.

Johnstone, R. (2010b). When private and public meet: Three CEDAW Committee views on intra-familial violence. In A. Di Stefano (Ed.), *Gender issues and international legal standards. Contemporary perspectives* (pp. 47–68). Catania: Edit Press.

Johnstone, R. (2011). Streamlining the constructive dialogue: Efficiency from the states' persectives. In M. C. Bassiouni & W. A. Schabas (Eds.), *New challenges for the UN human rights machinery. What future for the UN treaty body system and the Human Rights Council procedures?* (pp. 59–93). Cambridge: Intersentia.

Kabeer, N. (2005). Gender equality and women's empowerment: A critical analysis of the third millennium development goal. *Gender and Development, 13*(1), 13–24.

Kapur, R. (2006). Human rights in the 21st century: Take a walk on the dark side. *Sydney Law Review, 28*, 665–687.

Kardam, N. (2004). The emerging global gender equality regime from neoliberal and constructivist perspectives in international relations. *International Feminist Journal of Politics, 6*(1), 85–109.

Keck, M., & Sikkink, K. (1998). *Activists beyond borders. Advocacy networks in international politics.* Ithaca: Cornell University Press.

Keeley, J. F. (1990). Toward a Foucauldian analysis of international regimes. *International Organization, 44*(1), 83–105.

Kobayashi, Y. (2004). *A path toward gender equality: State feminism in Japan.* New York: Routledge.

Krasner, S. D. (1983). Structural causes and regime consequences: Regimes as intervening variables. In S. D. Krasner (Ed.), *International regimes* (pp. 1–21). Ithaca/London: Cornell University Press.

Kratochwil, F., & Ruggie, J. (1986). International organization: A state of the art or an art of the state. *International Organization, 40*(4), 753–775.

Kreisky, E., & Marion, L. (2009), Maskulinismus und Staat: Beharrung und Veränderung. In G. Ludwig, B. Sauer, & S. Wöhl (Eds.), *Staat und Geschlecht. Grundlagen und aktuelle Herausforderungen feministischer Staatstheorie* (pp. 75–88). Nomos: Baden-Baden.

Krivenko, E. Y. (2009). *Women, Islam and international law within the context of the Convention on the Elimination of All Forms of Discrimination against Women.* Leiden/Boston: Martinus Nijhoff.

Krook, M., & True, J. (2012). Rethinking the life cycles of international norms: The United Nations and the global promotion of gender equality. *European Journal of International Relations, 18*, 104–129.

Kroworsch, S. (2012). Article 25. In M. A. Freeman, C. Chinkin, & B. Rudolf (Eds.), *The UN Convention on the Elimination of All Forms of Discrimination against Women: A commentary* (pp. 547–556). Oxford: Oxford University Press.

La Morada, Comité Latinoamericano y del Caribe para la Defensa de los Derechos de la Mujer, Foro Abierto de Salud y Derechos Sexuales y Reproductivos, Center for Reproductive Law and Policy. (1999). *Women's rights in Chile: Alternative report to the III periodic report of Chile on the status of compliance with the women's convention: Compiled for the twenty-first session of the CEDAW-Committee.*

Lamarche, L. (2013). The Canadian experience with the CEDAW: All women's rights are human rights—a case of treaties synergy. In A. Hellum & H. S. Aasen (Eds.), *Women's human rights. CEDAW in international, regional, and national law* (pp. 358–384). Cambridge: Cambridge University Press.

Landman, T. (2005). *Protecting human rights. A comparative study*. Washington, DC: Georgetown University Press.

Laville, H. (2002). *Cold War women: The international activities of American women's organizations*. Manchester: Manchester University Press.

Leblanc, L. J., Huibregtse, A., & Meister, T. (2010). Compliance with the reporting requirements of human rights conventions. *The International Journal of Human Rights, 14*(5), 789–807.

Levitt, P., & Merry, S. (2009). Vernacularization on the ground: Local uses of global women's rights in Peru, China, India and the United States. *Global Networks, 9* (4), 441–461.

Levy, M., Young, O., & Zürn, M. (1995). The study of international regimes. *European Journal of International Relations, 1*(3), 267–330.

Liebowitz, D., & Zwingel, S. (2014). Gender equality oversimplified: Using CEDAW to counter the measurement obsession. *International Studies Review, 16*, 362–389.

Lijnzaad, L. (1995). *Ratify and ruin? Reservations to UN-human rights treaties*. Dordrecht/Boston/London: Martinus Nijhoff Publishers.

Liu, M., Hu, Y., & Liao, M. (2009). Travelling theory in China: Contextualization, compromise and combination. *Global Networks, 9*(4), 529–554.

Lombardo, E., Meier, P., & Verloo, M. (2009). Stretching and bending gender equality: A discursive politics approach. In E. Lombardo, P. Meier & M. Verloo (Eds.), *The discursive politics of gender equality. Stretching, bending and policy making* (pp. 1–18). London/New York: Routledge.

Londono, P. (2009). Developing human rights principles in cases of gender-based violence: Opuz v. Turkey in the European Court of Human Rights. *Human Rights Law Review, 9*(4), 657–667.

Lozner, S. L. (2004). Diffusion of local regulatory innovations: The San Francisco CEDAW ordinance and the New York City Human Rights Initiative. *Columbia Law Review, 104*, 768–793.

Mackay, F. (2014). *Global governance and UN women: Nested newness and the gendered limits of institutional reform*. Paper presented at the annual meeting of the International Studies Association, Toronto.

Mackie, V. (2001). The language of globalization, transnationality and feminism. *International Feminist Journal of Politics, 3*(2), 180–206.

Manokha, I. (2009). Foucault's concept of power and the global discourse of human rights. *Global Society, 23*(4), 429–452.

Marakowitz, E. (1996). Gender and national Identity in Finland. An exploration into women's policy agency. *Women's Studies International Forum, 19*(1/2), 55–63.

Massey, D. (1994). *Space, place, and gender.* Minneapolis: University of Minnesota Press.

Massey, D. (2005). *For space.* London/Thousand Oaks/New Delhi: Sage.

Mayer, A. E. (1999). Religious reservations to the Convention on the Elimination of All Forms of Discrimination against Women: What do they really mean? In C. Howland (Ed.), *Religious fundamentalisms and the human rights of women* (pp. 105–116). New York: St. Martin's Press.

Mazur, A. G. (2002). *Theorizing feminist policy.* Oxford: Oxford University Press.

McBride, D., & Mazur, A. G. (2006). Measuring feminist mobilization: Cross-national convergences and transnational networks in Western Europe. In M. Marx Ferree & A. M. Tripp (Eds.), *Global feminism. Transnational women's activism, organizing, and human rights* (pp. 219–246). New York/London: New York University Press.

McKean, W. (1983). The conventions and declarations: Equality of the sexes. In W. McKean (Ed.), *Equality and discrimination under international law* (pp. 166–193). Oxford: Clarendon Press.

McPhedran, M., Bazilli, S., Erikson, M., & Byrnes, A. (Eds.). (2000). *The first CEDAW impact study. Final report.* Toronto: Centre for Feminist Research, York University.

McQuigg, R. J. A. (2007). The responses of states to the comments of the CEDAW Committee on domestic violence. *International Journal of Human Rights, 11*(4), 461–479.

Mehra, M. (2013). India's CEDAW story. In A. Hellum & H. S. Aasen (Eds.), *Women's human rights. CEDAW in international, regional, and national law* (pp. 385–409). Cambridge: Cambridge University Press.

Melander, G. (2007). Important changes and further reforms needed. In H.-B. Schoepp-Schilling & C. Flinterman (Eds.), *The circle of empowerment. Twenty-five years of the UN Committee on the Elimination of Discrimination against Women* (pp. 345–349). New York: The Feminist Press.

Mendoza, B. (2002). Transnational feminisms in question. *Feminist Theory, 3*(3), 295–314.

Meron, T. (1990). Enhancing the effectiveness of the prohibition of discrimination against women. Editorial comments. *The American Journal of International Law, 84*, 213–217.

Merry, S. (2003). Constructing a global law—Violence against women and the human rights system. *Law and Social Inquiry, 28*, 941–977.

Merry, S. (2006). *Human rights and gender violence: Translating international law into local justice.* Chicago: Chicago University Press.

Meyer, M. (1999). Negotiating international norms: The Inter-American Commission on Women and the Convention on Violence against Women. In M. Meyer & E. Prügl (Eds.), *Gender politics in global governance* (pp. 58–71). Lanham: Rowman & Littlefield.

Meyer, M., & Prügl, E. (Eds.). (1999). *Gender politics in global governance.* Lanham: Rowman & Littlefield.

Meyer, J., Boli, J., Thomas, G., & Ramirez, F. O. (1997). World society and the nation-state. *American Journal of Sociology, 103*(1), 144–181.

Meyer-Ladewig, J. (1998). The control system of the UN human rights covenants from the point of view of a government representative. In E. Klein (Ed.), *The monitoring system of human rights treaty obligations: Colloquium, Potsdam, 22–23 November* (pp. 125–130). Berlin: Arno Spitz.

Miošić-Lisjak, N., Abrahamsdotter, E., Kovačević, O., & Milenković, N. (2009). *Accountability for the protection of women's human rights: Final report*, commissioned by UNIFEM regional programme for CEE.

Moala, K. (2015). How CEDAW impacts some Pacific cultures. *Pacific Institute of Public Policy.* http://pacificpolicy.org/2015/04/how-cedaw-impacts-some-pacific-cultures/. Date accessed 30 July 2015.

Moghadam, V. (2005). *Globalizing women. Transnational feminist networks.* Baltimore: John Hopkins University Press.

Mohanty, C. (1984). Under Western eyes. Feminist scholarship and colonial discourses. *Boundary 2, 12/13*(3/1), 333–358.

Molina, P. (2000). El Gobierno ante Beijing + 5. Las Políticas Frente a la Mujer Nuevamente al Banquillo. *El Mercurio, 4*, 1–5.

Moravcsik, A. (1995). Explaining international human rights regimes: Liberal theory and Western Europe. *European Journal of International Relations, 1*(2), 157–189.

Morgan, R. (Ed.). (1984). *Sisterhood is global: The international women's movement anthology.* New York: Anchor Press/Doubleday.

Morsink, J. (1991). Women's rights in the universal declaration. *Human Rights Quarterly, 13*(2), 229–256.

Mujica, R., & Meza, M. (2009). Women's rights in Peru: Insights from two organizations. *Global Networks, 9*(4), 485–506.

Murdoch, J. (2008). *The optional protocol to the United Nations Convention for the Elimination of All Forms of Discrimination against Women (CEDAW): The experience of the United Kingdom.* Technical report. UK Ministry of Justice, London.

Nagarajan, V., & Parashar, A. (2013). Space and law, gender and land: Using CEDAW to regulate for women's rights to land in Vanuatu. *Law Critique, 24*(1), 87–105.

Naples, N., & Desai, M. (Eds.). (2002). *Women's activism and globalization. Linking local struggles and transnational politics.* London/New York: Routledge.

Nash, K. (2002). Human rights for women: An argument for "deconstructive equality". *Economy and Society, 31*(3), 414–433.

National CEDAW Task Team/Masimanyane Women's Support Centre. (n.d.). *Request for an inquiry under the optional protocol of CEDAW*. Southernwood/ South Africa: Masimanyane Women's Support Centre.

Ndulo, M. (2009). The United Nations responses to the sexual abuse and exploitation of women and girls by peacekeepers during peacekeeping missions. *Berkeley Journal of International Law, 27*(1), 127–161.

Neumayer, E. (2005). Do international human rights treaties improve respect for human rights? *Journal of Conflict Resolution, 49*(6), 925–953.

Nousiainen, K., & Niemi-Kiesiläinen, J. (2001). Introductory remarks on Nordic Law and gender identities. In K. Nousiainen et al. (Eds.), *Responsible selves. Women in the Nordic legal culture* (pp. 1–22). Aldershot: Ashgate.

Nousiainen, K., & Pentikäinen, M. (2013). Rise and fall of the CEDAW in Finland: Time to reclaim its impetus. In A. Hellum & H. S. Aasen (Eds.), *Women's human rights. CEDAW in international, regional, and national law* (pp. 557–587). Cambridge: Cambridge University Press.

NYTKIS. (2008). *Submission to the United Nation's Committee on the Convention on the Elimination of All Forms of Discrimination against Women, Finland.*

NYTKIS. (2014). *Submission to the United Nation's Committee on the Convention on the Elimination of All Forms of Discrimination against Women, Finland.*

O'Flaherty, M., & Tsai, P.-L. (2011). Periodic reporting: The backbone of the UN treaty body review procedures. In M. C. Bassiouni & W. A. Schabas (Eds.), *New challenges for the UN human rights machinery. What future for the UN treaty body system and the Human Rights Council procedures?* (pp. 37–56). Cambridge: Intersentia.

O'Hare, U. (1999). Realizing human rights for women. *Human Rights Quarterly, 21*(2), 364–402.

OHCHR. (2005). The OHCHR plan of action: Protection and empowerment, Geneva. http://www2.ohchr.org/english/planaction.pdf. Date accessed 30 July 2015.

OHCHR. (2011). Resources in support of the human rights treaty body system, 11 May 2011. http://www2.ohchr.org/english/bodies/HRTD/docs/Sion BudgetPaper.pdf. Date accessed 30 July 2015.

OHCHR. (2015). *Optional protocol to the Convention on the Elimination of Discrimination against Women—Jurisprudence*. http://www.ohchr.org/EN/ HRBodies/CEDAW/Pages/Jurisprudence.aspx. Date accessed 30 July 2015.

OIC. (2015). Ministers in charge of women. http://www.oic-oci.org/oicv2/ page/?p_id=225&p_ref=71&lan=en. Date accessed 30 July 2015.

Olcott, J. (2010). Cold War conflicts and cheap cabaret: Sexual politics at the 1975 United Nations international women's tear conference. *Gender & History, 22*(3), 733–754.

Ombudsman for Equality. (2014). *Contribution to the United Nation's Committee on the Convention on the Elimination of All Forms of Discrimination against Women, seventh periodic report of Finland.*

OTD and IGLHRC. (2012). Violaciones de derechos humanos de las personas lesbianas, bisexuales y transexuales (LBT): Un informe sombra, Presentado a la Sesión n°53 de: La Convención Sobre la Eliminación de Todas Las Formas de Discriminación Contra la Mujer, Septiembre 2012, Chile.

Ouedraogo, A. (1999). Rapport final. Ateliers de formation et activites de sensibilisation relatifs a la Convention sur l'elimination de toutes les formes de discrimination a l'egard des femmes, Cotonou, Benin.

Parvikko, T. (1992). Conceptions of gender equality; similarity and difference. In M. Keränen (Ed.), *Gender and politics in Finland* (pp. 89–111). Aldershot/Brookfield: Avebury.

Pegg, S. (2009). Business and human rights. In D. P. Forsythe (Ed.), *Encyclopedia of human rights* (Vol. 1, pp. 220–231). Oxford/New York: Oxford University Press.

Pietilä, H. (2007). *The unfinished story of women and the United Nations.* New York: UN Non-Governmental Liaison Service. http://www.un-ngls.org/orf/pdf/UnfinishedStory.pdf. Date accessed 30 July 2015.

Pietilä, H., & Vickers, J. (1996). *Making women matter. The role of the United Nations* (3rd ed.). London: Zed Books.

Pradhan Malla, S. (2000). Nepal. In M. McPhedran et al. (Eds.), *The first CEDAW impact study. Final report* (pp. 77–122). Toronto: York University, Centre for Feminist Research.

Prasad, V. (2007). *The darker nations. A people's history of the Third World.* New York/London: The New Press.

Price, P. L. (1999). Bodies, faith, and inner landscapes. Rethinking change from the very local. *Latin American Perspectives, 26*(3), 37–59.

Pries, L. (2004). Transnationalism and migration: New challenges for the social sciences and education. In S. Luchtenberg (Ed.), *Migration, education and change* (pp. 20–39). London/New York: Routledge.

Pro tukipiste. (2014). *Submission to the Committee on the Elimination of All Forms of Discrimination against Women (CEDAW) 57th session*, 10–28 Feb 2014.

Prügl, E. (2013). Gender expertise as feminist strategy. In G. Çağlar, E. Prügl, & S. Zwingel (Eds.), *Feminist strategies in international governance* (pp. 57–73). New York: Routledge.

Quataert, J., & Roth, B. (2012). Guest editorial note. Human rights, global conferences, and the making of postwar transnational feminisms. *Journal of Women's History, 24*(4), 11–23.

Raday, F. (2012a). Article 4. In M. A. Freeman, C. Chinkin, & B. Rudolf (Eds.), *The UN Convention on the Elimination of All Forms of Discrimination against Women: A commentary* (pp. 123–139). Oxford: Oxford University Press.

Raday, F. (2012b). Article 11. In M. A. Freeman, C. Chinkin, & B. Rudolf (Eds.), *The UN Convention on the Elimination of All Forms of Discrimination against Women. A commentary* (pp. 277–309). Oxford: Oxford University Press.

Rajaram, N., & Zararia, V. (2009). Translating women's human rights in a globalizing world: The spiral process in reducing gender injustice in Baroda, India. *Global Networks, 9*(4), 462–484.

Rawstron, K. J. (2014). *CEDAW and sex segregation in education and employment: Australia, Japan and South Korea, 1970–2010*, thesis, School of Humanities and Social Inquiry, University of Wollongong, Wollongong.

Razavi, S. (2013). Governing the economy for gender equality? Challenges of regulation. In G. Çağlar, E. Prügl, & S. Zwingel (Eds.), *Feminist strategies in international governance* (pp. 217–232). London: Routledge.

Real Women of Canada. (2015). About us. http://www.realwomenofcanada.ca/about-us/. Date accessed 30 July 2015.

Red de Salud de las Mujeres Latinoamericanas y del Caribe. (2002). Apoyo a protocolo facultativo de la CEDAW en Chile. http://www.convencion.org.uy/lang/es/apoyo-a-protocolo-facultativo-de-la-cedaw-en-chile. Date accessed 15 Aug 2015.

Rehof, L. (1993). *Guide to the Travaux Préparatoires of the United Nations Convention on the Elimination of All Forms of Discrimination against Women.* Dordrecht: Martinus Nijhoff Publishers.

Reilly, N. (2007). Linking local and global feminist advocacy: Framing human rights as women's rights in the Republic of Ireland. *Women's Studies International Forum, 30*, 114–133.

Reilly, N. (2009). *Women's human rights: Seeking gender justice in a globalising age.* Cambridge: Polity Press.

Reiman, K. (2006). A view from the top: International politics, norms, and the worldwide growth of NGOs. *International Studies Quarterly, 50*, 45–67.

Richter, D. (2011). Das Frauenrechtsübereinkommen der Vereinten Nationen (CEDAW): Universelle Geltung und Verschiedenheit der Vertragsstaaten im Spiegel der Praxis. In U. Rust & J. Lange (Eds.), *CEDAW vor dem Zwischenbericht 2011. Handlungsspielräume und –erfordernisse der UN-Frauenrechtskonvention* (pp. 151–195). Rehburg-Loccum: Evangelische Akademie Loccum.

Risse, T., Ropp, S., & Sikkink, K. (Eds.). (1999). *The power of human rights. International norms and domestic change.* Cambridge: Cambridge University Press.

Risse, T., S. Ropp, and K. Sikkink (eds.) (2013) *The Persistent Power of Human Rights. From Commitment to Compliance* (Cambridge: Cambridge University Press).

Roald, A. S. (2009). Islamists in Jordan: Promoters of or obstacles to female empowerment and gender equality? *Religion and Human Rights, 4*, 41–63.

Roerink, A., & I. van Dijk (2000). Netherlands. In M. McPhedran, et al. (Eds.), *The first CEDAW impact study. Final report* (pp. 123–134). Toronto: Centre for Feminist Research, York University.

Rosen, M., & Yoon, D. (2009). Bringing coals to Newcastle? Human rights, civil rights and social movements in New York City. *Global Networks, 9*(4), 507–528.

Rosenblum, D. (2011). Unsex CEDAW, or what's wrong with women's rights. *Columbia Journal of Gender and Law, 20*(2), 98–194.

Ross, S. D. (2008). *Women's human rights. The international and comparative law casebook*. Philadelphia: University of Pennsylvania Press.

Rucht, D. (1996). Multinationale Bewegungsorganisationen: Bedeutung, Beding ungen, Perspektiven. *Forschungsjournal Neue Soziale Bewegungen, 2*, 24–49.

Rudolf, B. (2011). CEDAW und die Europäische Union. In U. Rust & J. Lange (Eds.), *CEDAW vor dem Zwischenbericht 2011. Handlungsspielräume und -erfordernisse der UN-Frauenrechtskonvention* (pp. 75–92). Rehburg-Loccum: Evangelische Akademie Loccum.

Ruggie, J. (2007). *State responsibilities to regulate and adjudicate corporate activities under the United Nations' core human rights treaties, individual report on the United Nations Convention on the Elimination of All Forms of Discrimination against Women. Prepared for the special representative of the secretary-general on human rights and transnational corporations and other business enterprises.* Geneva: United Nations.

Rupp, L. (1997). *Worlds of women. The making of an international women's movement.* Princeton: Princeton University Press.

Sabat, R. (2013). Translating international norms: Filters to combating violence against women in Lebanon. In G. Çağlar, E. Prügl, & S. Zwingel (Eds.), *Feminist strategies in international governance* (pp. 141–160). London: Routledge.

Sadasivam, B. (1997). The impact of structural adjustment on women: A governance and human rights agenda. *Human Rights Quarterly, 19*(3), 630–665.

Sandler, J., & Rao, A. (2012). *Strategies of feminist bureaucrats: United Nations experiences (with a preface by Rosalind Eyben)* (IDS Working Paper 2012/ 397). Brighton: Institute of Development Studies.

Savery, L. (2007). *Engendering the state. The international diffusion of women's human rights.* London/New York: Routledge.

Schild, V. (2013). Care and punishment in Latin America: The gendered neoliberalization of the Chilean state. In M. Goodale & N. Postero (Eds.), *Neoliberalism, interrupted. Social change and contested governance in contemporary Latin America* (pp. 195–224). Stanford: Stanford University.Press.

Schöpp-Schilling, H.-B. (1999). Effektivität von Abkommen zum Schutz der Menschenrechte am Beispiel der CEDAW. *Die Friedens-Warte, 74*(1–2), 204–228.

Schöpp-Schilling, H.-B. (2007a). The nature and scope of the convention. In H.-B. Schöpp-Schilling & C. Flinterman (Eds.), *The circle of empowerment, twenty-five years of the UN Committee on the Elimination of Discrimination against Women* (pp. 10–29). New York: The Feminist Press.

Schöpp-Schilling, H.-B. (2007b). Treaty body reform: The case of the Committee on the Elimination of Discrimination against Women. *Human Rights Law Review, 7*(1), 201–224.

Schöpp-Schilling, H.-B. (2007c). The nature and mandate of the committee. In H.-B. Schöpp-Schilling & C. Flinterman (Eds.), *The circle of empowerment. Twenty-five years of the UN Committee on the Elimination of Discrimination against Women* (pp. 248–261). New York: The Feminist Press.

Schöpp-Schilling, H.-B., & Flinterman, C. (Eds.). (2007). *The circle of empowerment. Twenty-five years of the UN Committee on the Elimination of Discrimination against Women*. New York: The Feminist Press.

Schuller, M. (2012). *Killing with kindness. Haiti, international aid, and NGOs*. New Brunswick: Rutgers University Press.

Schwarz, R. (2004). The paradox of sovereignty, regime type, and human rights compliance. *International Journal of Human Rights, 8*(2), 199–215.

Sen, A. (1999). *Development as freedom*. New York: Oxford University Press.

Sen, G. (2005). *Neolibs, neocons and gender justice. Lessons from global negotiations* (Occasional paper no. 9). Geneva: United Nations Research Institute for Social Development.

Sen, G., & Grown, C. (1988). *Development, crisis and alternative visions. Third World women's perspectives*. London: Earthscan Publications Limited.

Sepper, E. (2008). Confronting the "sacred and unchangeable": The obligation to modify cultural patterns under the women's discrimination treaty. *University of Pennsylvania Journal of International Law, 30*(2), 585–639.

SETA—LGBTI Rights in Finland. (2014). *NGO submission to the 57 session (10–28 Feb 2014) of United Nation's Committee on the Convention on the Elimination of All Forms of Discrimination against Women related to the consideration of the seventh periodic report submitted by Finland under Article 18 of the convention*, 16 Jan 2014.

Shahani, L. (2004). The UN, women, and development: The world conferences on women. In A. Fraser & I. Tinker (Eds.), *Developing power: How women transformed international development* (pp. 26–36). New York: The Feminist Press.

Shalev, C. (2001). China to CEDAW: An update on population policy. *Human Rights Quarterly, 23*(2), 119–147.

Shin, H. (2007). CEDAW and violence against women: Providing the "missing link". In H.-B. Schoepp-Schilling & C. Flinterman (Eds.), *The circle of empowerment. Twenty-five years of the UN Committee on the Elimination of Discrimination against Women* (pp. 223–233). New York: The Feminist Press.

Shivdas, M., & Coleman, S. (Eds.). (2010). *Without prejudice. CEDAW and the determination of women's rights in a legal and cultural context*. London: Commonwealth Secretariat.

Sikkink, K. (2011). *The justice cascade. How human rights prosecutions are changing world politics*. New York: W.W. Norton.

Simmons, B. (2009). *Mobilizing for human rights. International law in domestic politics*. Cambridge: Cambridge University Press.

Sinegiorgis, K. (2007). Challenges and impacts. In H.-B. Schoepp-Schilling & C. Flinterman (Eds.), *The circle of empowerment. Twenty-five years of the UN Committee on the Elimination of Discrimination against Women* (pp. 276–280). New York: The Feminist Press.

Sjorup, L. (1995). *Negotiating ethics: The Holy See, its allies and contesting actors in Beijing* (CDR working papers no. 96.1). Copenhagen: Centre for Development Research.

Skard, T. (2009). Gender in the malestream—Acceptance of women and gender equality in different United Nations Organisations. *Forum for Development Studies, 36*(1), 155–191.

Smith, J., Pagnucco, R., & Lopez, G. A. (1998). Globalizing human rights: The work of transnational human rights NGOs in the 1990s. *Human Rights Quarterly, 20*(2), 379–412.

Smith-Cannoy, H. (2012). *Insincere commitments. Human rights treaties, abusive states, and citizen activism.* Washington, DC: Georgetown University Press.

Sokhi-Bulley, B. (2006). The optional protocol to CEDAW: First steps. *Human Rights Law Review, 6*(1), 143–159.

Spivak, G. C. (2004). Righting wrongs. *The South Atlantic Quarterly, 103*(2/3), 523–581.

Staab, S. (2012). Maternalism, male-breadwinner bias, and market reform: Historical legacies and current reforms in Chilean social policy. *Social Politics, 19*(3), 299–332.

Stachursky, B. (2013). *The promise and perils of transnationalization. NGO activism and the socialization of women's human rights in Egypt and Iran.* New York: Routledge.

Stamatopoulou, E. (1995). Women's rights and the United Nations. In J. Peters & A. Wolper (Eds.), *Women's rights, human rights: International feminist perspectives* (pp. 36–48). London/New York: Routledge.

Stevenson, L. S. (2012). The Bachelet effect on gender-equity policies. *Latin American Perspectives, 39*(4), 129–144.

Stienstra, D. (1994). *Women's movements and international organizations.* New York: St. Martin's Press.

Sudduth, J. (2009). CEDAW's flaws: A critical analysis of why CEDAW is failing to protect a woman's right to education in Pakistan. *The Journal of Law and Education, 38*(4), 563–592.

Sulkunen, I. (2007). The general strike and women's suffrage. Centenary of women's full political rights in Finland. http://www.helsinki.fi/sukupuolentutkimus/aanioikeus/en/articles/strike.htm. Date accessed 14 Aug 2015.

Sweeney, S. (2004). *Global transformations, national institutions, and women's rights: A cross-national comparative analysis.* Paper presented at the annual conference of the American Political Science Association, Chicago.

Tallberg, J. (2002). Paths to compliance: Enforcement, management and the European Union. *International Organization, 56*(3), 609–643.

Tanaka-Naji, H. (2009). *Japanische Frauennetzwerke und Geschlechterpolitik im Zeitalter der Globalisierung* (Deutsches Institut für Japanstudien, Band 44). München: Iudicum.

Tang, K., & Cheung, J. T. (2003). Realizing women's human rights in Asia: The UN convention and the optional protocol. *Asian Journal for Women's Studies, 8* (4), 9–37.

Tavarez da Silva, M. R., & Ferrer Gomez, Y. (2007). The Juárez murders and the inquiry procedure. In H.-B. Schoepp-Schilling & C. Flinterman (Eds.), *The circle of empowerment. Twenty-five years of the UN Committee on the Elimination of Discrimination against Women* (pp. 298–308). New York: The Feminist Press

Thayer, M. (2010). *Making transnational feminism. Rural women, NGO activists, and Northern donors in Brazil.* London/New York: Routledge.

The Women's Institute for Leadership Development for Human Rights. (2008). *Respect, protect, fulfill. Raising the bar on women's rights in San Francisco*, authored by D. J. Liebowitz. http://www.drew.edu/wp-content/uploads/sites/109/Final-CEDAW-SF-Report.pdf. Date accessed 30 July 2015.

Tickner, A. (2001). *Gendering world politics. Issues and approaches in the post-Cold War era.* New York: Columbia University Press.

Timothy, K., & Freeman, M. A. (2000). The CEDAW convention and the Beijing platform for action: Reinforcing the promise of the rights framework. http://www1.umn.edu/humanrts/iwraw/Freeman-Timothy.html. Accessed 30 July 2015.

Tønnessen, L. (2011). Feminist interlegalities and gender justice in Sudan: The debate on CEDAW and Islam. *Religion and Human Rights, 6*, 25–39.

Towns, A. (2010). *Women and states. Norms and hierarchies in international society.* Cambridge: Cambridge University Press.

Trebilcock, A. (2010). Labour issues and the Convention on the Elimination of All Forms of Discrimination against Women. In A. Di Stefano (Ed.), *Gender issues and international legal standards. Contemporary perspectives* (pp. 139–181). Catania: Edit Press.

Tripp, A. (2006). Challenges in transnational feminist mobilization. In M. Marx Ferree & A. M. Tripp (Eds.), *Global feminism. Transnational women's activism, organizing, and human rights* (pp. 296–312). New York/London: New York University Press.

True, J., & Mintrom, M. (2001). Transnational networks and policy diffusion: The case of gender mainstreaming. *International Studies Quarterly, 45*, 27–57.

True, J., & Parisi, L. (2013). Gender mainstreaming strategies in international governance. In G. Çağlar, E. Prügl, & S. Zwingel (Eds.), *Feminist strategies in international governance* (pp. 37–56). New York: Routledge.

Tsing, A. (1997). Transitions as translations. In C. Kaplan, J. W. Scott, & D. Keates (Eds.), *Transitions, environments, translations* (pp. 255–258). London/New York: Routledge.

UNDP. (2010). *Género. Los desafíos de la igualdad.* Country: Chile. http://hdr.undp.org/en/content/género. Date accessed 15 Aug 2015.

UNDP. (2015). Gender Inequality Index (GII). http://hdr.undp.org/en/content/gender-inequality-index-gii. Date accessed 15 Aug 2015.

UNFPA/UNICEF. (2011). *Women's and children's rights. Making the connection.* New York: UNFPA/UNICEF.

UNICEF. (2003). Children have rights. http://www.unicef.org/why/why_rights.html. Date accessed 30 July 2015.

UNICEF/The Academy for Peace and Development. (2002). Women's rights in Islam and Somali culture. http://www.unicef.org/somalia/resources_11626.html. Date accessed 30 July 2015.

UNIFEM. (1998). *Bringing equality home. Implementing the Convention on the Elimination of All Forms of Discrimination against Women.* New York: UNIFEM.

UNIFEM. (2001). *Turning the tide: CEDAW and the gender dimensions of the HIV/AIDS pandemic.* New York: United Nations Development Fund for Women.

UNIFEM. (2006). *CEDAW and security council resolution 1325: A quick guide.* New York: United Nations Development Fund for Women.

UNIFEM. (2007). *CEDAW and the human rights based approach to programming. A UNIFEM guide*, by Lee Waldorf. New York: United Nations Development Fund for Women.

UNIFEM. (2008). *Budgeting for women's rights. Monitoring government budgets for compliance with CEDAW*, By Diane Elson. New York: United Nations Development Fund for Women.

UNIFEM. (2010). UNIFEM. Annual report 2009–2010. New York: UNIFEM.

UNIFEM/Universalia Management Group. (2008). *UNIFEM Programme. Facilitating CEDAW Implementation in Southeast Asia (CEDAW SEAP). Evaluation report.* New York: United Nations Development Fund for Women.

United Nations. (1996). *The United Nations and the advancement of women 1945–1996* (Blue Book Series, Vol. 6). New York: United Nations Department of Public Information.

United Nations. (2010). *The world's women 2010. Trends and statistics.* New York: United Nations.

United Nations/DAW. (2000a). *The optional protocol: Text and materials.* New York: United Nations.

United Nations/DAW. (2000b). *Bringing international human rights law home. Judicial colloquium on the domestic application of the Convention on the Elimination of All Forms of Discrimination against Women and the Convention on the Rights of the Child.* New York: UN.

United Nations/ESCAP. (2000). *Using CEDAW at the grass roots: Convention on the Elimination of All Forms of Discrimination against Women in the Pacific.* New York: UN.

UN Women. (2015a). About UN women. http://www.unwomen.org/en/about-us/about-un-women. Date accessed 30 July 2015.

UN Women. (2015b). What we do. http://www.unwomen.org/en/what-we-do. Date accessed 30 July 2015.

UN Women. (2015c). CEDAW Southeast Asia programme. http://www.unwomen-eseasia.org/projects/Cedaw/index.html. Accessed 30 July 2015.

UN Women. (2015d). Technical cooperation programmes. http://www.un.org/womenwatch/daw/TechnicalCooperation/tcprog.htm. Date accessed 30 July 2015.

Valdés, T. (2010). El Chile de Michelle Bachelet ¿Género en el poder? *Latin American Research Review, 45*(Special Issue), 248–273.

Valdés, T. (2013). The CEDAW and the state of Chile: Old and new debts with the gender equality. *Anuario de Derechos Humanos, 9*, 171–181.

Valenzuela, A. (1999). Chile: Origins and consolidation of a Latin American democracy. In L. Diamond, J. Hartlyn, J. J. Linz, & S. M. Lipset (Eds.), *Democracy in developing countries: Latin America* (pp. 191–247). Boulder/London: Lynne Rienner.

van der Vleuten, A., van Eerdewijk, A., & Roggebrand, C. (Eds.). (2014). *Gender equality norms in regional governance. Transnational dynamics in Europe, South America and Southern Africa.* Houndsmills: Palgrave MacMillan.

van Kersbergen, K., & Verbeek, B. (2007). The politics of international norms: Subsidiarity and the imperfect competence regime of the European Union. *European Journal of International Relations, 13*(2), 217–238.

Verloo, M. (Ed.). (2007). *Multiple meanings of gender equality: A critical frame analysis of gender policies in Europe.* Budapest: Central European University Press.

Verloo, M., & Lombardo, E. (2007). Contested gender equality and policy variety in Europe: Introducing a critical frame analysis approach. In M. Verloo (Ed.), *Multiple meanings of gender equality: A critical frame analysis of gender policies in Europe* (pp. 21–50). Budapest: Central European University Press.

Vertovec, S. (1999). Conceiving and researching transnationalism. *Ethnic and Racial Studies, 22*, 447–462.

Visvanathan, N., & Yoder, K. (2011). Women and microcredit: A critical introduction. In N. Visvanathan, L. Duggan, N. Wiegersma, & L. Nisonoff (Eds.), *The women, gender and development reader* (2nd ed., pp. 47–54). New York/London: Zed Books.

von Braunmühl, C. (2013). A feminist analysis of UN Security Council resolution on women, peace, and security. In G. Çağlar, E. Prügl, & S. Zwingel (Eds.), *Feminist strategies in international governance* (pp. 163–180). New York: Routledge.

Waldorf, L. (2009). Making human rights for women a reality. *Open Democracy*. http://www.opendemocracy.net/5050/lee-waldorf/making-human-rights-for-women-reality

Waylen, G. (1996). Democratization, feminism and the state in Chile: The establishment of SERNAM. In S. M. Rai & G. Lievesley (Eds.), *Women and the state. International perspectives* (pp. 103–117). London: Taylor & Francis.

WEDO. (2005). *Beijing betrayed women worldwide report that governments have failed to turn the platform into action*. New York: WEDO.

Weiss, A. (2003). Interpreting Islam and women's rights: Implementing CEDAW in Pakistan. *International Sociology, 18*(3), 581–601.

West, L. (1999). The United Nations women's conferences and feminist politics. In M. Meyer & E. Prügl (Eds.), *Gender politics and global governance* (pp. 177–193). Lanham: Rowman & Littlefield.

Wichterich, C. (2007). Transnationale Frauenbewegungen und Global Governance. *gender…politik…online*. http://www.fu-berlin.de/sites/gpo/int_bez/globalisierung/Transnationale_Frauenbewegungen/wichterich.pdf. Date accessed 30 July 2015.

Wilkinson, C., & Langlois, A. J. (Eds.). (2014). Special issue: Not such an international human rights norm? Local resistance to lesbian, gay, bisexual, and transgender rights. *Journal of Human Rights, 13*(3).

Williams, M. (2013). A perspective of feminist international organizing from the bottom up. The case of IGTN and the WTO. In G. Çağlar, E. Prügl, & S. Zwingel (Eds.), *Feminist strategies in international governance* (pp. 92–108). London: Routledge.

Wing, S. (2012). Human rights-based approaches to development: Justice and legal fiction in Africa. *Polity, 44*(4), 504–522.

Winslow, A. (Ed.). (1995). *Women, politics, and the United Nations*. Westport: Greenwood Press.

Wittkopp, S. (2012). Article 7. In M. A. Freeman, C. Chinkin, & B. Rudolf (Eds.), *The UN Convention on the Elimination of All Forms of Discrimination against Women. A commentary* (pp. 197–219). Oxford: Oxford University Press.

World Conference on Human Rights. (1993). Vienna declaration and program of action. http://www.ohchr.org/en/professionalinterest/pages/vienna.aspx. Date accessed 30 July 2015.

Yoneda, M. (2000). Japan. In M. McPhedran, et al. (Eds.), *The first CEDAW impact study. Final report* (pp. 63–76). Toronto: Centre for Feminist Research, York University.

Young, B. (2013). Structural power and the gender biases of technocratic network governance in finance. In G. Çağlar, E. Prügl, & S. Zwingel (Eds.), *Feminist strategies in international governance* (pp. 267–282). New York: Routledge.

Zearfoss, S. (1991). Note, the Convention on the Elimination of All Forms of Discrimination against Women: Radical, reasonable or reactionary? *Michigan Journal of International Law, 12*, 903–942.

Zwingel, S. (2005a). From intergovernmental negotiations to (sub)national change: A transnational perspective on the impact of the CEDAW convention. *International Feminist Journal of Politics, 7*(3), 400–424.

Zwingel, S. (2005b). How do international women's rights become effective domestic norms? An analysis of the Convention on the Elimination of All Forms of Discrimination against Women. http://www-brs.ub.ruhr-uni-bochum.de/netahtml/HSS/Diss/ZwingelSusanne/. Date accessed 30 July 2015.

Zwingel, S. (2013a). Translating international women rights norms: CEDAW in context. In G. Çağlar, E. Prügl, & S. Zwingel (Eds.), *Feminist strategies in international governance* (pp. 111–126). London: Routledge.

Zwingel, S. (2013b). International feminist strategies: Strengths and challenges of the rights-based approach. *Politics and Gender, 9*(3), 344–351.

UN Document

A/34/107, General Assembly, 34th Session, 107th Plenary Meeting, 18 December 1979.

A/41/45, Report of the Committee on the Elimination of Discrimination against Women, Fifth session, 1986.

A/41/608, Status of the Convention on the Elimination of All Forms of Discrimination against Women, Report of the Secretary General, 1986.

A/42/38, Report of the Committee on the Elimination of Discrimination against Women, Sixth session, 1987.

A/43/38, Report of the Committee on the Elimination of Discrimination against Women, Seventh session, 1988.

A/44/38, Report of the Committee on the Elimination of Discrimination against Women, Eighth session, 1989.

A/47/38, Report of the Committee on the Elimination of Discrimination against Women, Eleventh session, 1992.

A/48/38, Report of the Committee on the Elimination of Discrimination against Women, Twelfth session, 1993.

A/49/38, Report of the Committee on the Elimination of Discrimination against Women, Thirteenth session, 1994.

A/50/38, Report of the Committee on the Elimination of Discrimination against Women, Fourteenth session, 1995.

A/52/38, Report of the Committee on the Elimination of Discrimination against Women, Sixteenth and Seventeenth sessions, 1997.

A/53/38, Report of the Committee on the Elimination of Discrimination against Women, Eighteenth and Nineteenth sessions, 1998.

A/54/38, Report of the Committee on the Elimination of Discrimination against Women, Twentieth and Twenty-first sessions, 1999.

A/55/38, Report of the Committee on the Elimination of Discrimination against Women, Twenty-second and Twenty-third sessions, 2000.

A/56/38, Report of the Committee on the Elimination of Discrimination against Women, Twenty-fourth and Twenty-fifth sessions, 2001.

A/57/38, Report of the Committee on the Elimination of Discrimination against Women, Twenty-sixth, Twenty-seventh and exceptional sessions, 2002.

A/59/38, Report of the Committee on the Elimination of Discrimination against Women, Thirtieth and Thirty-first sessions, 2004.

A/60/38, Report of the Committee on the Elimination of Discrimination against Women, Thirty-second session and Thirty-third session, 2005.

A/61/38, Report of the Committee on the Elimination of Discrimination against Women, Thirty-fourth, Thirty-fifth, and Thirty-sixth session, 2006.

A/62/38, Report of the Committee on the Elimination of Discrimination against Women, Thirty-seventh, Thirty-eighth, and Thirty-ninth session, 2007.

A/63/38, Report of the Committee on the Elimination of Discrimination against Women, Fortieth and Forty-first session, 2008.

A/64/38, Report of the Committee on the Elimination of Discrimination against Women, Forty-second and Forty-third session, 2008-2009.

A/64/342, Status of the Convention on the Elimination of All Forms of Discrimination against Women, Report of the Secretary-General, September 2009.

A/65/38, Report of the Committee on the Elimination of Discrimination against Women, Forty-forth and Forty-fifth session, 2009-2010.

A/66/38, Report of the Committee on the Elimination of Discrimination against Women, Forty-forth and Forty-fifth session, 2009-2010.

A/66/175, Report of the Chairs of the Human Rights Treaty Bodies on their Twenty-third meeting, July 2011.

A/67/38, Report of the Committee on the Elimination of Discrimination against Women, Forty-ninth, Fiftieth, and Fifty-first session, 2011-2012.

A/67/222, General Assembly 67th session, Implementation of Human Rights Instruments, Note by the Secretary General, August 2012.

A/68/38, Report of the Committee on the Elimination of Discrimination against Women, Fifty-second, Fifty-third and Fifty-forth session, 2012-2013.

A/69/38, Report of the Committee on the Elimination of Discrimination against Women, Fifty-fifth, Fifty-sixth and Fifty-seventh session, 2013-2014.

A/C.3/34/SR. 70-73, General Assembly, 34th Session, Third Committee, 70th, 71st, 72nd, and 73rd Meeting, December 1979.

A/C.3/42/SR. 22, 26-28, 30, General Assembly, 42nd Session, Third Committee, Summary Records 22nd, 26-28th and 30th Meeting, October 1987.

A/HRC/4/104, Report of the Secretary-General on the implementation of resolution 2005/42, integrating the human rights of women throughout the United Nations system, February 2007.

A/HRC/20/28, Report of the Working Group on the issue of discrimination against women in law and in practice, April 2012.

A/Res/62/218, General Assembly Resolution 62/218, Convention on the Elimination of all Forms of Discrimination against Women, 2007.

CEDAW/2003/II/ WP.3, Committee on the Elimination of Discrimination against Women, Twenty-ninth session, Working paper for the Committee on the Elimination of Discrimination against Women on how the other treaty bodies have dealt with sexual orientation as it relates to discrimination and the enjoyment of human rights, May 2003.

CEDAW/C/5/Add. 56, Consideration of Reports Submitted by States Parties under Article 18 of the Convention, Initial Reports of States Parties, Finland, 1988.

CEDAW/C/7, Guidelines for the preparation of initial reports prepared by the Committee on the Elimination of All Forms of Discrimination against Women, 1983.

CEDAW/C/34/D/8/2005, Communication No. 8/2005, Kayan v. Turkey, Decision adopted by the Committee at its Thirty-fourth session.

CEDAW/C/36/D/3/2004, Communication No. 3/2004, Dung Thi Thuy Nguyen v. Netherlands, Views, Thirty-sixth session.

CEDAW/C/36/D/4/2004, Communication No. 4/2004, A.S. v. Hungary, Views, Thirty-sixth session.

CEDAW/C/38/D/10/2005, Communication No. 10/2005, N.S.F. v. UK, Decision adopted by the Committee at its Thirty-eighth session.

CEDAW/C/39/D/5/2005, Communication No. 5/2005, Goekce (deceased) v. Austria, Views, Thirty-ninth session.

CEDAW/C/39/D/6/2005, Communication No. 6/2005, Yildirim (deceased) v. Austria, Views, Thirty-ninth session.

CEDAW/C/39/D/7/2005, Communication No. 7/2005, Munoz-Vargas y Sainz de Vicuna v. Spain, Decision adopted by the Committee at its Thirty-ninth session.

CEDAW/C/42/D/15/2007, Communication No. 15/2007, Zheng v. Netherlands, Decision adopted by the Committee at its Forty-second session.

CEDAW/C/44/D/12/2007, Communication No. 12/2007, *Groupe d'Intérêt pour le Matronyme* v. France, Decision adopted by the Committee at its Forty-fourth session.

CEDAW/C/44/D/13/2007, Communication No. 13/2007, *SOS Sexisme* v. France, Decision adopted by the Committee at its Forty-fourth session.

CEDAW/C/46/D/18/2008, Communication No. 18/2008, Tayag Vertido v. Philippines, Views, Forty-sixth session.

CEDAW/C/49/D/17/2008, Communication No. 17/2008, Pimentel v. Brazil, Views, Forty-ninth session.

CEDAW/C/49/D/20/2008, Communication No. 20/2008, V.K. v. Bulgaria, Views, Forty-ninth session.

CEDAW/C/49/D/23/2009, Communication No. 23/2009, Abramova v. Belarus, Views, Forty-ninth session.

CEDAW/C/50/D/22/2009, Communication No. 22/2009, T.P. F. v. Peru, Views, Fiftieth session.
CEDAW/C/50/D/26/2010, Communication No. 26/2010, Herrera Rivera v. Canada, Decision adopted by the Committee at its Fiftieth session.
CEDAW/C/51/D/25/2010, Communication No. 25/2010, M.P.M. v. Canada, Decision adopted by the Committee at its Fifty-first session.
CEDAW/C/51/D/28/2010, Communication N0. 28/2010, R.K.B. v. Turkey, Views, Fifty-first session.
CEDAW/C/52/D/32/2011, Communication No. 32/2011, Jallow v. Bulgaria, Views, Fifty-second session.
CEDAW/C/53/D/31/2011, Communication No. 31/2011, V.P.P. v. Bulgaria, Views, Fifty-third session.
CEDAW/C/55/D/33/2011, Communication No. 33/2011, M.N.N. v. Denmark, Decision adopted by the Committee at its Fifty-fifth session.
CEDAW/C/55/D/35/2011, Communication No. 35/2011, M.E.N. v. Denmark, Decision adopted by the Committee at its Fifty-fifth session.
CEDAW/C/55/D/40/2012, Communication No. 40/2012, M.S. v. Denmark, Decision adopted by the Committee at its fifty-fifth session.
CEDAW/C/57/D/34/2011, Communication No. 34/2011, R.P.B. v. Philippines, Views, Fifty-seventh session.
CEDAW/C/57/D/36/2012, Communication No. 36/2012, De Blok et al. v. Netherlands, Views, Fifty-seventh session.
CEDAW/C/57/D/39/2012, Communication No. 39/2012, N. v. Netherlands, Decision adopted by the Committee at its Fifty-seventh session.
CEDAW/C/58/D/47/2012, Communication No. 47/2012, Angela González Carreño v. Spain, Decision adopted by the Committee at its fifty-eighth session.
CEDAW/C/59/D/49/2013, Communication No. 49/2013, S. O. v. Canada, Decision adopted by the Committee at its fifty-ninth session.
CEDAW/C/60/D/48/2013, Communication No. 48/2013, E. S. and S. C. v. United Republic of Tanzania, Decision adopted by the Committee at its sixtieth session.
CEDAW/C/2014/II/CRP, Report of the Committee on the Elimination of Discrimination against Women, Fifty-eighth session, 30 June–18 July 2014.
CEDAW/C/2014/III/CRP, Report of the Committee on the Elimination of Discrimination against Women, Fifty-ninth session, 20 October–7 November 2014.
CEDAW/C/CHI/1, Consideration of reports submitted by States Parties under article 18 of the Convention on the Elimination of All Forms of Discrimination against Women, Initial reports of States Parties, Chile, 1991
CEDAW/C/CHI/3, Consideration of reports submitted by States Parties under article 18 of the Convention on the Elimination of All Forms of Discrimination against Women, Third periodic reports of States Parties, Chile, 1999.

CEDAW/C/CHI/4, Consideration of reports submitted by States Parties under article 18 of the Convention on the Elimination of All Forms of Discrimination against Women, Fourth periodic reports of States Parties, Chile, 2004.

CEDAW/C/CHL/CO/4, Concluding comments of the Committee on the Elimination of Discrimination against Women: Chile, August 2006.

CEDAW/C/CHL/CO/5-6, Consideration of reports submitted by States Parties under article 18 of the Convention on the Elimination of All Forms of Discrimination against Women, Fifth and sixth periodic reports of States Parties, Chile, 2011.

CEDAW/C/CHL/CO/5-6, Concluding observations on the fifth and sixth periodic reports of Chile, adopted by the Committee at its fifty-third session (1–19 October 2012).

CEDAW/C/CHL/CO/5-6/Add.1, Concluding observations on the combined fifth and sixth periodic reports of Chile, Addendum, Information provided by Chile in follow-up to the concluding observations, April 2015.

CEDAW/C/DMA/CO/AR, Concluding observations of the Committee on the Elimination of Discrimination against Women, Dominica, January 2009.

CEDAW/C/FIN/2, Consideration of Reports Submitted by States Parties Under Article 18 of the Convention, Second Periodic Reports of States Parties, Finland, 1993.

CEDAW/C/FIN/3, Consideration of Reports Submitted by States Parties under Article 18 of the Convention, Third Periodic Reports of States Parties, Finland, 1997.

CEDAW/C/FIN/4, Consideration of Reports Submitted by States Parties under Article 18 of the Convention, Fourth Periodic Reports of States Parties, Finland, 2000.

CEDAW/C/FIN/5, Consideration of Reports Submitted by States Parties under Article 18 of the Convention, Fifth Periodic Reports of States Parties, Finland, 2004.

CEDAW/C/FIN/6, Consideration of Reports Submitted by States Parties under Article 18 of the Convention, Sixth Periodic Reports of States Parties, Finland, 2007.

CEDAW/C/FIN/CO/6, Concluding Observations of the Committee on the Elimination of Discrimination against Women: Finland, July 2008.

CEDAW/C/FIN/CO/6/Add.1, Information provided in follow-up to the concluding observations of the Committee, Finland, 2010.

CEDAW/C/FIN/7, Consideration of Reports Submitted by States Parties Under Article 18 of the Convention, Seventh Periodic Reports of States Parties, Finland, 2012.

CEDAW/C/FIN/Q/7/Add.1, List of issues and questions in relation to the seventh periodic report of Finland, Addendum, Replies of Finland, November 2013.

CEDAW/C/FIN/CO/7, Concluding Observations of the Committee on the Elimination of Discrimination against Women: Finland, March 2014.

CEDAW/C/OP.8/PHL/1, Summary of the inquiry concerning the Philippines under article 8 of the Optional Protocol to the Convention on the Elimination of All Forms of Discrimination against Women, April 2015.

CEDAW/C/OP.8/CAN/1, Report of the inquiry concerning Canada of the Committee of the Elimination of Discrimination against Women under article 8 of the Optional Protocol to the Convention on the Elimination of All Forms of Discrimination against Women, March 2015.

CEDAW/C/UK/CO/6/Add.1, Response by the United Kingdom of Great Britain and Northern Ireland to select recommendations of the Committee on the Elimination of Discrimination against Women following the examination of the fifth and sixth periodic reports of the United Kingdom of Great Britain and Northern Ireland on 10 July 2008, November 2009.

CEDAW/SP/1995/2, Meeting of the States Parties to the Convention on the Elimination of All Forms of Discrimination against Women, Eighth Meeting, Report of the States Parties, 1995.

CEDAW/SP/1996/5, Meeting of the States Parties to the Convention on the Elimination of All Forms of Discrimination against Women, Ninth Meeting, Report of the States Parties.

ECOSOC Resolution 1325 (XLIV), Voluntary reporting system on the implementation of the Declaration on the Elimination of Discrimination against Women, 10 June 1968

ECOSOC Resolution 1985/17, Review of the composition, organization and administrative arrangements of the Sessional Working Group of Governmental Experts on the Implementation of the International Covenant on Economic, Social and Cultural Rights

E/1989/22, Annex III, Committee on Economic, Social and Cultural Rights, General Comment No. 1, 1989.

E/1996/26, Annex III, Summary of exchange of views on elements contained in suggestion 7 held in the open-ended working group in 1996, Report of the Commission on the Status of Women at its fortieth session, 11-22 March 1996

E/1999/27, Annex II, Interpretive statements on the draft optional protocol to the Convention on the Elimination of All Forms of Discrimination against Women, Report of the Commission on the Status of Women at its forty-third session, 1-12 March and 1 April 1999.

E/CN.4/2005/68, Updated report of the Secretary-General on integrating the human rights of women throughout the United Nations system, January 2005.

E/CN.6/575/ Rev. 1, Status of Women and Family Planning: Report of the Special Rapporteur appointed by the Economic and Social Council under resolution 1326 (XLIV), United Nations, Department of Economic and Social Affairs, 1975.

E/CN.6/1996/10 and Add. 2, Views submitted by Governments, intergovernmental and non-governmental organizations on the elaboration of a draft optional protocol to the Convention on the Elimination of All Forms of Discrimination against Women. Report of the Secretary-General submitted to the Commission on the Status of Women at its fortieth session, 11-22 March 1996.

GA Resolution 1921 (XVIII), Draft declaration on the elimination of discrimination against women, 1274th plenary meeting, 5 December 1963.

HRI/MC/1998/6, Integrating the gender perspective into the work of UN human rights treaty bodies, Tenth meeting of persons chairing the human rights treaty bodies, Report by the Secretary-General.

HRI/MC/2006/3, Harmonized Guidelines on Reporting under the International Human Rights Treaties, Including Guidelines on a Common Core Document and Treaty-Specific Documents, 5th Inter-Committee Meeting, June 2006.

ST/CSDHA/5, The Work of CEDAW, Reports of the Committee on the Elimination of Discrimination against Women (CEDAW), Sales No. E. 89. IV. 4, January 1990, Vienna.

Index

S. Zwingel, *Translating International Women's Rights*, Gender and Politics, DOI 10.1057/978-1-137-31501-4

Printed by Printforce, the Netherlands